MRS J. JACKSON-COX

40.00

Green Reporting

Green Reporting

Accountancy and the challenge of the nineties

Edited by
Dave Owen

Senior Lecturer in Accounting
University of Leeds

CHAPMAN & HALL
University and Professional Division

London · New York · Tokyo · Melbourne · Madras

Published by Chapman & Hall, 2–6 Boundary Row, London SE1 8HN

Chapman & Hall, 2–6 Boundary Row, London SE1 8HN, UK

Chapman & Hall, 29 West 35th Street, New York NY10001, USA

Chapman & Hall Japan, Thomson Publishing Japan, Hirakawacho Nemoto Building, 7F, 1-7-11 Hirakawa-cho, Chiyoda-ku, Tokyo 102, Japan

Chapman & Hall Australia, Thomas Nelson Australia, 102 Dodds Street, South Melbourne, Victoria 3205, Australia

Chapman & Hall India, R. Seshadri, 32 Second Main Road, CIT East, Madras 600 035, India

First edition 1992

© 1992 Chapman & Hall

Typeset in 10/12 Times by Mews Photosetting, Beckenham, Kent
Printed in Great Britain by St. Edmundsbury Press, Bury St. Edmunds, Suffolk

ISBN 0 412 40130 4

British Library Cataloguing in Publication Data
Green reporting: Accountancy and the challenge of
the nineties.
  I. Owen, Dave
  657

  ISBN 0-412-40130-4

Library of Congress Cataloging-in-Publication data
Green reporting : accountancy and the challenge of the nineties /
  edited by Dave Owen – 1st ed.
      p. cm.
    Includes bibliographical references and index.
    ISBN 0-412-40130-4
      1. Corporations—Great Britain—Accounting. 2. Environmental
  protection—Great Britain—Accounting. I. Owen, Dave.
  HF5686.C7G56 1992
  657'.95'0941—dc20
                                                    91–18119
                                                    CIP

∞ Printed on paper which is acid-free to ANSI archive quality. It is chlorine-free, contains no added brighteners and is manufactured using only selected waste-wood fibre and environmentally-friendly fillers as opacifying agents. The paper is completely recyclable. The manufacturers consistently monitor their environmental situation and ensure that the paper is ecologically neutral. Little or no use is made of chemicals, water is recirculated as much as possible and waste is recycled.

CONTENTS

PART FOUR   THE FURTHER DEVELOPMENT OF GREEN REPORTING

CONTRIBUTORS

Richard Adams
Director of New Consumer, previously Founder and Managing Director of Traidcraft plc.

Roger Adams
Head of Technical Services and Research, The Chartered Association of Certified Accountants.

Hilary Benn
Research Officer, Manufacturing Science Finance.

Andrew J. Blaza
Head of the Environment Management Unit, The Confederation of British Industry.

Janice Buck
Economic Research Executive, The Institute of Directors.

Anthony Carey
Deputy Director of the Research Board of the Institute of Chartered Accountants in England and Wales, and Secretary of its Environment Research Group.

Malcolm Cooper
Head of Research, Carnegie International.

Roger Cowe
Financial Correspondent, *The Guardian*.

Gilly Filsner
Financial Analyst, Carnegie International.

Mike Geddes
Principal Research Fellow and Research Manager, The Local Government Centre, University of Warwick, and co-editor of *Social Audit Network News* (SANE).

Rachel Griffith
Senior Researcher, Ethical Investment Research Service (EIRIS).

Paul Hackett
Policy Advisor on Energy and Environment, The Trades Union Congress.

George Harte
Lecturer in Accounting, University of Edinburgh.

Brian Ing
Management Consultant, Computer Management Group (CMG).

Alan Jackson
Assistant National Officer (Water Section), NALGO.

Keith Lester
Chairman of the Audit Committee, The British Institute of Management.

Alan Miller
Ethical Investment Consultant and Founding Chairman of the UK Social Investment Forum, previously a Director of Bromige & Partners.

Dave Owen
Senior Lecturer in Accounting, University of Leeds.

Lesley Phillips
Technical Officer (Public Affairs) and Secretary of the Environmental Accounting Working Group, The Chartered Institute of Management Accountants.

Clare Roberts
Lecturer in Accounting, University of Glasgow.

Clive Wicks
Senior Industrial Policy Executive, World Wide Fund for Nature.

PREFACE

The past couple of years have seen green issues, or to put it more simply a concern with the future of the planet, intrude into the public consciousness and subsequently the political agenda in a big way. It is also becoming increasingly apparent that ever growing trends in green awareness, evidenced by legislative developments together with the mounting influence of environmental pressure groups, the rise of green consumerism and the first stirrings of a green investment movement, have tremendous financial implications for business. Indeed, as environmental legislation becomes ever stricter its impact on corporate financial statements, and hence the accounting function, becomes ever more clear.

The premise underpinning this book is that Green Reporting provides the fundamental challenge facing accountants today. Evidence that this is not an entirely eccentric viewpoint is perhaps provided by the plethora of recent articles on green accounting issues in professional journals, the active involvement of major professional accounting bodies in terms of funding research and establishing working parties, to say nothing of the strenuous efforts of leading international accounting firms to corner the environmental audit market. At the same time it must be acknowledged that the development of green reporting practice is not a task that can be accomplished by the accounting profession alone. Disastrous experiences with inflation accounting and more recently issues such as brand names and goodwill should at least counsel a little humility. Rather, there is a pressing need for accountants to show a willingness to enter into debate with various groups in society having an interest in the development of green reporting. In drawing on contributions from industry and commerce, the investment community, the trade union movement, prominent pressure groups, the accounting profession and academia, this book aims to stimulate just such a debate.

The book is structured as follows:

Part One	Charts emerging issues in the environmental and social spheres and draws out their potential impact on the accounting function.
Part Two	Elicits views on the future of green reporting from the perspectives of industry and commerce, the trade union movement, the accounting profession, prominent pressure groups and the investor.
Part Three	Surveys current trends in green reporting both in the United Kingdom and Western Europe. A series of short case studies is utilized to highlight the activities of particularly innovative companies in terms of management information systems developments. Finally, the opportunity is also taken to study developments outside the corporate reporting function as evidenced by the work of the Social Audit and Green Investment movements.
Part Four	Discusses some of the practical implications of introducing green reporting systems.

There are a number of individuals whose assistance in getting this project off the ground is worthy of acknowledgment. First and foremost of course I must thank the various contributors who spared time in busy schedules to make an input. Additionally a number of people made helpful comments on the original proposal which were invaluable in enabling me to develop what I hope is a coherent format for the book. In particular I owe a debt of gratitude to Rob Gray of the University of Dundee, a long-time collaborator on many projects, in this particular regard. Rob's contribution to the development of the greening of accountancy is indeed clearly highlighted in the number of references to his research report prepared for the Chartered Association of Certified Accountants, *The Greening of Accountancy: The Profession After Pearce*, appearing throughout the book. A major motivation in carrying out this project has been to add some practical insights to the theoretical material contained in that report. In this context long conversations with three senior members of staff at Clark Whitehill, Chartered Accountants – Derek Haynes, Richard Derwent and Brian Ing (now of CMG) – during the initial stages of the project were of immeasurable help. Throughout the course of preparation of the final manuscript Alan Nelson of Chapman and Hall has been unfailingly encouraging and supportive as well as accepting, apparently cheerfully, the inevitable delays that have accompanied the finalization of a work drawing on the contributions of some twenty different busy individuals. Last, but by no means least, I must thank Pat Greenfield, for not only typing various parts of the manuscript but also for coping with the mound of correspondence generated by this project.

One final word of warning. Books inevitably become dated and it is my heartfelt wish that this book dates more quickly than most. Such an outcome would mean that many new initiatives will have been launched to cope with the growing environmental crisis in addition to those described in the following pages!

Dave Owen

Part One

THE BACKGROUND TO GREEN REPORTING

Chapter One

THE IMPLICATIONS OF CURRENT TRENDS IN GREEN AWARENESS FOR THE ACCOUNTING FUNCTION: AN INTRODUCTORY ANALYSIS

DAVE OWEN

During the 1980s an ever increasing emphasis on the pursuit of financial efficiency and value for money as the keys to achieving social prosperity led inevitably to accounting, and indeed accountants, occupying a position of prime importance in the public policy arena. As Anthony Hopwood (1984) puts it:

> Accounting has . . . been implicated in a more positive shaping and influencing of that which is regarded as problematic, the forms which public debates take and the options seemingly available for management and public action (p. 168).

However, at the end of the decade a dramatic change in public mood took place – the United Kingdom went 'green'. This was particularly evidenced in the surge of support for the Green Party in the 1989 European elections, which, whilst in itself being apparently short-lived, suddenly led to environmental issues becoming central to the political, economic and business agendas. In particular, major reservations increasingly being expressed over the impact of economic activity on the quality of life, reflected in public concern over issues such as natural resource depletion, unacceptably high levels of pollution, global warming, acid rain and deforestation amongst others, have given rise to a fundamental questioning of private profit as an adequate measure of organizational success.

The business community has been quick to react to the new climate of opinion. Not only have an ever growing number of companies felt the need to parade their green credentials but also prominent organizations such as the Confederation of British Industry, the British Institute of Management and the Institute of Directors have launched a series of green initiatives. (These latter responses are outlined in the contributions of Andrew Blaza, Keith Lester and Janice Buck respectively to the next chapter of this book.) Furthermore, environmental consultancy is taking off in a big way and indeed is bidding fair to replace value for money and efficiency studies as the growth area of the 1990s.

Such developments would seem to have considerable repercussions for the accounting function, particularly as companies increasingly view their annual report and accounts as an essential medium of communication in respect of environmental and social issues, and management information systems are developed which are designed to promote the green dimension to a central position within the corporate decision-making process. Clearly, for accounting to maintain its prominent position within the aforementioned public policy and corporate decision-making arenas the profession must grasp the nettle of green reporting sooner rather than later. The nature of the challenge facing the accounting profession has recently been forthrightly stated by no lesser personage than the President of the Institute of Chartered Accountants in England and Wales. Writing in the January 1991 issue of *Accountancy*, Mike Lickiss unequivocally states that:

> In responding to the challenges posed by the environment, which is our natural wealth, all aspects of accountancy including financial reporting, auditing, management accounting and taxation will have to change. In doing so, there will be an impact on all members of the Institute whether in public practice or in commerce and industry and whether working at home or abroad.

That this view is shared by the other major UK accounting bodies, the Chartered Association of Certified Accountants (ACCA) and the Chartered Institute of Management Accountants (CIMA), is made quite clear by the contributions of Roger Adams and Lesley Phillips in Chapter 4. Indeed, it should be pointed out that these latter two bodies have responded far more speedily in practical terms to the emerging green agenda than has the ICAEW, notwithstanding the stirring words of Mike Lickiss!

My main task in this chapter is to draw attention to the actual and potential repercussions upon the accounting function, in the areas of internal reporting (management information systems), external reporting and auditing, of current increased levels of green awareness. Before doing this it would be useful very briefly to outline recent developments in the public policy arena which are increasingly setting out the terms of the green agenda for business, and thereby inevitably the accountant, in the 1990s.

PUBLIC POLICY INITIATIVES: TOWARDS A NEW BUSINESS CLIMATE

The Pearce Report

The first real manifestation of government concern with green issues appeared with the then Environment Secretary, Chris Patten's, enthusiastic endorsement of the Pearce Report, published in the summer of 1989. Embracing the concept of sustainable development, which had earlier featured centrally in the work of the Brundtland Commission (World Commission on Environment and Development, 1987), and the principle of 'the polluter pays', the report placed major emphasis on the role of financial quantification and market-based incentives in achieving environmental objectives. Such an emphasis is clearly in tune with current economic thinking, not just within the United Kingdom but throughout the European Community, and one can anticipate the conceptual basis underpinning the report exerting a substantial influence on the course of future green legislation. Whilst the Pearce Report is essentially concerned with issues of macroeconomic policy, as Rob Gray (1990) has pointed out in an influential research study conducted under the auspices of the ACCA, *The Greening of Accountancy: The Profession After Pearce*, further implementation of the ideas it puts forward will probably not be possible without both a voluntary response from organizations and, especially, some new environmental accounting systems to support them.

The Environmental Protection Act 1990

This recently enacted legislation takes the first steps towards practical implementation of the polluter pays principle, particularly in establishing a system of integrated pollution control. Amongst other requirements, companies will have to meet the charges that are gradually being phased in to pay for regulatory and control bodies to inspect them and will face heavy financial penalties for breaking specified emission limits. Furthermore, industry will have to foot the bill for environmental impact assessments which will be required in the case of new developments such as factories and shopping centres. Perhaps of most significance for the accounting function, however, in terms of costing out new pollution control methods, is the legal obligation imposed to minimize waste production utilizing what is called the 'Best Available Technology Not Entailing Excessive Cost' (BATNEEC) principle. Interestingly, a similar emphasis on applying concepts of cost effectiveness in the field of pollution control is apparent in a series of Department of Trade and Industry publications concerned with 'business and the environment'.

    When considered in conjunction with provisions imposing tighter controls over waste disposal companies, which will inevitably force up costs to the customer, the financial implications for industry of the Act are clearly considerable. A final feature worthy of note, not only in terms of additional costs for companies in self-monitoring pollution but also having potential implications for external reporting practice, lies in the Act's commitment to greater openness in giving the public access to information concerning the operations of polluting industries via registers kept by enforcing authorities.

The White Paper *This Common Inheritance*

September 1990 saw the launch of the much heralded White Paper on the environment, a glossy 291 page effort containing some 350 different proposals. However, for most commentators the document signalled a significant retreat by the government on environmental issues with attention being drawn to a distinct lack of positive commitments laid down, particularly an absence of firm proposals for harnessing market forces to environmental ends. The general reaction is neatly summarized in press headlines such as 'Not Just White But Deathly Pallid' (*The Guardian*), 'Faint Tinge of Green' (*The Times*) and, perhaps most damningly, 'Missed Chance For Cleaner UK' (*The Independent*). Nevertheless a number of issues addressed in the White Paper do have potential implications for industry, for example the outlining of various steps to promote more efficient use of energy in order to help combat global warming; the laying down of a tentative strategy to return carbon dioxide levels to 1990 levels by the year 2005; a continued commitment to stricter control of air and water pollution including extended monitoring of air pollution together with increased fines for water polluters; and the promise of further steps being taken to reduce industrial waste. In sum, it might be argued that the White Paper at least ensured a continued place for environmental issues at the forefront of political debate whilst admittedly failing to fulfil heightened public expectations largely created as a result of government action over the preceding twelve months.

The European Community

Developments within the European Community are, of course, having an ever increasing influence on UK business practices. It is therefore of no little significance to note that the Single European Act makes it clear that environmental considerations are to be fully integrated into moves towards establishing an internal market. Indeed, there are already more than 200 extant EC directives concerning the control of air and water pollution, and further ones in the pipeline dealing with issues such as freedom of access to information on the environment and the problems of waste disposal. However, the most recent development, and one of great potential significance for the accounting profession, is the circulation for discussion of a draft directive calling for the compulsory environmental auditing of companies whose activities have a significant impact on the environment.

As a recent survey into UK corporate attitudes towards environmental issues conducted by Touche Ross Management Consultants (1990) points out, EC inspired environmental legislation is set to have an increasingly significant impact on all industrial and commercial activity in the future. It is therefore surely a cause for great concern that the same survey indicates a surprisingly high level of unawareness on the part of UK companies of the extent of EC initiatives in the area.

The above summary, although of necessity very brief, indicates not only the tremendous pace of recent developments in the public policy arena in respect of environmental issues, but also points to the signficant current impact, together with an even more significant future impact, on business activity. Furthermore, environmental issues are now firmly placed at the forefront of political debate with all the major parties having issued detailed policy statements. The activities of green pressure groups, the increasing influence of green consumerism and indeed the first stirrings of a green investment movement all tend to indicate that they will remain there for the foreseable future. Clearly, there are tremendous financial implications for business arising from ever increasing trends in environmental awareness and hence, inevitably, repercussions for the accounting profession – a point highlighted by a number of contributors to this book. It is to a consideration of these repercussions, both in terms of current and possible future developments, that we shall now turn our attention.

GREEN AWARENESS AND THE ACCOUNTING FUNCTION

Internal reporting

Perhaps the most obvious role for the accountant in the initial stages of the 'greening' of organizations, and one highlighted by Lesley Phillips (Chapter 4), will lie in the area of developing information systems capable of capturing the cost effect of adopting environmentally friendly practices. However, it would be unduly restrictive to see the accountant's role merely in terms of concentrating on financial implications. Indeed, Rob Gray (1990) has cogently argued that accountants tend to overestimate their abilities in the realm of attaching financial numbers to various aspects of business activity whilst, at the same time, probably underestimating their most important talent – that of the design of, recognition of, assessment of and control of information systems in an organization. As Roger Adams (Chapter 4) succinctly puts it, 'Systems and controls are the accountants bread and butter.'

Much recent discussion has centred on how best accountants may employ these latter talents in the development of what is becoming a prime tool for managing corporate environmental performance, the environmental audit. Roger Adams, in fact, goes so far as to suggest that:

In order for credible environmental audits to take place, the process must borrow wholesale from the experience and expertise which accountants and the accounting/auditing profession have developed over the years.

Environmental auditing has been defined by the International Chamber of Commerce (1989) as being:

A management tool comprising a systematic, documented, periodic and objective evaluation of how well environmental organisation, management and equipment are performing with the aim of helping to safeguard the environment by:

(i) facilitating management control of environmental practices.
(ii) assessing compliance with company policies, which would include meeting regulatory requirements.

The series of short case studies presented by Andrew Blaza in Chapter 9 indicates the extent to which leading companies are beginning to employ environmental audit, or review/monitoring, techniques. Further evidence for their increasing prevalence throughout British industry, particularly amongst large firms, is provided in surveys published by the World Wide Fund for Nature (Elkington, 1990) and *Green Magazine* (Grant, 1990), with names such as Lever Brothers, RTZ and Shell figuring prominently. Keith Lester (Chapter 2) outlines the many different types of audit that may be conducted ranging from reviews of particularly problematical sites or activities to a comprehensive audit of the entire business. John Elkington's (1990) description of current practices employed by BP gives an interesting insight into the practical application of such an approach.

Essentially, environmental auditing methodology is largely derived from longer established operational (or internal) and external audit processes developed and refined over many years by the accounting profession. Indeed, as Brian Jenkins (1990), Head of Audit at Coopers & Lybrand Deloitte, points out in outlining the approach adopted by his firm, just as is the case with the more traditional financial audit the environmental auditor operates most effectively by tracking laid down management procedures and assessing both whether they are likely to achieve their objectives and whether they are being followed. Thus it is by virtue of their experience and expertise in the realm of information systems and control procedures generally that accountants can make a considerable contribution in the environmental auditing field, notwithstanding their lack of detailed technical and scientific knowledge in respect of the environmental issues themselves.

Whilst the overwhelming majority of the literature on the development of internal environmental accounting and information systems, and particularly descriptions of practical corporate initiatives undertaken (see, for example Elkington, 1990), has focused on environmental auditing and review techniques, there are a number of other ways in which the accounting function can contribute towards organizations becoming more environmentally sensitive. One would anticipate, for example, the accountant playing a major role in emerging corporate procedures described by Andrew Blaza (Chapter 9) such as environmental impact assessments, the development of waste management strategies and improvement plans and establishing performance measurement systems which entail the setting up of mechanisms for collecting, collating and transmitting quantitative data.

The material introduced in Chapter 9 adds a practical flavour to much of the theoretical material presented in Rob Gray's (1990) study. Interestingly, Gray goes on to anticipate further developments which begin to go beyond the collection and dissemination of information and more directly integrates this information into the organization's day-to-day activities. Among his suggestions, all of which have clear accounting implications, are the following.

Environmental budgets

In order to integrate environmental awareness fully within traditional financial and marketing objectives one needs to be able to rank environmental criteria on some comparable level with the more traditional performance measures employed. One possibility is to allocate levels of environmental activity along with other levels of budget allocation to activity centres and, furthermore, to tie in an element of the reward and penalty system to the satisfaction of allocated budget level. Interdivisional transfers could be dealt with, in principal, by a system of financial charges (perhaps tradeable pollution permits) or the budgetary system kept in physical units and environmental interdependencies recorded accordingly.

Environmental hurdle rates for new investments

The conventional approach to discounting, whereby uncertainty is handled by employing short-term payback criteria and inflated discount rates, arguably discriminates against giving a fair weighting to environmental factors. For example, as Paul Hackett (Chapter 3) points out, the future cost of safe disposal at the end of an asset's useful life may not be taken fully into account, whilst environmental projects with long gestation periods and low values in current prices, such as reforestry, are undervalued. Using lower discount rates for particular environmental benefits would ensure that a significant present value would attach to them, even if they were to occur many years in the future.

Additionally it will be necessary to build qualitative criteria into investment hurdle rates. The previously mentioned Environmental Protection Act's espousal of the BATNEEC concept indicates that organizations will need increasingly in the future to provide both quantitative and qualitative analysis of a chosen project's environmental impact and be able to justify hurdle rates used. Thus one can anticipate accountants becoming increasingly concerned with the theoretical and applied development of investment appraisal methodologies capable of incorporating environmental factors.

Environmental asset maintenance

Assets essentially fall into three classes: critical natural capital (such as the ozone layer or the rainforests) that can only be expended with dire consequences, other natural capital (such as agricultural products or minerals) which can be renewed or substituted for use value, and man-made capital. Accounting techniques wedded to notions of private ownership and prices tend to encourage exploitation of the first two categories of capital and hence mitigate against environmental enhancement. Much critical natural capital is not owned and is therefore treated as a free good by traditional accounting systems whereas ownership of natural capital (and indeed some critical natural capital such as the rainforests) seemingly confers the right to abuse and deplete these assets. In Gray's analysis the notion of property rights inherent in the concept of ownership has to be amended towards a recognition that ownership involves stewardship, which entails a responsibility to care for and maintain the assets owned on behalf of this and future generations, whilst similar concepts of capital maintenance must be applied to non-owned critical natural assets.

The task for the accounting information system is to categorize the assets owned by and under the control of the organization, to keep track of transfers between categories and hence to indicate the extent to which each category of capital is being maintained. Some natural capital, i.e. the priced element, can be accounted for using historic cost accounting techniques, whilst much critical natural capital will be included as something like intangible assets (i.e. the estimated value to the organization of non-priced natural facilities). In the latter case reliance will have to be placed on a variety of media including description and physical quantities as well as financial additions and benefits/depletions and transfers. In sum, the aim is to simply inform decision-makers of the extent to which their particular organization is depleting the planet's capital!

The latter suggestions considered above clearly raise severe problems in terms of practical application. Nevertheless for environmental issues to become central to the corporate decision-making process experimentation along these lines, which raises issues starting to go to the heart of the organizational accounting system, is surely called for. One might further hope that organizations at the forefront of innovatory practice in developing environmental accounting systems are prepared to share their ideas and experiences. In Rob Gray's words:

(i) the issues are too important to let everyone . . . duplicate efforts behind closed doors and continually re-invent wheels: and (ii) the issues are considerably more important than trying to get a 1% market advantage over one's nearest competitor (p. 134).

As Andrew Blaza's contribution to this book makes clear, many organizations are active in developing information systems designed to promote good environmental performance but details released into the public domain are unfortunately somewhat superficial.

A further vital element of openness in the sphere of corporate environmental initiatives is that of keeping employees fully informed on issues of company policy and what the information system is seeking to achieve, as Janice Buck acknowledges in Chapter 2. Trade unions have an important role to play here, which is plainly spelt out by the contributions in Chapter 3. Paul Hackett points to the unions having decades of experience in consistent work for greater health and safety at the work place, which is clearly of relevance in the tackling of wider community problems, and spells out the fact that, 'Environmental protection will only succeed where there is transparency of information and open access. Consensus will be unachievable and preventive strategies unworkable when decisions are made in secret and verification denied.' Hilary Benn outlines the work his union, Manufacturing Science Finance (MSF), is undertaking in seeking improved dialogue between union and employers but also points to the prevalence of an unhelpful attitude on the part of government and many employers. Further evidence of an apparent unwillingness to involve trade unions more fully in discussion concerning the environmental aspects of organizational performance is provided by Alan Jackson's description of NALGO's campaign against water privatization.

Given that labour issues, in addition to strictly environmental concerns, are central to the green critique of modern industrial society, and figure prominently in European-wide debate over the quality of life ramifications of corporate activity as exemplified in the proposed EC Social Charter, Chapter 3 raises worrying implications in the context of the greening of British industry. We are, however, beginning to stray somewhat from a consideration of the accounting implications of increasing green awareness with which this chapter is essentially concerned. Nevertheless, we shall remain very much with the theme of the need for openness as we turn our attention to the external corporate reporting function.

External reporting

Survey evidence reviewed by George Harte and Dave Owen in Chapter 8 strongly suggests that UK companies in general currently give a low priority to the reporting of social, and more particularly environmental, information. Some interesting trends in disclosure practice on the part of companies identified as 'good disclosers' are, however, noted in the chapter. In particular there is a move towards publishing statements of objectives which encompass social and environmental issues in addition to the purely financial together with an increased prevalence for the usage of (potentially auditable) specific narrative, with, in some cases, external reference points being introduced in reporting on performance. Nevertheless, even on the part of the more innovative companies, information provision tends to be highly selective and largely public relations driven. In particular there appears to be a virtually universal reluctance to disclose bad news.

The slow response on the part of UK companies towards heightened public concern over issues of corporate social and environmental impact in terms of developments in external reporting practice is unfortunate in view of the fact that external reports are extremely valuable as a means of promoting public accountability, the need for which is central to the emerging green agenda. Furthermore, as Clare Roberts (Chapter 7) indicates, UK companies are generally failing to keep up with best European, most particularly German, practice.

One might expect pressure for UK companies to adopt a more rigorous and less partial approach, particularly in the area of reporting on the environmental impact of their activities, to come from a number of sources, in particular the following.

Domestic legislative developments

Whilst no statutory standards appear to be immediately on the horizon, the Environmental Protection Act and subsequent White Paper have, as has already been noted, demonstrated the beginnings of a commitment to greater openness. Pressures for extending this openness into the formal corporate annual reporting mechanism are already being felt. For example, the Labour opposition tabled an amendment to the 1989 Companies Bill during its committee stage which would, had it been successful, have required companies to explain their policy regarding control of pollution and to report any fines or other penalties incurred in respect of breaches of legislation. More recently the Campaign for Freedom of Information and Citizen Action Compensation Campaign have been actively lobbying for a private member's bill to force companies to disclose in annual reports details of environmental and safety offences together with information on compensation payments made to accident victims.

Supranational influence

We have already remarked on the rapid pace of developments within the European Community in terms of issuing directives on environmental matters. Obviously such developments will have a continuing influence, and indeed an increasing influence from 1992, on domestic legislation.

Perhaps more remotely in terms of immediate practical implementation, the United Nations Intergovernmental Working Group of Experts on International Standards of Accounting and Reporting (a Committee of the UN's Economic and Social Council) have, as Roger Cowe notes in Chapter 6, turned their attention to issues of environmental disclosure. Amongst their initial suggestions is a call for companies to disclose:

- environmental policy;
- environmental expenditure in the accounting period;
- future expenditure (contingent liabilities together with voluntary and semi-voluntary clean-up and restoration costs);
- activity and performance (for example, emission levels, noise levels, toxic waste, etc.) measured against statutory and internally generated targets.

The subject of environmental disclosure is firmly established as a continuing interest of the group. Their recent work in further refining the above broad recommendations is outlined by Anthony Carey in Chapter 4 who suggests that it could well prove a useful starting point in developing a more systematic approach towards the reporting of environmental issues.

Influential user and pressure groups

Consumer and investor pressure is clearly recognized as a major force that business has to reckon with by the representatives from the three major UK business organizations contributing to Chapter 2. The growing power of green consumerism is further discussed at some length by Richard Adams (Chapter 5) and has indeed apparently already exerted some influence on the corporate reporting function, particularly amongst companies in the retailing sector as the illustrations from the Body Shop and Tesco reports included in Chapter 8 indicate. However, one might anticipate that investor pressure is likely to prove a yet more potent force in bringing about changes in external reporting practice.

The latter half of the 1980s saw the concept of ethical or social investment rise to a position of some prominence in the United Kingdom. Its most visible manifestation is the recent proliferation of ethical and environmental unit trusts which, in addition to looking for a financial return, seek to base their investment portfolios on a number of social criteria – typically environmental performance, enlightened personnel policies, avoidance of relations with repressive regimes and absence of involvement in armaments manufacture, alcohol or tobacco products. In charting the emergence of the social investment movement on both sides of the Atlantic, Alan Miller (Chapter 11) notes that the establishment of such trusts in the United Kingdom has mirrored earlier trends in the United States. He goes on to point to signs that the wider institutional and more activitist approach to social investment over there is also beginning to take off here. This is particularly evidenced by the growing number of pension funds showing an interest in the social ramifications of their investment strategy, the establishment of support groups (such as EIRIS and PIRC) providing information and research backup for social investors and, most recently, the launching of a UK Social Investment Forum to further promote and encourage the development and positive impact of socially responsible investment.

Rachel Griffith, in a postscript to Chapter 11, highlights the serious limitations in the provision of information useful for the ethical, or social, investor within UK annual reports and suggests a number of improvements, particularly in terms of providing data on employment issues and corporate environmental impact. As the social investment movement continues to grow in size and influence one might expect it to exert increasing pressure on accounting policy-makers to take action in these areas. Significantly, deficiencies in the provision of environmental information within annual reports seems to be a concern shared by the more traditional, solely profit-seeking investor. Malcolm Cooper and Gilly Filsner (Chapter 6) argue that financial logic must take its place in the assessment of candidates for investment and the investor needs to know how environmental issues affect the 'bottom line'. In other words information should be provided which enables the investor to assess the savings being pursued and the costs involved in a strongly environentally aware corporate policy and which clarifies the current and future financial situation. Their view is that the profit motive will be more effective in furthering the green cause than the adoption of any ideological stance. Whilst the motivations are therefore very different, it nevertheless appears that the purely profit-seeking and the social investor share the same need for the provision of hard data on corporate environmental performance. Together their influence on the policy-makers is potentially considerable.

Corporate self-interest

As noted earlier, provision of information on environmental and social issues on the part of UK companies seems at the present time to be highly selective and largely public relations driven. This distinct tendency to err on the side of self-congratulation inevitably carries with it the risk of eliciting an increasingly cynical response from any intended audience. Indeed, one recent reaction has been the establishment by Friends of the Earth of a 'Green Con' award for companies making the most misleading claims! The most potent defence against corporate critics (for example, the Social Audit Movement, the development of which is described in some detail by Mike Geddes in Chapter 10) must surely lie in rigorous disclosure. Furthermore, as increasingly onerous environmental legislation imposes ever higher financial costs on companies, the scale of which is, for example, indicated by ICI's announcement in November 1990 that it intended to spend £200 million a year over the next five years on cleaning up its operations, it would seem eminently sensible to report fully in order to justify expenditure incurred. Certainly there appears to be a growing demand on the part of investors for such information to be provided, as we have just seen. Arguably, therefore, simple corporate self-interest represents the most immediate pressure for change in responding to current heightened levels of green awareness.

Possible developments in reporting practice

Two contributors in particular devote considerable attention to possible changes in external reporting practice so that the environmental dimension of performance may be captured. Rachel Griffith (Chapter 11), whilst being essentially concerned with a whole range of social issues of relevance to the ethical investor, makes a number of suggestions for the inclusion of information that would help the report user assess corporate environmental impact. In particular she suggests that companies could provide details on:

- consumption of energy and any measures being taken to reduce it;
- transport – information on size and make up of car and goods vehicles fleet and measures being taken to reduce usage of the road network;
- steps being taken to replace usage of hazardous substances, particularly those coming within the ambit of international agreement, such as the Montreal Protocol, or domestic restrictions, with more environmentally friendly alternatives;
- information on licences held, such as those for animal testing.

Roger Cowe (Chapter 6) also calls for the provision of specific data on the company's use of energy and physical resources together with information on waste output. Additionally, in order to make up a comprehensive environmental reporting package he highlights the need for:

- general improvements in reporting as envisaged in the Financial Report

(Arnold, Cooper and Shaw, 1990), which would in particular ensure that companies provide more meaningful information on objectives and plans and give report users more chance of assessing progress other than in a purely financial fashion;

- financial reporting of environmental expenditure and liabilities as recommended in the UN study referred to earlier;
- an environmental report indicating the company's broader impact on the environment and consisting of valuations of man-made and natural assets, transfers between these categories, and data on the maintenance of assets.

This latter suggestion clearly raises major practical problems, as we noted earlier in considering the issue of environmental asset maintenance in the context of developments in internal reporting systems. However, as Roger Cowe points out, the other proposals do not require the development of new measurement principles and could be reported tomorrow by companies which are environmentally sensitive.

Whilst Rachel Griffith and Roger Cowe point the way towards practical change in reporting practice which is largely achievable in the short term, Richard Adams (Chapter 5) highlights, in the latter part of his contribution, the immense task inherent in attempting to develop a comprehensive green reporting system encompassing the issues of renewable resource use, non-renewable resource use, pollution control and pro-environmental activities. Whether accountants have much of a role to play in developing reporting along these latters lines is, of course, highly debatable. In any event the issues raised in this latter contribution point the way to developments in the far distant future. Changes in reporting practice in the short term are more likely to be along the lines we have just been considering, where, as the contribution of Clare Roberts (Chapter 7) indicates, there is a growing wealth of European experience to draw on, and, I suspect, will also focus on the financial implications of heightened green awareness. As such these changes are likely to involve accountants who have, of course, traditionally been at the forefront of developments in external corporate reporting practice.

Auditing

Roger Adams (Chapter 4) raises the possibility that corporate environmental disclosures may not be considered credible by readers of the annual report unless the data is externally audited. He then goes on to suggest that it is within the capabilities of the accounting profession to assist in the development of both the methodology and the reporting framework of such an audit exercise. As we note earlier in considering issues of internal reporting, it is largely by virtue of their experience and expertise in the realm of information systems and control procedures generally that accountants can make a contribution in the environmental auditing field. Support for this view is forthcoming from a Gallup survey commissioned by Coopers & Lybrand Deloitte (1990) which sought to elicit views from finance directors and chief accountants in 108 large companies concerning the extent to which they considered environmental matters an issue for business, and more particularly the finance function. When questioned as to whether they would value commentary from their auditors on matters of environmental concern to the company over half (58%) suggested it would be helpful if comment was to be made on how good the company's management information systems and processes were in respect of environmental issues, compared to practice elsewhere.

A number of contributors to this book raise the issue of companies making publicly available the results of environmental auditing exercises, with Janice Buck (Chapter 2) mentioning the possibility of annual environmental audits not only being given equal status to, but also being incorporated within, the financial audit. Significantly, writing from the perspective of the purely profit-seeking and ethical investor respectively, the contributions of Malcolm Cooper and Gilly Filsner (Chapter 6) and Alan Miller (Chapter 11) both lend support to the notion of a published environmental audit report appearing with the annual report and accounts. The report published by Caird Group in their 1989 accounts, which is reproduced in Chapter 8, possibly provides a model for other companies to follow in this context.

Whilst one might confidently predict that environmental audits will become very much the norm for companies operating in particularly sensitive industrial sectors (the developments within the European Community discussed earlier will see to that) and that the accounting profession could well make a substantial contribution to developing appropriate auditing methodology, the environmental ramifications of corporate activity are also of more immediate relevance to the financial auditor. As Clive Wicks (Chapter 5) points out, there is little point in certifying the accounts of an apparently profitable company if it goes into bankruptcy shortly afterwards due to a failure to insure itself against claims for the environmental damage caused by its products or processes.

The fact that auditors have a responsibility to consider environmental issues in the context of carrying out the statutory financial audit, as these issues can have financial consequences which potentially impact on the true and fair view, is spelt out by David Pimm of Coopers & Lybrand Deloitte in a paper presented to a Workshop on Environmental Accounting organized by the European Institute for Advanced Studies in Management in December 1990. Amongst potential financial consequences listed in the paper are the following:

- obsolete stock arising from shifts in consumer preference, for example away from aerosols containing CFCs;

- a permanent diminution in value of production assets consequent upon such shifts in consumer preference, or indeed changes in legislation leading to a major process of the business being no longer economically viable in its present form;
- site abandonment costs, provision for which is common practice in the case of mining or oil and gas companies, may become a burden for many other companies, particularly those in the chemical industry, consequent upon European Community proposals to tighten up on the liabilities of business polluting land;
- contingent liabilities, the range of which in respect of environmental short-comings is unending, with particularly large liabilities deriving from health hazards where compensation claims can be enormous.

Additionally, the paper points out that a further area of potential financial consequence arises in respect of illegal acts, the auditor's responsibility in relation to which has recently been the subject of an exposure draft published by the Auditing Practices Committee. Broadly there appears to be two circumstances in which the auditor may have to undertake some work to assess the risk of material misstatement arising from breaches of legislation: first, in industries where failure to comply with environmental legislation can be expected to affect fundamentally the operations of the company – such a situation is most likely to occur in businesses where a high standard of environmental performance is required (e.g. the water industry) and those which are a major potential source of pollution or face high risks of environmental accident; secondly, and quite simply, in any business when in the course of carrying out his or her duties the auditor becomes aware of environmental shortcomings.

To sum up, increasing public (and legislative) concern with environmental issues has major potential repercussions for the auditor and the auditing function. In the long term one might expect the auditing profession to make a not inconsiderable contribution to the development of environmental auditing methodology *per se*. However, and of more immediate impact, the fact that environmental issues, and particularly company shortcomings in response to these issues, have ever-increasing financial consequences for business means that the financial auditor must pay due regard to them now in the conduct of current statutory audits.

THE DEBATE OVER ACCOUNTING'S ROLE IN PROMOTING GREEN AWARENESS: RADICALS vs. REFORMISTS

The above discussion concerning possible repercussions on the accounting function of current heightened levels of green awareness adopts very much what might be labelled a 'technocentrist' approach. In other words, there

is underpinning the analysis, a belief that the way to tackle our current environmental and social problems is by a process of objective analysis based on
the provision of 'better' information. Furthermore, it is largely assumed that
such problems can be accommodated within the prevailing socio-political
system, utilizing a free-market economy approach or, at most, a gradualist
liberal reform of the market system. Overall, little challenge is therefore posed
to prevailing economic orthodoxy, perhaps most notably propounded by the
Brundtland Commission (World Commission on Environment and Development, 1987) suggesting that industry is both central to the economies of modern
societies and an indispensable motor of growth. As such, the analysis appears
to be very much in tune with the overwhelming consensus of views expressed
by the wide range of contributors to this book.

One jarring note to this consensus is, however, struck by Mike Geddes
(Chapter 10). In a detailed analysis of the work of the social audit movement, the extent of which will no doubt be a surprise to many readers, he
particularly underlines the opposition of the movement to the economics and
politics of the market. In particular he stresses that, 'Social audit attempts
to challenge the hegemony of money over both the productive economy and
society, and of accountants – the technicians of money – over economic, social
and political decisions.' This latter 'radical' view has much in common with
the so called 'dark' green strand of environmentalist thought, from which
perspective accounting may be considered as being a craft, or discipline, which
is simply reflective of our current economic and political system – a system
obsessed with the necessity for economic growth. In a particularly penetrating
analysis the French philosopher André Gorz, for example, points out that:

> ... once you begin to measure wealth in cash, enough doesn't exist.
> Whatever the sum, it could always be larger. Accountancy is familiar with
> the categories of 'more' and of 'less' but doesn't know that of enough (Gorz,
> 1989, p. 112).

In other words, accounting is unable to cope with notions such as
'sustainable' or 'sufficient' and therefore is of very little relevance to the central
issues raised in the current green debate. The fundamental concern in Gorz's
analysis, then, becomes one of defining limits within which economic
rationality, and thereby associated accounting techniques, is to operate, rather
than permitting its seemingly never ending expansion. In particular, it is
necessary to reclaim areas of human activity as the preserve of moral or
aesthetic criteria and to deny the relevance of economic calculations when
essentially ethical principles are at stake. The call for a spiritual reawakening
is indeed central to much radical green analysis, a point which is clearly
recognized in critiques of traditional economic thought, such as those provided by Schumacher (1973) and Daley and Cobb (1990), which locate current
environmental problems in the spiritual failings of western society and

offer a new paradigm for economic and public policy issues underpinned by an insistence on the very need for a spiritual reawakening.

It may come as something of a relief to the reader to learn that I don't intend to pursue the spiritual angle any further, but would rather draw attention to the other major point of departure for a prescriptive analysis of society's current environmental and social malaise from a radical ecology perspective – its rejection of the pursuit of economic growth as an essential societal goal. As the authors of the influential Club of Rome report, *The Limits to Growth* (Meadows *et al*, 1972) point out, the proposal for some sort of non-growing state for human society is hardly a new one. Discussion of the concept can be traced back to the writings of Plato and Aristotle, through to those of Malthus and John Stuart Mill in the eighteenth and nineteenth centuries respectively, and on to modern economists such as Boulding and Mishan. More recently, the seminal work of Schumacher (1973) has inspired further development and analysis by a succession of contributors to 'The Other Economic Summit' (see Ekins, 1986). In sum, the radical ecologists' position is neatly encapsulated in Jonathon Porritt's (1984) comment that:

> If you want a simple contrast between green and conventional politics, it is our belief that quantitative demand must be reduced, not expanded (p. 136).

For the radical ecologist the route towards reducing quantitative demand lies in the economic system gearing itself towards meeting real need rather than satisfying demands expressed in the market-place, demands which the market system positively encourages and cultivates. Mike Geddes' discussion of 'needs auditing' gives a flavour of the type of analysis that may be employed in this particular context, although it must surely be acknowledged that there is currently a distinct lack of an adequate framework for distinguishing real needs from mere wants (a point addressed at some length by Andrew Dobson (1990) in his highly readable introduction to the ideas underpinning green politics). Thus, it may appear that the problem of reducing economic demand may well at the moment appear intractable. Nevertheless there does appear to be a large measure of consensus amongst radical green opinion, as exemplified in the work of writers such as Ryle (1988), Gorz (1989) and Seabrook (1990), that the achievement of such an end entails making a sustained assault on the market system, the basic flaw of which lies in its ineluctably expansive tendency.

In providing a particularly penetrating analysis of this point, Gorz (1989) draws attention to the fact that maximum efficiency in the valorization of capital within the market economy necessitates the finding of purchasers for ever increasing levels of production and thereby the expansion of consumption well beyond the satisfaction of actually felt needs. In particular, in order to place consumption in the service of production, commercial advertising techniques are continually employed to induce a craving on the part of consumers to have what others appear to possess. Furthermore, under the market system there is very little incentive to tackle the problem of prevailing levels of poverty, as merely eliminating needs – which are limited – cannot assure indefinite growth in production whereas wants and superfluous desires are, by contrast, potentially unlimited.

While still on the subject of satisfying needs, rather than gratifying wants, it must of course be pointed out that many people living on this planet, notably in the Third World but also only too clearly in the West, do indeed live in real need. In pursuing the ideal of sustainability (the current buzz word!), which entails shifting resources from current to future production, it would seem only equitable that the major sacrifices in consumption be borne by the wealthy, who do after all consume the bulk of our material sources. Such a notion, in addition to its probable political unacceptability in a country such as the United Kingdom driven by consumerist values and a ruthless materialistic philosophy, calls into question the strategies of green consumerism and socially responsible investment, as put forward by two contributors to this book. Alan Miller (Chapter 11), for example, stresses that socially responsible investment is an additional consideration in investment, not a substitute for sound commercial judgment, in other words making money. Richard Adams (Chapter 5) in turn underlines the fact that green consumerism appeals to the affluent who choose to afford the extra cost of environmentally benign products. Under such eco-consumerist strategies, as David Pepper (1989) has noted, the poor, far from being favoured, seem to be effectively disenfranchised as the power of the purse comes to represent the quintessential vote in the capitalist world economy. Additionally, of course, such strategies, with their emphasis on individual action, arguably underrate and consequently don't square up to, the power of vested material interests to block change.

Essentially the radical critique outlined above calls into question the view generally advocated by contributors to the following part of this book that one can successfully pursue social or environmental and traditional financially orientated goals largely simultaneously within the workings of the market economy. Instead the assault on the market system that is advocated goes beyond a mere critique of the rules of economics, or indeed accountancy, and requires nothing less than the invention of new institutions for a different, non-market economy. Unfortunately radical critique doesn't extend to the elaboration of new 'accounting' systems which would operate in such an economy. However, there is a clear denial of the efficacy of applying the principles of neoclassical economics, via market-based incentives such as those advocated in the Pearce Report, towards solving environmental problems, or indeed of seeking to develop an accounting response within this particular framework.

Whilst acknowledging the strength of the above outlined radical critique the line taken in this particular chapter, and which indeed pervades the book as a whole, is largely informed by notions of pragmatism. In essence the approach may be labelled 'reformist'. A reformist perspective noting accounting's newly won position of prime importance in the public policy arena, an observation indeed made at the beginning of this chapter, suggests that, like it or not, accounting information is therefore vitally important in moulding perceptions of what constitutes good and bad organizational performance. As Anthony Hopwood (1984) so cogently puts it, accounting's strength lies in its ability to make visible and discipline performance. However, in focusing on issues of profit and efficiency whilst ignoring the social and environmental dimensions of organizational performance, conventional accounting techniques are heavily implicated in the current environmental mess we've got ourselves into. Interestingly, a similar observation was made by the famous economist John Maynard Keynes some sixty years ago when he noted that, 'Under the peculiar logic of accountancy, the men of the nineteenth century built slums rather than model cities because slums paid' (Keynes, 1933). The reformist, therefore, goes on to argue that there is a pressing need to reform accounting practice so that the wider aspects of performance are captured, and hence enter into the decision-making process. A similar motivation, incidentally, underpinned the efforts of accounting researchers in the 1970s who sought to develop workable social accounting measures and reporting techniques (see Gray, Owen and Maunders, 1987).

A further major justification for the adoption of a reformist perspective lies in the observation that whereas radical ecology provides us with a fundamental critique of current patterns of consumption and production, very little serious thinking seems to have gone into developing actual strategies for change, a point particularly drawn to our attention by commentators such as Frankel (1987) and Dobson (1990). The fact that many of the environmental issues now exhibiting such a hold on public consciousness have been continually brought to our attention by environmentalists, perhaps most starkly in the Club of Rome report referred to earlier, over the past twenty-odd years would suggest strong grounds for believing that our current environmental and social malaise is of such a magnitude that abstract theorizing provides an insufficient response. Certainly this is the impression conveyed by environmental blockbusters such as Bill Mckibben's (1990) widely acclaimed *The End of Nature*. In suggesting that nature has already been irredeemably altered and that the ecological holocaust is indeed already happening Mckibben minces no words noting, for example, that:

> The choice of doing nothing . . . is not a choice, in other words. It will lead us, if not straight to hell, then straight to a place with a similar temperature (p. 134).

Recent press reports suggesting that damage caused by acid rain and the destruction of the ozone layer are both of a far greater magnitude than previously envisaged should make us wary of dismissing too lightly such warnings. Indeed it would appear that in the United Kingdom particularly we have little cause for complacency in view of Greenpeace's (1990) highly detailed analysis indicating that Britain very much remains the 'dirty man of Europe'. Amongst no fewer than 17 reasons advanced for the retention of this undesired title are allegations that Britain is both the largest sulphur dioxide polluter and largest producer of ozone destroying chemicals in Western Europe, one of the world's largest importers of radioactive waste, lags behind most major Western European countries in cutting carbon dioxide emissions and continually delays or reneges on joint agreements to control various polluting activities. Whether or not one is entirely convinced by such allegations there are clearly grounds for suggesting that practical change is an urgent necessity. At the very least, by starting to move away from the exclusive emphasis on short-term financial performance prevailing throughout most of the past decade within the United Kingdom economy the reformists do begin to point the way towards practical change.

PROBLEMS IN IMPLEMENTING AN ACCOUNTING RESPONSE

Whilst it is possibly unfortunate to have to conclude this chapter on a somewhat pessimistic note, we do have to face the fact that pursuing practical change along the lines suggested by a reformist perspective does pose fundamental problems in terms of calling forth innovations in accounting theory and practice. A flavour of the scale of the practical problems encountered is given by Brian Ing's analysis in the concluding chapter. However, the scale of change in accounting methodology that would be necessary in order to fully embrace green issues is arguably much greater still.

As the chequered history of past attempts to develop social accounting practice indicates, a major stumbling block is encountered in the accountant's traditional obsession with, and insistence on, objectively verifiable and largely financially based measurement techniques. Schumacher (1973) in his seminal work *Small Is Beautiful* effectively pinpoints the danger of seeking to press what are essentially non-economic values into the framework of economic calculus:

> All it can do is to lead to self deception or the deception of others; for to undertake to measure the immeasurable is absurd and constitutes but an elaborate method of moving from pre-conceived notions to foregone conclusions: all one has to do to obtain the desired results is to impute values to the immeasurable costs and benefits. The logical absurdity, however, is not the greatest fault of the undertaking: what is worse, and

destructive of civilisation, is the pretence that everything has a price, or in other words, that money is the highest of all values (p. 38).

The need to get to grips with the problem of developing non-financial social, or quality of life, indicators in measuring economic performance is indeed drawn to our attention by both Paul Hackett (Chapter 3) and Mike Geddes (Chapter 10). Simply then, what is called for if accounting is to make a real contribution to the green debate is nothing less than a fundamental re-examination of the marginalist and neoclassical economic underpinnings of the accounting craft whereby accounting can only seemingly operate when prices are generated by transfer of property rights in the market place. As noted earlier such a re-examination is absolutely necessary in tackling the concept of environmental asset maintenance.

In addition to moving away from an exclusive emphasis on financially quantified 'bottom line' performance measures, the necessity for which arises from the recognition that not all 'values' are quantifiable, other aspects of the traditional accounting framework stand in need of basic change in order to incorporate a green dimension. Roger Cowe (Chapter 6) alludes to a number of these aspects of which three in particular – the emphasis on single time period, historic performance measurement and the concentration on the economic entity as the focus of reporting – are clearly fundamentally flawed in the context of developing green accounting. The point here of course is that ecological issues are long term in nature and particularly affect future generations whilst environmental impacts are 'externalities' as far as the entity itself is concerned. This latter aspect highlights a major difference between the accountant's conceptual framework and that of the ecologist which Rob Gray (1990) particularly draws attention to. Put very simply the accountant's perceptual field is constrained by reference to events that directly impinge on the particular economic entity he or she is dealing with and that can generally be described in financial terms. By contrast ecology is a holistic discipline dealing with a complex interreacting set of systems which support life. Clearly therefore some recognition of the importance of systems theory and concepts is vital if accounting is to succeed in truly gaining a green dimension.

For such a fundamental rethink as that suggested above to take place green concerns must be incorporated centrally within the accounting standard setting process rather than being treated as merely peripheral. The recently outlined work programme for the newly constituted Accounting Standards Board suggests that this is unlikely to occur. However, as is noted by a number of contributors, a more modest piecemeal approach towards tackling some of the issues raised by the emerging green agenda in terms of developments in the accounting function is eminently feasible. Much will depend upon the will of the accounting profession to push for some form of environmental report to be added to company reporting packages. Perhaps significantly, Roger

Cowe (Chapter 6) expresses strong doubts whether such a will exists. This viewpoint is perfectly understandable when one recalls a notable previous attempt by the accounting profession to re-examine financial reporting in the light of modern needs and conditions – *The Corporate Report* (Accounting Standards Steering Committee, 1975) – where the profession saw fit to inject little urgency into the debate following the publication of that document and broadly adopted a posture of sitting on the fence.

In view of the subject matter of this book it is of some interest to note the view expressed by Basil Jeuda (1980) that the real problem with *The Corporate Report*, as far as the profession was concerned, lay in its espousal of the concept of public accountability and promotion of the needs of other user groups in addition to capital providers. Further evidence that the traditional concern of the accountant with the needs of finance capital may prove a major stumbling block in terms of incorporating a green dimension into accounting practice is provided by Colwyn Jones (1990). A programme of interviews he conducted with 57 accountants working in six large manufacturing and merchanting firms elicited the overwhelming response that, in their view, profit is the prime, if not only, goal of business and social responsibilities are deserving of a very low level of priority!

SUMMARY AND CONCLUSIONS

Following a review of some of the major recent developments in the public policy arena which are increasingly setting out the terms of the green agenda for business it was noted that, in terms of the reformist perspective which underpins these developments, the accountant can make a not inconsiderable contribution in essentially two areas:

- Developing management information systems to assist organizations in responding at the micro level to the various macro level initiatives which have recently taken place, most notably those introduced by the Pearce Report.
- Developing external reporting practice, including the auditing function, in order to promote public accountability, the need for which is clearly central to the emerging green agenda.

A major stumbling block encountered in developing green accounting may, however, lie in both the nature of the accounting craft and the 'world view' exhibited by its practitioners.

It may well be apposite to recall here the view expressed by the authors of *The Corporate Report* in 1975 that what they termed 'social' accounting ' . . . will be an area of growing concern to the accounting profession and one in which it has an opportunity to help develop practical reporting techniques'.

Unfortunately this particular opportunity is one which the profession has not seen fit to grasp. A continued lack of responsiveness to renewed public concern over the environmental and social ramifications of business activity would, in my view at least, do little to enhance the prestige of the profession. Indeed, as Anthony Carey (Chapter 4) clearly acknowledges, being part of a profession implies having a concern for the public interest, and therefore being prepared to address the main issues facing society. If, as suggested earlier in this chapter, our methods of accounting are implicated in the present environmental crisis it is no less than our duty in the public interest to attempt to contribute to the reversal of that crisis. The overall tone of the contributions that follow is that accounting can indeed make a contribution. The ball is in the accounting profession's court!

REFERENCES

Accounting Standards Steering Committee (1975) *The Corporate Report*, London, ASSC.
Arnold, J.A., Cooper, M.J.D. and Shaw, J.C. (eds) (1990) *Financial Reporting – The Way Forward*, London, The Institute of Chartered Accountants in England and Wales.
Coopers & Lybrand Deloitte (1990) *Environment and the Finance Function: A Survey of Finance Directors*, London, Coopers & Lybrand Deloitte.
Daley, H.E. and Cobb, J.G. Jnr. (1990) *For the Common Good: Redirecting the Economy Towards Community, the Environment and a Sustainable Future*, London, Greenprint.
Department of the Environment (1990) *This Common Inheritance*, DoE White Paper, London, HMSO.
Dobson, A. (1990) *Green Political Thought*, London, Unwin Hyman.
Ekins, P. (ed) (1986) *The Living Economy: A New Economics in the Making*, London, Routledge & Kegan Paul.
Elkington, J. (1990) *The Environmental Audit: A Green Filter for Company Policies, Plants, Processes and Products*, London, Sustainability/WorldWide Fund For Nature.
Frankel, B. (1987) *The Post Industrial Utopians*, Cambridge, Polity Press.
Gorz, A. (1989) *Critique of Economic Reason*, London, Verso.
Grant, G. (1990) 'Environmental audit: cradle to grave', *Green Magazine*, Summer, pp. 53–7.
Gray, R.H. (1990) *The Greening of Accountancy: The Profession After Pearce*, London, Chartered Association of Certified Accountants.
Gray, R.H., Owen, D. and Maunders, K. (1987) *Corporate Social Reporting: Accounting and Accountability*, London, Prentice Hall International.
Greenpeace (1990) *Why Britain Remains the Dirty Man of Europe: A Report for Greenpeace by Media Natura*, London, Greenpeace.
Hopwood, A. (1984) 'Accounting and the pursuit of efficiency', in Hopwood, A.

and Tomkins, C. (eds), *Issues in Public Sector Accounting*, Oxford, Philip Allan.

International Chamber of Commerce (1989) *Environmental Auditing*, Paris, ICC.

Jenkins, B.G. (1990) *Environmental Audit: An Auditors Perspective*, text of a talk given at Glaziers Hall, London, 27 March 1990, London, Coopers & Lybrand Deloitte.

Jeuda, B. (1980) 'Deserving a better fate – The Corporate Report', *Accountancy*, February, pp. 76–8.

Jones, C. (1990) 'Corporate social accounting and the capitalist enterprise', in Cooper, D.J. and Hopper, T.M. (eds), *Critical Accounts*, London, Macmillan.

Keynes, J.M. (1933) 'National self sufficiency', *Yale Law Review*, Vol. 22, pp. 755–763.

Lickiss, M. (1991) 'Measuring up to the environmental challenge', *Accountancy*, January, p. 6.

Mckibben, B. (1990) *The End of Nature*, London, Penguin.

Meadows, D.H., Meadows, D.L., Randers, J. and Behrens, W.W. (1972) *The Limits to Growth*, London, Earth Island.

Pearce, D., Markandya, A. and Barbier, E.B. (1989) *Blueprint for a Green Economy*, London, Earthscan Publications.

Pepper, D. (1989/90) 'Green consumerism – Thatcherite environmentalism', *New Ground*, Winter, pp. 18–20.

Pimm, D. (1990) *The Environment and the Auditor*, paper presented to a workshop on Environmental Accounting organized by the European Institute for Advanced Studies in Management, December, London.

Porritt, J. (1984) *Seeing Green: The Politics of Ecology Explained*, Oxford, Basil Blackwell.

Ryle, M. (1988) *Ecology and Socialism*, London, Radius.

Schumacher, E.F. (1973) *Small is Beautiful*, London, Blond and Briggs.

Seabrook, J. (1990) *The Myth of the Market: Promises and Illusions*, Bideford, Green Books.

Touche Ross Management Consultants (1990) *Head in the Clouds or Head in the Sands? UK Managers' Attitudes to Environmental Issues – A Survey*, London, Touche Ross.

World Commission on Environment and Development (1987) *Our Common Future*, Oxford, Oxford University Press.

Part Two

THE FUTURE OF
GREEN REPORTING

Chapter Two

INDUSTRY AND COMMERCE

Environmental reporting – a view from the CBI
Andrew J. Blaza, The Confederation of British Industry

Green awareness: an opportunity for business
Janice Buck, The Institute of Directors

Protecting the environment:
a new managerial responsibility
Keith Lester, The British Institute of Management

ENVIRONMENTAL REPORTING – A VIEW FROM THE CBI

Andrew J. Blaza

As a means of ensuring a more stable basis for long-term business planning, the CBI has for some time advocated a move away from a purely *reactive* approach to environmental issues, beyond just responding to new legislation. With the publication in 1986 of its booklet, *Clean up – it's good business*, companies were given guidance based on case studies of how good environmental performance could bring significant benefits to the business and to the environment.

In 1989 as environmental issues became positioned at the top of the business and political agendas and with the prospect of further potentially restrictive legislation, the case for a proactive approach to environmental protection and enhancement was even more convincing. Accordingly, the CBI published its Environmental Action Plan for the 1990s incorporating advice to business on key environmental issues.

Many large companies had already formulated their own internal policies on environmental management, some of which had been published in annual reports or through separate bulletins.

For others, particularly the small to medium sized companies which did not have the internal capability for monitoring the constantly changing environmental situation, it was proving increasingly difficult to focus on precisely what were their potential impacts on the environment.

There had been much criticism of industry's lack of response to the increasing demands of environmentalists, the 'green consumer' and indeed the public in general. Industry was seen as the cause of the problem without recognizing the fact that it is clearly the source of any solutions.

Within this atmosphere of confrontation, many smaller companies were finding it difficult to respond, particularly in the absence of sound and well-balanced information, often only available to larger companies with the resources to keep up to date.

Organizations faced with the apparently ever-increasing costs of responding to environmental legislation are tending to concentrate on the burdens to the business which these seemingly cause. Clearly a new way of approaching the problem is required with the focus switching away from costs and burdens to concentrate on opportunities and benefits, thereby enabling companies to tackle environmental issues in a more positive, proactive manner.

Having shown them how to focus on their potential environmental impacts and identity problem areas, the solutions can be found and, more importantly, implemented.

Prior to 1990, although there had been a number of excellent publications on the system of environmental auditing, few if any offered really practical advice on how smaller companies could implement a system of positive environmental management within their organizations.

In mid-1990, as part of the Environmental Action Plan, the CBI published its guidelines on environmental auditing, although the process described in this publication went beyond 'auditing' or 'reviewing' to include a system for implementing the necessary improvement plans. To help companies unfamiliar with the process, the guidelines incorporated a preliminary checklist of ten areas of company activities with simple questions, the answers to which highlight those areas requiring further action.

One of the problems during 1990 which distracted attention away from real progress in implementing corporate environmental management systems was the confusion of environmental auditing with financial auditing, the latter being seen as a one-off external validation resulting in a relatively brief reference in the company annual report but with little emphasis on action.

There have been many definitions of environmental auditing but all agree on one point which is that the process, far from being a single act, involves a thorough and continuous internal review of all the potential impacts of an operation on the environment. What is more, the process should be voluntary, not conducted in response to legislation with the potential for restricting the scope of the exercise to defensive compliance with whatever elements managed to survive the process of introducing such legislation.

The CBI view has always been to encourage companies to conduct the exercise voluntarily using as inducements the considerable benefits which can accrue to the business. In the guidelines, environmental auditing is defined as:

> The systematic examination of the interactions between any business operation and its surroundings. This includes all emissions to air, land and water; legal constraints; the effects on the neighbouring community, landscape and ecology; and the public's perception of the operating company in the local area.

Although compliance with legislation clearly forms part of the review process, it does not stop there but goes beyond to consider factors within the business not covered by the legislation. Furthermore, it is not a mere 'green-washing' public relations exercise as many perceived it in the first instance. Of course done well, it could considerably enhance the public's image of the organization, which is why companies are prompted to publish the results at the end.

Essentially environmental auditing is a total strategic approach to the organization's activities which some have described as a 'cradle to grave' approach. This seems not to go far enough, since by the 'cradle' stage much of the fate of the product or process has already been determined. A more thorough expression as defined in the CBI guidelines is 'conception to resurrection', meaning design to recycling.

Clearly the term environmental auditing has been much in use (some would say misuse) and in view of its potential for confusion with financial auditing, the term *environmental reviewing* is tending to be used instead.

However, whatever term is used to describe the process, no amount of 'auditing' or 'reviewing' will produce any lasting benefit to the business or the environment without a sound management structure within the organization for implementing, monitoring and revision of the improvement plans which are generated as a result.

Fundamental to business success in the current climate of operation is the ability to respond, not just to new legislation, which in any case is no longer seen as the main pressure for change on environmental issues, but to the various demands of customers, investors and the general public. In fact for many companies, market pressures are now the main driving force on the environment. Those companies which can identify the relevant factors at an early stage and act on them can gain considerable competitive advantage: for example, in the development of new products and services; in demonstrating to customers that quality products are matched by equally good environmental performance in their manufacture and marketing; and ultimately, in a highly competitive situation, in ensuring long-term viability of the business operation.

Such a response requires a different and much more strategic approach to environmental performance than mere 'compliance with legislation'. Not that legal compliance is unimportant but rather, by taking action in advance of legislation – for example by designing in new technology from the start rather than resorting to expensive retro-fitting at a later stage – there will be considerable benefits to the business and the environment.

One of the other problems of 1990 which hindered progress in corporate environmental performance was the tendency in some quarters to promote the idea that the environment as a business issue was different and required a special approach. This is clearly untrue. The key to long-term business success is good management performance and the environment is just one of the key issues which management should be addressing.

Vital to the success of the operation is the ability to identify the factors affecting the business, the collection and assessement of data, reporting to management in such a way that decisions can be taken and actions defined and incorporated into strategic business plans.

By adopting a proactive stance, the management will be better placed to consider the environment, not as an additional cost burden but rather as an opportunity for gaining competitive advantage. In many areas which will be covered by the process of environmental management there will be significant cost savings, for example in the areas of waste minimization and energy efficiency. In other cases, opportunities for new products and services, enhanced image with customers, investors, employees and the general public, reduced risk and liability, will all add to the continuing viability of the business and provide a more stable basis for long-term business planning.

In conclusion, therefore, environmental reporting in the future should go beyond a 'compliance led' process, with its emphasis on costs and burdens, to a market-driven voluntary approach which identifies opportunities and benefits on which management can base long-term business plans.

A sound internal management system will need to be established as for any business issue with the following key features for assessing and improving environmental performance:

1. Setting corporate objectives based on a thorough knowledge of the business *and* its potential impact on the environment. This will involve collection, assessment and reporting of data on those factors in the market which affect the business and its environmental performance, which will include, but not be restricted to, current and future legislation. Management will use this information to formulate and publish as appropriate, the objectives in the form of a *Corporate Environmental Policy Statement.*
2. Reviewing performance against these objectives in order to measure variances and identify ways of reducing or eliminating the variances, to be reported to management for inclusion in strategic business plans (*Environmental Audit* or *Review*).
3. Implementation of business plans and continuous monitoring to ensure that the goals identified in these plans are being achieved in the timescales set. Again variances from plan will be reported to management so that revisions can be made (*Environmental Strategy*).

GREEN AWARENESS: AN OPPORTUNITY FOR BUSINESS

Janice Buck

The Institute of Directors (IOD) has a membership of nearly 39 000 individual company directors and business leaders (32 000 in the UK and 7000 overseas). It has no corporate membership and no political affiliation. The Institute's membership reflects the demography of companies in the UK economy which comprises 3500 quoted companies and some one million private companies and also reflects the sectoral make-up of the economy. It is, therefore, in a unique position to represent the general interest rather than that of any particular sector of the economy.

As owners of a stake in the country and its future, company directors enjoy a great privilege. Hand in hand with this goes the responsibility to ensure that by their actions they will not have reduced the quality of life available to their children and grandchildren.

While the last century has seen economic development which has created great and continuing increases in material wealth, there can be little dispute that the sources of that development are unsustainable into the next century. Resources such as air and sea and forests cannot continue to be exploited at the current rate. Something must be done to ensure a future for our planet and for our descendants.

Surveys of members conducted by the IOD have shown an awakening awareness of the need to take action now to prevent irrevocable damage to the environment. In a survey conducted in July 1990, of the sample of directors interviewed, 49 % said that their board's activities have changed in the last twelve months to reflect growing environmental concern and 43 % indicated that their company has a specific environmental policy.

The responses to environmental concerns and the actions taken are varied. Many smaller, service based companies do not yet see 'green' issues as being relevant to them although they too are polluters. The leading edge of good environmental behaviour is found in those industries which have traditionally been the most visibly polluting industries: oil and chemicals. Multinational corporations also tend to be further down the road because they must comply with the most stringent requirements in the world in one or other of their subsidiaries.

What then can be done to raise the awareness and then the behaviour of all companies to the level necessary to ensure the future of our planet and its ability to continue to play host to mankind? This section examines some ways in which this may be achieved, bearing in mind that a thing done willingly will be far better done than one done unwillingly.

It is vital that more businesses follow the example of the leading companies and take on the responsibility of self-regulation. Many companies are beginning to accept the concept of product stewardship. The good company is not responsible for one brief episode in the life of a product – it has a cradle-to-grave responsibility for the product. This acceptance needs to be extended to more areas and more businesses.

Once the corporate philosophy is in place, there is a base for the company to undertake annual environmental audits. These should be given equal status with financial audits – even incorporated within them – if industry does not want to be accused of putting profits ahead of their responsibilities. It is not enough to set targets for environmental improvement – companies must ensure that the targets are met if they are to have any significance. Having said that, companies must be aware of the dangers involved in legislation imposing environmental auditing. There are simply not enough people qualified to undertake this type of work for all companies to comply with any such regulation. The basis for success in financial auditing lies in the common body of accounting rules which must be obeyed. There is no such common ground in diverse production processes.

The ultimate aim of environmental auditing is the disclosure of information about production processes and their by-products. To the extent that it is not commercially sensitive, businesses could be proactive in providing this information to the public. Companies engaged in processes or storage operations which are, or are perceived to be, potentially dangerous or unpleasant or degrading should adopt a policy of openness towards and dialogue with the local communities in the vicinity of the sites concerned. Current US legislation gives local citizens the right to information – as does the 1990 UK Environmental Protection Act – and to visit sites. Openness is crucial to obtaining planning permission for future sites and the local public can help as a watchdog to keep companies on their toes. If the information is provided voluntarily then there is less reason to pass legislation forcing firms to comply. It can also be a useful learning process for the company to find out exactly what they do produce in the way of emissions and waste.

Research is vital for staying ahead, both of the opposition and of global degradation. Good companies do it already. It is the quality of the research which is important. This is not a problem to be solved by throwing money at it – especially money from the public sector. Research should be market driven and with the rise of the green consumer and broad-brush ambient standard regulation it should be a source of business opportunity to most companies rather than a threat to their existence.

There are many other business opportunities arising from the move to make the world a better place to live in. There is much to be done to clean up existing blighted areas. This will provide opportunities for businesses engaged in that line. The forward-thinking company will spend money now to prevent pollution rather than spend vast amounts later to try to clean up the problems that it is causing.

One industry which is taking its responsibilities seriously is the advertising industry. It is aware of the power of the 'environmentally friendly' tag on anything that is for sale. For many consumers there is so much seemingly contradictory information available that labelling and advertising are really their only way of differentiating between products. It is in the interests of the advertisers to retain control of the regulation of their industry so they are ensuring that members take strict notice of any claims that are made about the properties of various goods before incorporating them into an advertisement.

This is becoming more important as consumers become more educated and more discerning in their buying habits. If the market place is allowed to work efficiently with accurate price signals and information, catering to the green consumer can provide the marketing edge for the proactive company. For the reactive company the green consumer can provide the market policing.

It is clear that although self-regulation can be used to a certain extent, there will come a time when regulation must also be considered. Producer-orientated regulations need to be carefully tailored to the realities of producers' corporate structures. Overwhelmingly these will be limited companies; this always poses problems as to where penalties, whether civil or criminal, should fall. As economic entities companies are easy to expose to economic penalties, whether compensatory or punitive. However, given the possible scale of penalty that might be awardable in environmental cases, there is a clear case for ensuring that such penalties should be limited to a company's shareholders' funds, shareholders being the only parties who have voluntarily assented to the assumption of a company's general risks. Without such a provision, an award which led to a company's liquidation would fall on creditors, who do not necessarily have any responsibility whatsoever for the contravention.

Many punitive regulatory provisions which apply to companies are given additional teeth by making liable to penalties any director, manager, secretary or officer of the company who consents to or connives at a corporate offence. In the case of an offence of strict liability, this exposure is extended to any such officer to whose neglect the occurrence of the offence is attributable. The inclusion of a provision to this effect appears to be standard practice in all new statutes of a regulatory nature. Such an approach is not objectionable *per se* in that it places personal responsibility for ensuring compliance with the people who are recognized as the company's directing 'mind and will'. There are, however, restrictions on the value of this approach. Although it encourages directors to take a positive attitude to compliance at the strategic level, it would not necessarily prevent disaster at the operating level. While it may be politically attractive to punish companies and directors, general requirements as to environmental safety imposed on those directly in charge of operations might be more effective (cf. health and safety legislation or the responsibility of masters of vessels).

The existing regulations as laid out in the Environmental Protection Act specify BATNEEC (best available technology not entailing excessive cost) as an objective in the control of air pollution. However, the definition of BATNEEC is left to HM Inspectorate of Pollution which is seriously under-resourced for its present workload. There is concern among businesses on two levels: first, that BATNEEC will rapidly become simply BAT whether or not it is affordable; and secondly, that easy problems will be fixed first accompanied by a show of strength. More difficult problems will be left and will probably be the more environmentally damaging processes. This approach would do nothing to level the playing field for industry.

Because of this problem of inadequate regulatory staff in the foreseeable future, encouragement should be given to firms to regulate themselves to the greatest extent possible. The adoption by companies of a voluntary code of environmental good behaviour should be encouraged. Many firms are already finding that energy conservation and waste reduction are actually economically as well as environmentally beneficial. This message should be driven home to a much greater extent. The IOD's philosophy is that private ownership of resources gives not only the right to their use, but also the responsibility for their stewardship. In this way regulation and self-regulation can be made synergistic.

In any action that is taken it must be remembered that industry alone is the creator of wealth. One has only to look at the worst examples of pollution in Eastern Europe and the Third World to realize that poverty breeds environmental damage. It is only when people are freed from their daily struggle for personal survival that they have the time or effort available to think about the survival of the planet in a form fit to support future generations. It is only through industry that world incomes can be raised to a level where all people can raise their aspirations.

There are important employment considerations for businesses as well. A company which has a good record as an employer and as a protector of the environment is likely to find it easier to recruit staff than one with a poor image. At times of skills shortage this is very important and may compensate in the long term for any initial rise in production costs due to new health and safety standards.

It is essential that a company's environmental policy fits into the company's overall business strategy. Although there is a great deal that companies can do to protect the environment within the employment field these are matters for the company and not for government legislation.

As environmental concerns become more important for business there will be an increasing need for education and training in this field to equip employees to implement both company policy and national legislation. In many cases massive damage can be done by one bored, alienated or unaware employee. The case of Perrier water is a spectacular example of how the failure of one employee to change one filter can have international repercussions. Employees must realize that everyone has the responsibility to care for the environment, but they will need training to understand how their job performance can make a difference. This too is likely to lead initially to increased employment costs but may well have long-term benefits.

Increasing awareness of the environment should be seen by business as an opportunity rather than a threat. In addition to the opening up of new areas of activity, environmental protection will provide benefits such as clean water and air as inputs to production, and cost savings from measures such as increased energy efficiency. While concern for the environment may be seen at the moment as a marketing edge to attract the green consumer, in time it will become the price of entry into the market.

In conjunction with the concept of individual responsibility there should be the widest possible extension of private ownership to give people a stake in the environment. Individual stewardship of the air, the waters, the seas and the land can only help to ensure the improvement of their quality.

PROTECTING THE ENVIRONMENT: A NEW MANAGERIAL RESPONSIBILITY

Keith Lester

The British Institute of Management has recently drawn up a policy statement regarding management and the environment and is in the process of identifying ways in which the policy can be implemented in order to ensure environmentally friendly management.

Management is about the effective use of resources and the art of optimizing their use, treating the environment as a resource. Caring for the environment requires the right attitude of mind and a long-term view.

The objectives of individual managers pursuing the goals of the organization for which they work may conflict with the policies needed for proper consideration for the environment. This dilemma is only eliminated when organizations adopt and follow a policy which does give proper regard to the needs of the environment. That such policies are adopted may depend upon regulation resulting from legislation. This in turn is a function of 'short termism' centring on the necessity to obtain votes through the ballot box thereby enabling political parties to exercise power in government.

BACKGROUND

The major problem facing our civilization has now been widely recognized as the threat to the natural systems that sustain life on the planet. The environment is now seriously threatened by the by-products of many industrial processes as well as the products themselves. We are currently polluting the air we breathe, the water we drink, wash and swim in, the soil that produces our crops, the animals we farm and the fish we eat. Our current lifestyle is unsustainable and will be disastrous for our planet unless appropriate changes are made.

Man has already become an endangered species in many countries. One billion people are suffering from malnutrition and starvation now, and 20 million of these die each year from starvation or related diseases, at least half being children under four years of age.

Unless we manage our planet's resources sustainably it is estimated that we will have 2 billion starving people by the year 2020. This may include 200 million refugees from low-lying areas which could be flooded as the seas rise, assuming that predictions of global warming materialize. The annual death toll through starvation and related diseases could rise to 30 million. This will not be just a Third World problem, but will affect the lives of many millions in the developed world as well. The costs of environmental mismanagement have been estimated as at least 6% of the gross national product of most industrialized countries.

The cost of environmental damage is usually underestimated. In 1979 the OECD ministers estimated that it represented between 3% and 6% of the gross national product of the OECD member states. The German government has taken the lead in trying to establish the financial losses caused from environmental destruction (Table 2.1).

The estimate of an atmospheric pollution cost of £16 500 million represents a figure calculated through a household survey in Berlin on the willingness to pay for purer air grossed up to the total German (FDR) population. The willingness to pay reflects a 'loss of enjoyment caused by air pollution'. It covers some of the less tangible costs such as impaired well-being.

However, this balance sheet is still not a sufficiently comprehensive enumeration of the costs of environmental pollution as it gives minimum figures and the actual damage is much higher. Nevertheless in 1984 this was equivalent to over £35 billion and represented 6% of the German (FDR) gross national product.

Table 2.1 Federal Democratic Republic of Germany: the cost of environmental pollution

Damage category	Cost (£ million per year)
Atmospheric pollution:	Approx. 16500
– health damage	Over 800–2000
– material damage	Over 800
– damage to crops	Over 35
– woodland and forest damage	Over 1900–3000
Water pollution:	Well in excess of 6000
– damage to rivers and lakes	Over 5000
– damage to North and Baltic Seas	Well over 100
– damage to ground water	Over 1000
Soil damage:	Well in excess of 1800
– Chernobyl and Chernobyl prevention costs	Over 800
– disposal of inherited pollution	Over 600
– habitat and species conservation costs	Over 350
– token entry: miscellaneous soil contamination	Well in excess of 35
Noise:	In excess of 1100
– loss of residential value	Over 1000
– loss of productivity	Over 100
– noise-induced welfare payments	Over 140
Total damage:	Well in excess of £35 800 million

Source: Industry and the Environment (June 1990) paper by Clive Wicks of the World Wide Fund for Nature (with acknowledgements to Raymond Carlisle, *Environmental Business Journal* (December 1989) and George Winter (EEC book), *Business and the Environment*).

MAJOR CONCERNS

There are three interrelated areas of concern, namely resources, pollution and population. In each case the use or generation of these must be balanced by the ability of the environment to accommodate the increase or decrease. These three matters need to be managed sustainably at all levels and times.

Resources

Resources like timber, land, fresh water and wildlife that at some time in the past could all have been considered inexhaustible are now no longer so, and in addition there is now concern about light, wind, waves and oceans as well. The conclusion is therefore that at some future date resources considered inexhaustible today may become exhaustible. It is therefore imperative to move to reduce the utilization of non-renewable resources. Furthermore, there is a requirement to recycle where possible and not to squander resources, but rather to seek sustainable development instead.

Pollution

In addition to conserving the quantity of resources on the Earth, there is clearly also a need to maintain their quality. Ideally, each manufacturing industrial operation should be a closed cycle, producing as far as possible the minimum of waste products and, even then, they should be environmentally benign. Effluents, for example, discharged into rivers and seas should not adversely affect the ecosystem into which they are being discharged. The same philosophy applies to pollution and waste products from transport systems, which themselves are part of contemporary industrial society. A further example relates to domestic waste, whether sewage outlets to the sea or dry waste which is dumped in waste-fill sites. These latter take up valuable areas of land to bury potentially useful raw materials, and there is the attendant risk of chemicals leaching into the soil – and hence into the ground water – and producing potentially noxious gases.

Population

Mankind must also face the fact that projected population figures will exceed the 'carrying capacity' of the Earth, using currently known systems. People must be given the opportunity, education and resources to manage their numbers in a sustainable way. We must meet the needs of the present without compromising future generations' ability to meet their needs, and through the use of advancements in knowledge and selective investment seek sustainable development.

Not only is the human race multiplying at an enormous rate as a whole but a few industrial countries consume a disproportionately large share of the resources and create most of the pollution and waste. People are also a resource within the environment and should be treated as such, for example by making better use of the skills of older members of our society.

CURRENT RESPONSES

Some organizations are declaring a commitment to the environment by formulating an environmental policy, setting overriding environmental goals within an organizational policy statement. One, for example, commits the company concerned to 'reduce to a minimum the ecological impact of all its activities'; another aims to protect the health and safety of its employees, customers and others in the conduct of its activities, and to limit the adverse effects on the environment in which these activities are carried out.

Organizations in the public sector have made environmental issues a cornerstone of their policies and have adopted 'green charters' which cover, for instance, the promotion of conservation and sustainable use of natural resources and the limitation of pollution to meet environmental standards.

The European Community has already started to take action against countries which ignore new environmental legislation. A recent report from the Confederation of British Industry, written in conjunction with PA Consulting Group, indicates that companies see local authorities, consumers and pressure groups as the major influences on their environmental policies, and notes that local authorities and other governmental organizations are growing less likely to grant licences for certain activities unless they meet appropriate environmental standards.

Consumer pressure is demonstrably a force to be reckoned with. Supermarkets and cosmetic manufacturers are taking heed of 'green' issues and finding their actions good for business. Many multinational companies have already taken this problem seriously while most smaller and medium sized companies have not, and will lose market share unless they react quickly.

Finance houses are under pressure to be more selective in their investments and organizations can no longer expect insurance companies to reimburse every loss where environmental damage could have been avoided. These matters do have a major impact on finance, costs and profits. No manager can afford to ignore them.

GUIDING PRINCIPLES

Already a powerful and growing coalition of environmental interests and investment fund managers are soliciting organizations to subscribe to a set of wide-ranging environmental, health and safety measures. Based broadly on the Valdez Principles, named after the Exxon tanker accident in Alaska, they are defined below:

- Restoration and protection of the biosphere.
- Sustainable use of resources.
- Reduction, recycling, conversion and safe disposal of waste.
- Wise use of safe energy resources.
- Reduction of environmentally related risks.
- Marketing of safe products and services.

- Development of economic and financial models that include the full costs of compensation for damage to or restoration of the environment.
- Public disclosure of environmental health or safety hazards.
- Appointing environmental directors and managers.
- Assessment of environmental practices and annual environmental audit.

ACTIONS FOR MANAGEMENT

What should management do today to safeguard tomorrow's environment and how should it be monitored and reported? Attention should be given to three areas: operational management, a comprehensive overview, and safety control and risk management.

Operational management

Environmental guidelines can be drawn up for every organization which create an awareness in the organization of the needs of the environment. Managers' responsibilities with respect to the environment will be defined, while consumer pressures will determine whether such leadership is an adequate environmental response. The following list of actions has been based upon the CEFIC environmental guidelines for the European Chemical Industry Federation in conjunction with the Environmental Guidelines for World Industry established by the International Chamber of Commerce:

- Prepare and regularly review at the highest management level company environmental policies and establish procedures for their implementation.
- Foster among employees at all levels an individual sense of responsibility for the environment and the need to be alert to potential sources of pollution associated with their operations.
- Assess in advance the environmental implications of new processes, products and other activities, and monitor the effects of current operations on the local environment.
- Minimize adverse environmental effects of all activities and take steps to minimize waste and conserve energy.
- Take the necessary measures to prevent avoidable accidental releases of pollution.
- In cooperation with the public authorities establish and maintain contingency procedures to minimize the effect of accidents that may occur.
- Provide the public with the information necessary to enable them to understand the potential environmental effects of an organization's operations and be prepared to respond positively to expressions of public concern.

- Provide the public authorities with the relevant information and assist them in establishing well-founded environmental regulations.
- Provide appropriate advice to employees and customers on safe handling, use and disposal of the company's products.
- Ensure that contractors working on the organization's behalf apply acceptable environmental standards.
- In transferring technology to another party, provide the information necessary to ensure that the environment can be adequately protected, avoiding the transfer of environmental problems.
- Promote research into the development of environmentally sound processes and products.

Comprehensive overview

An in-house environmental review should establish the current position and allow plans to be prepared with respect to all resources used. These reviews should quantify the parameters involved and set measurable goals, maximizing usage and minimizing waste. The environmental audit may be an internal or independent review.

Environmental audits will increasingly feature as part of an organization's activities. These may include site audits, making spot checks on activities and areas where there has been a history of environmental problems or where difficulties might be anticipated. Some audits may relate to activities such as transport where the activity crosses the boundaries of different businesses. In other circumstances the audit of an entire business may be carried out, possibly using the organization's statutory auditors and other expertise external to the organization, or staffed completely from resources internal to the organization. Legislation will undoubtedly increase the impact of compliance audits to ensure adherence to prescribed regulations. There will be 'duty of care' audits, for example, regarding waste disposal. In addition there are possibilities of audits of companies which act as agents outside the UK, and of audits on individual topics such as air pollution which review the effectiveness of the company in handling the chosen topic.

The environmental audit will concentrate on key questions. The initial question, and first step, will be to establish whether there is an environmental policy for the organization. Examination of different areas of the business will reveal where business activities currently produce, or have the potential to produce, environmental impacts which do not conform to the organization's policy, or are otherwise unacceptable. Investigations into the way in which the actual or potential problems are being handled and ways recommended for improvement to meet current and expected standards will take place. Historical and future trend patterns will be reviewed to identify changes in the organization's perceived environmental performance, or other organizations similar to itself.

Safety control and risk management

To mitigate possible environmental disasters plans should be prepared which are strategically proactive, as opposed to being operationally reactive, with full commitment from the board, management and staff. Most man-made disasters are avoidable.

A POLICY FOR MANAGEMENT AND THE ENVIRONMENT

The policy for management being considered by the members of the British Institute of Management is set out in Table 2.2.

Table 2.2 A policy for management and the environment

Management should:

- Recognize its obligations to owners, employees, suppliers, customers, users, society and the environment.
- Appoint directors or managers with responsibilities that include environmental issues.
- Educate and train all employees in environmental excellence.
- Make the most effective use of all natural resources and safe energy sources for the benefit of the organization and the overall public interest.
- Promote the use of sustainable resources and minimize the use of finite resources.
- Reduce the amount of waste, avoid harmful pollution and find ways of reprocessing or converting waste materials into useful products and safely disposing of the residue.
- Actively seek to restore and protect the biosphere.
- Reduce environmentally related risks.
- Market products, services and processes which create the minimum environmental damage.
- Be willing to exercise influence and skill for the benefit of the society within which the organization operates.
- Ensure that all public communications are true and unambiguous, with full disclosure of environmental, health and safety issues.
- Develop economic and financial models where appropriate which include the full cost compensation of damage or restoration to the environment.

As part of the implementation of the policy there will be enhanced reporting and monitoring requirements at all levels. Increasing legislation will continue to add pressure for organizations to implement policies appropriate to the environment. During the past twenty years there has been the development of elements of social disclosure in statutory accounts through company legislation, but so far little progress has been made on environmental reporting. However, the situation could change quite rapidly during the next decade covering some of the topics discussed earlier.

The organizational response to implementation will be governed by what it is seeking to achieve and, for example, something may be done only when the costs and penalties of not acting are too high. Such penalties might be the closure of the business and/or the directors being imprisoned. On the other hand an environmentally friendly response by the organization may influence customers, employees and regulatory authorities in favour of the organization.

To assist in promoting a wider understanding of environmental matters the British Institute of Management in particular, and other organizations, are providing courses and brochures and applying resources to the development of training programmes.

In the longer term the continued habitation of the planet will depend upon the effective use of sustainable resources and the adoption of practices which will enable the aspirations of future generations to be realized. This may be expressed briefly as 'good management of the environment is good management'. To achieve this, management and reporting systems will have to be modified or developed to provide the newly demanded information.

REFERENCES

Whilst literature citations in the text have been kept to a minimum in the interests of readability, I have drawn heavily on the following sources in preparing this contribution.

British Institute of Management (1979) *The Environment – Management's Responsibility*, BIM Management Checklist No. 63.

Carlisle, Raymond J. (1989) 'Environmental stewardship', *Environmental Business Journal*, December.

Confederation of British Industry, *Clean Up, It's Good Business*, CBI, Centre Point, New Oxford Street, London WC1.

Confederation of British Industry, *Managing Waste – Guidelines for Business*, CBI (see address above).

Conseil Européen des Fédérations de l'Industrie Chimique, *Industrial Waste Management*, CEFIC, Avenue Louise 250/71, B1050, Brussels, Belgium.

Elkington, John (1989) *The Green Capitalists*, Victor Gollancz.

Gray, R.H. (1990) *Trends in Corporate Social and Environmental Accounting*, Paper prepared for the British Institute of Management.

Jackson, T. and Roberts, S. (1989) *Getting Out of the Greenhouse*, Friends of the Earth, 26–28 Underwood Street, London N1 7JQ (Tel: 071-490 1555). Price: £2.50. A checklist on the environment is also available.

Winter, G., *Business and the Environment*, Commission of the European

Communities, 8 Storey's Gate, London SW1. Contains 22 environmental checklists for practical use.

World Wide Fund for Nature, *The British Response to the Brundtland Report*, WWF, Panda House, Weyside Park, Catteshall Lane, Godalming, Surrey GU7 1XB (Tel: 0403 42644).

World Wide Fund for Nature, *The Environmental Audit – A Green Filter for Company Policies, Plants, Processes and Products*, WWF (see address above). Price: £20.

World Wide Fund for Nature, *Managing Environmental Issues in Organizations*, WWF (see address above). Free from WWF.

ACKNOWLEDGEMENTS

In preparing this chapter acknowledgement is given to the members of the committee who prepared the paper *Management and the Environment* for the British Institute of Management:

Arthur Barber, BSc, MSc, MBIM, AIIS, Director, Disaster Management Ltd

Chris Bennett, BSc (Eng), DMS, AIPM, FBIM, Consultant, Macmillan Davies Consultancy

Robert Gilchrist, BA, MSc, ABIM, AIIS, Director, Disaster Management Limited

Ged Lawrenson, BSc (Econ), DipTP, DMS, MRTPI, MBIM, Chief Planner, Merton Borough Council

Hazel Prowse, BSc (Physics), DMS, MBIM

Alan West, BSc, CEng, FIGasE, FInst E, MBIM

Clive Wicks, FBIM, MCIM, MIEx, Dip Ex, Industrial Policy Executive, World Wide Fund for Nature.

Chapter Three

THE TRADE UNION MOVEMENT

Developing a trade union charter for
the environment
Paul Hackett, The Trades Union Congress

The trade union as environmental campaigner:
the case of water privatization
Alan Jackson, NALGO

Green negotiating: the MSF approach
Hilary Benn, Manufacturing Science Finance

DEVELOPING A TRADE UNION CHARTER FOR THE ENVIRONMENT

Paul Hackett

A series of national and international disasters, growing scientific evidence of world-wide hazards, first-hand experience of new pollution effects on water, food and personal health are among key factors producing a public awareness that the quality of life on this planet is at risk.

The TUC identifies itself with that feeling and accepts the challenge to play a leading part in raising alarm about the present situation, and turning a general commitment to the environment into practical and urgent action. In doing so, and in working with others who share that feeling, the trade unions do not come to the task as newcomers. Decades of consistent work for greater health and safety at the workplace have led trade unionists to seek also to tackle community problems – by pressing for better housing, cleaner air, smoke-free cities and in countering pollution arising from the effect of transportation of hazardous wastes or substances used at work.

The results of a diminution of public protection and regulation, the process of privatization and an intensification of competition have brought new dangers. Urgent government action – at home and internationally – and public expenditure are necessary. Employers must meet their responsibilities, accepting the principle of 'the polluter must pay'. Multinational companies must not be permitted to be predators of the world's environment.

But the trade union movement accepts its responsibilities to act, too. Precisely because we have done so much, we are aware of how much needs to be done. To this end, Congress in 1989 adopted the General Council's statement 'Towards a Charter for the Environment', a central feature of which entailed the establishment of an Environment Action Group (EAG). The Group has made significant progress on the agenda set out at the 1989 Congress in not only laying down a clear policy framework for action but also in beginning to bring the environmental challenge into the workplace. In particular, the Group has raised awareness of the social dimension to the environmental debate and made it clear that trade unions have a special responsibility and a positive contribution to make.

The work of the EAG is outlined in a report presented to the 1990 Congress at Blackpool. It deals in turn with the major global issues, the main national and local concerns and the response at government, corporate and workplace level. The Group has sought to identify the issues, and develop policies for action. Where the issues are global in nature, notably those of climate change, acidification and ozone depletion, the Group has taken on a special responsibility in establishing its international role as the collective value of trade unions in Britain.

A key element of the EAG Report is the outlining of 'A Policy Framework for the 1990s'. A number of aspects of the framework have major implications for the accounting function and it is to these that we now turn our attention.

A POLICY FRAMEWORK FOR THE 1990s

Sustainable development

The central policy problem in the 1990s will be how to reconcile growth, environmental protection and the quality of life. The Group endorse the views of reports such as those of Brundtland[1] and Pearce[2] that economic and environmental growth are compatible. The Group believe that this can be achieved by adopting the concept of sustainable development, as recommended

---

1. World Commission on Environment and Development (1987) *Our Common Future*, Oxford, Oxford University Press.
2. Pearce, D. Markandya, A. and Barbier, E.B. (1989) *Blueprint for a Green Economy*, London, Earthscan Publications.

by the above reports, i.e. that the environmental impact of growth is managed in such a way that future generations are able to sustain living standards and make further progress. The Pearce Report was commissioned by the government to identify how economic and industrial policies could be developed in a way which would reflect the full cost of using environmental resources, which are for the most part used more or less as free. The report's main recommendations, which are likely to form the basis of further action by the government, were:

- economic and environmental objectives should be integrated in future policy-making;
- environmental policies should anticipate future problems, not just react to problems already with us;
- environmental resources should be measured by physical and monetary national accounts; and
- the 'polluter pays' principle should be the basis for future policy initiatives.

While accepting the merits of the Report's recommendations, the Group considered a more qualitative approach was needed. As such the Group added six important reservations to the main recommendations proposed by the Pearce Report.

First, there is no working, agreed and practical definition of sustainable development. Nor will it be easy to develop one without improved national accounts which measure both in physical and money terms the stock of environmental assets. The Group believe that a definition must include reference to the *quality of life* by using a number of indicators, such as air and water quality or educational qualifications. But above all it must be seen as *credible and practical* if it is to be taken seriously in future policy-making, and if it is to be widely accepted by employers, trade unions, and the general public.

Secondly, sustainable development rightly focuses attention on future generations, and the need to pass on to our children the means to maintain and improve living standards. But the Group give equal importance to *fairness and equitable solutions* to today's environmental problems. At the global level this means fair treatment of the concerns of developing nations by the industrialized world. At the national level, the poor and low paid should not be expected to shoulder an unfair share of the cost of environmental improvement.

Thirdly, the concept of sustainable development is now widely accepted in principle in many industrialized countries, but some – notably the United States – are far less committed to coming to terms with the *practical implications*, such as the cost of meeting environmental targets. The view that economic growth and environmental protection are compatible is also less commonly accepted in Japan than other industrialized countries. Many developing countries are rightly worried that concerns about the consequences of pollution by the industrialized world will restrain their own development and living standards, and divert resources from traditional aid programmes.

Fourthly, the Group believe that some environmental assets can – and almost inevitably will be – run down. These must be offset by *technological advances* and by improvements in *education and training*, if future generations are to tackle environmental problems successfully. While acknowledging that some assets are so sensitive and for practical purposes irreplaceable, the Group do not believe it is realistic to talk as if the current environment can be handed over unchanged and intact.

Fifthly, the Pearce Report in particular has done much to show policy-makers and commentators how to work towards placing a value on the environment and hence give practical expression to the concept of sustainable development. But the Group believe that there are also considerable limits to this approach, which must be recognized. Not all assets can be valued and in many cases – for example, when life or health is concerned – a *monetary measure* does not seem to be appropriate.

Finally, Pearce and other reports have supported the 'polluter pays' principle, whereby industrial and other polluters pay for the amount of environmental damage concerned. The Group acknowledge this is likely to be adopted by international bodies such as the EC Commission and the OECD and feature in UK government policy, but believe this approach also has drawbacks which need to be taken into account. Without more research and accurate environmental accounting it will be difficult if not impossible to assess the damage each polluter causes accurately and to set the penalty cost correctly. Moreover, there are some pollutants which are so dangerous that their elimination or strict control by statutory regulation is essential.

National accounts, cost-benefits and discounting

The Group believe that practical first steps can be taken to make sure environmental assets and resources are more fully reflected in policy-decisions. This will require improvements and changes in national accounting procedures and in the use of cost-benefit analysis and discounting techniques in assessing particular projects.

The national accounts as they exist do not properly measure environmental damage. The oil spill from the *Exxon Valdez* could actually boost US GDP because while the environmental damage is not counted other factors such as clean-up costs are. Similarly, there has been a long standing problem in measuring the value of public services and public sector productivity which add to the quality of life, such as education and health care.

The public sector already often uses cost-benefit analysis to decide which projects should go ahead. This should be extended and developed. The failure of the government to face up to environmental impacts of road and rail on a comparable basis has been one reason why the proposed high speed rail link to the Channel Tunnel can find no private sector investor, and is contributing to under-investment in the rail system elsewhere in the country. Cost-benefit analysis could also be useful in regulating both private and public sectors by showing which regulatory regime could achieve the desired standard in the most cost-effective way.

The conventional use of 'discounting' gives a rate of return over a project's life, and is essential in setting priorities for which projects ought to be tackled first. But this conventional approach discriminates against environmental concerns. The future cost of safe disposal at the end of the asset's life is not fully taken into account. Moreover, it undervalues environmental projects with long 'gestation' periods and low values in current prices, such as reforestry. The whole issue of 'sustainable development' raises the fundamental question of how investment decisions giving environmental benefits can take account of the interests of future generations. Some international studies suggest that a discount rate far lower than the conventional rate is needed. 'Zero time preference', whereby a benefit in the year 2050 or 2100 is as valuable as a benefit today, is impracticable. However, as a number of studies have shown, if a discount rate of about 2% was used for certain environmental benefits, then significant present value would attach to the value of such benefits even if they only occurred fifty years from now. Institutions such as the newly created East–West Bank (BERD), to be located in London – which will be largely concerned with investments in infrastructure and the environment among other matters – could usefully be an innovator in this field if it could draw on national funds on this basis.

This Group believe that conventional practices and measures must be improved and changed so that environmental concerns are more accurately reflected in policy-decisions. The Group therefore recommends:

- separate *national* accounts on environmental assets should be drawn up, as recommended by the Pearce Report;
- better instruments should be developed to identify and measure the contribution of *public services* to the quality of life;
- above work to be overseen by an *independent advisory committee* working with the Central Statistical Office and professional accountancy bodies and able to commission independent research;
- more *flexible use of cost-benefit and discounting criteria* especially for major public sector projects with very long lifetimes, taking full account of environmental concerns and closure and disposal costs; and
- development of *'compensation funds'* to deal with closure and disposal problems.

An environment action plan

The government invited a debate on environmental issues which should feature in the White Paper eventually published in September 1990. The Group's initial response to this invitation was a submission, *Environmental Issues and Policy Implications: Towards the White Paper* (TUC, March 1990) which addressed itself to some of the basic concepts and principles which it was felt ought to feature in the White Paper.

The Group's submission called for a three stage approach to tackling environmental problems. First, there should be *sound and independent scientific research* to identify the scale, nature and seriousness of the problem. Secondly, these should be a public debate on the scientific evidence, aimed at developing *a consensus view* on the need for action and the targets and standards which should be adopted. Thirdly, there should then be consideration of what *mix of policy instruments* would best achieve the agreed goals – using regulation, market mechanisms (such as taxes) and planning.

The Group argued that this approach should be based on a clear commitment to a number of principles:

- independent, objective and balanced *research*;
- open and free access to *information* on environmental issues;
- encouragement of public debate and consultation as a basis for *consensus and agreement*;
- adequate *enforcement* inspection;
- recognition of value of *public services* to the quality of life;
- development of *new rights* in the workplace;
- seek *international agreement* on standards and enforcement;
- underpin policies by *transfer of resources* to the developing world.

To put these into effect, the government should draw up an Environment Action Plan for the 1990s and beyond, based on public discussion and consultation. A coordinated approach to the environment is called for covering central and local government and environmental protection agencies. The main features such a plan could cover are as follows:

Aim:	set down environmental objectives, targets and timescales;
Assessment:	impact on economy and quality of life and industrial implications, especially for jobs, training, competitiveness and health and safety;
Means:	policy mix needed to achieve objectives using pollution charges, taxes, subsidies, regulation and planning;
Responsibilities:	clear responsibility for taking action between central and local government and environment protection agencies;
Financing:	implications of financial costs and revenues and who is expected to pay for what.

INSIDE AND OUTSIDE THE WORKPLACE

Trade unions and the environment

The EAG believe that the working and living environments are intimately linked, and that action to improve the former benefits the latter. In the face of growing public concern over both global and local environmental issues the Group have emphasized that:

- trade unions have a special role and responsibility because most external environmental concerns originate in the workplace – giving unions a frontline environmental responsibility;
- traditional trade union concerns about the advancement of living standards and quality of life should be part of policies aimed at combating environmental pollution;
- trade unions must fully participate in the decision-making process at every level; and
- the trade union role must involve environmental rights as well as obligations.

The Group have begun to develop a workplace response, in part building on the experience of trade unions in the traditional health and safety field. Where appropriate, the Group have looked towards extending and integrating health and safety into new workplace environmental areas. Attention has also focused on devising joint strategies with employers on questions of mutual concern, such as raising employee awareness and the effects on the workplace of introducing control technologies and complying with new pollution standards. In particular, the Group have worked on the trade union response to environmental audits, on training and retraining strategies, on improving information flow, communications and participation both inside and outside the factory gate, and on devising education courses on the environment for union officers and lay officials.

Environmental audits

Environmental auditing is a relatively new development, prompted by the need to improve environmental performance and ensure compliance with company policy, laws and regulations. Although initially a preserve of firms operating in high-risk sectors such as chemicals, the concept, if not the practice, of environmental auditing has since spread to virtually all industries as well as public services and local government.

There is now an emerging consensus that environmental audits represent a practical and effective way of relating environmental problems and issues directly to the workplace. The ILO says that 'environmental auditing is an effective means to manage the working environment in the framework of tripartite cooperation'. Some of Europe's largest conglomerates consider the systematic auditing of environmental processes and systems, along with environmental impact assessment (which considers potential rather than current environmental effects) as central to their environmental management system. The Integrated Pollution Control measures introduced under the Environmental Protection Bill may force thousands of UK manufacturers to submit some form of environmental audit statement when applying for an authorization permit. The European Commission, meanwhile, is currently drafting a framework law requiring companies in all EC countries to carry out a systematic examination of the environmental effects of their operations, including all emissions to air, land and water, and the impact on the local community.

At the UNECE Bergen Conference governments, industry and unions agreed on the need for more widespread use of environmental auditing. The Bergen 'Joint Agenda for Action' which the UK is party to, stated that:

> In drawing up environmental audits employers should consult workers and their trade union representatives; in particular, information should be provided on those environmental regulations and standards which will affect the pattern of our work, or the viabilty of the plant.

The EAG believe that environmental auditing provides an opportunity for active trade union involvement at the plant, sector and local level. Particular consideration has been given to ensuring that attempts to control pollutants inside the workplace as they affect workers (i.e. in terms of health and safety) are compatible with standards relating to emissions and discharges. Building on the knowledge and experience of trade unions in conducting workplace health and safety audits and the widespread recognition among employers that employee involvement is crucial to the success of an environmental audit, the EAG have undertaken work on three key aspects of auditing: the approach to audits and the process of union involvement, the objectives of audits, and the scope of subjects to be covered. Joint consultation with employers and environmental groups on all three aspects is currently under way with the intention of publishing clear TUC-approved guidelines for union officers and lay officials. In addition, the EAG will continue to press the case at national and international level for proper union involvement in environmental auditing.

Attention is also being given to increasing awareness of such audits, both inside and outside the workplace. In particular, the Group believes that management and unions should seek to ensure that relevant information contained in an audit passes into the public domain.

The issues and procedures arising from local authority or public service audits will naturally differ, though the EAG consider that environmental

Table 3.1 Trade unions and environmental audits

Approach to audit
- Does the company have an environmental policy? How does it relate to health and safety policy?
- Who in the company is responsible for environmental policy and what monitoring and assessment is being conducted?
- What steps have been taken to raise company awareness of environmental issues?
- Is the company prepared to set up a joint union/management group on environmental auditing or bring the issue under the umbrella of existing health and safety committees?
- Is the company prepared to negotiate an Environment Agreement on auditing which sets out the union role, joint procedures, methods and issues to be addressed?

Objectives of audit
- Determine and improve overall environmental performance of production processes, facilities and equipment.
- Verify and improve compliance with international, national or local laws and regulations.
- Assess and improve compliance with company (or joint union-company) policies, standards and targets.
- Provide information on all aspects of environmental protection (including employment and training implications).

Scope of audit
Pollution control and compliance
- What pollutants are produced (e.g. water discharges, air emissions)? What monitoring and compliance procedures are in place?
- What processes, products and materials are used which offer potential for switching to less/non–polluting alternatives?
- How are hazardous materials stored and transported? How is solid/liquid waste disposed of? Are CFCs and asbestos present?
- What procedures are in place to prevent/deal with pollution accidents?

- Do company vehicles use lead free petrol and are there plans to fit catalytic converters? Does the company encourage/assist employees to use public transport?
- What policies are in place to develop environmental training and retraining?
- Is pollution and environmental information available to all employees and the local community?
- Is the company's health and safety policy consistent with environmental policy? Has a health and safety audit been conducted?
- Has the company carried out assessments under the Control of Substances Hazardous to Health Regulations 1988?

Energy efficiency and recycling
- Does the company assess energy use and is there scope to enhance energy efficiency/conservation? What level of priority/awareness is given to energy efficiency?
- Is energy conservation taken into account when buildings are constructed or refurbished? What insulation standards are used?
- What ventilation/comfort problems are likely to arise from energy savings?
- Is energy efficiency a factor in vehicle and equipment purchasing?

Others
- What is the scope for waste capture and recycling?
- Are products over-packaged and are biodegradable materials used?
- Does the investment policy of the company, including that of the pension fund, involve environmental considerations?

Public consultation
- Incorporate into local planning procedures.
- Joint meeting with local authority.
- Careful consideration to observations by public.
- Feedback of above into audit assessment.

Source: TUC General Council's Report to Congress (1990), p. 53.

auditing is as applicable to the NHS as to ICI. However, the scope for effective auditing is limited where management systems and responsibilities have been fragmented as a result of privatization and contracting out.

Table 3.1 indicates the sort of approach, objectives and items that unions may consider when seeking involvement in company-based environmental auditing.

IN CONCLUSION

Free and open access to information on all aspects of pollution abatement and compliance is central to achieve a wider understanding and essential to effective enforcement. The 'right to know' should extend from the individual consumer, to the local community and into the workplace. Management and unions have a special responsibility to ensure that environmental information is accessible, understandable and open for discussion. Environmental protection will only succeed where there is transparency of information and open access. Consensus will be unachievable and preventative strategies unworkable when decisions are made in secret and verification denied. The TUC believes that the 'right to know' must also be matched by the 'right to participate' and the 'right to influence'. For the unions, seeking to raise standards inside the workplace, this means building on existing health and safety rights and engaging in constructive and open dialogue with their employers across the entire range of environmental policies and issues.

THE TRADE UNION AS ENVIRONMENTAL CAMPAIGNER: THE CASE OF WATER PRIVATIZATION

Alan Jackson

NALGO's interest in the environment depends partly upon the services we represent. Our largest membership group, local government, has an obvious interest in environmental matters, not least because the government department overseeing local government is the Department of the Environment. We have environmental interests via our other services, such as water, electricity, health, gas and higher education. In the wider sense all our members

Table 3.2 Environment policy approved at NALGO's 1990 Annual Conference

Conference believes that the protection of the environment and the protection of life on earth is the most fundamental issue currently facing humanity and notes, in particular, changes in the weather and rises in sea-level arising from the greenhouse effect, and recognizes the need to reduce the emission of the gases responsible, for our own benefit and as a duty to our children.

As a major trade union it is essential that NALGO plays a leading role in environmental issues and this should be one of the top priorities within NALGO's annual work programme.

Conference condemns the hypocrisy of the government's declarations of awareness of the greenhouse effect and totally deplores its accompanying policies on energy and transport which will inevitably make the problem worse.

Conference therefore instructs the NEC to:

1. examine NALGO policy decisions in respect of their effect, or potential effect, on the environment;
2. initiate and participate in campaigns aimed at raising the awareness of both members and employers;
3. furthering initiatives aimed at encouraging employers to adopt good environmental practices.

Conference also notes with approval the Friends of the Earth environmental charter for local government and resolves:

1. to campaign for the realization of its aims and objectives;
2. to devise a national strategy to encourage branches to negotiate these objectives as a long-term aim;
3. that during the interim period branches should use the document as a guideline in all relevant negotiations at branch level;
4. to campaign for central government to make available the funds necessary for the implementation of the aims and objectives of the Charter, including the restoration of grant cuts, in real terms, which have taken place since 1979.

Conference further calls for:

1. increased public spending to promote energy conservation, and a legal requirement for the power industries to adopt it as a major objective;
2. increased subsidies for public transport, in line with our European partners;
3. the diversion of funds from new motorway building to improving road networks and increased maintenance of existing roads;
4. the further development by local authorities of traffic calming and pedestrianization schemes along with improved provision for cyclists.

Furthermore, Conference calls on NALGO's TUC General Council members to use their best endeavours to ensure that the TUC's environmental action group makes real progress.

have environmental concerns that we seek to reflect. Apart from being members of a trade union they are also members of the public, as concerned as anyone else about the environment. Because of this diversity of interest, responsibility for environmental matters within the union does not rest with one person, but is spread across departments and individuals.

Whilst pursuing environmental interests over a number of years, NALGO policy was restated at our 1990 annual conference. The resolution, reproduced in Table 3.2, gives some idea of the general direction of these policies.

In the water section, where we represent approximately 25 000 employees in the industry, our interest in the environment and contact with environmental groups developed as early as 1984 when the government announced its intention to privatize the industry.

THE CAMPAIGN AGAINST PRIVATIZATION

The joint water industry trade unions organized a campaign against water privatization. We appreciated very early on that a broad range of concerns and interests were involved, therefore we sought to pull together a broad church of opposition, of which we were only one part. Our intention was to act as a catalyst, but with the ability to work with and support other groups, organizations and individuals.

The impact of privatization on the environment was an issue that quickly became established as one of the main elements of the campaign. Water authorities, as they were then known, owned vast areas of land. The provision of wholesome water, and the disposal of sewage, has obvious environmental implications. In addition to all this their raw material – water and sewage – by its very nature is of the utmost environmental importance.

Another major issue in the campaign was the financial implications of water privatization. This is a multi-billion pound industry, with vast assets, estimated as worth over £5.5 billion pounds (though this was not the price at which the government sold it!). This campaign therefore brought together two issues – environment and finance.

As trade unions one of our difficulties was that we were neither environmental or financial experts, therefore we had to contact others who were. Eventually we were working with all the major environmental groups and interests, including Friends of the Earth, Greenpeace, the Council for the Protection of Rural England, Royal Society for the Protection of Birds, Marine Conservation Society, Earth Resources and many more. We also worked closely with other individuals and organizations with environmental interests – the European Commission, politicians, colleges, universities, etc. To cover the financial aspects of the campaign we contacted various financial and academic experts, some with a long and intimate knowledge of the water industry.

We also arranged and sponsored a number of seminars. A seminar at Leeds University was devoted to the environment. The London School of Economics hosted a seminar bringing together stockbrokers and City analysts. At NALGO we held a conference with representatives from local authorities. We also organized two large conferences at the Royal Commonwealth Society in London, and invited everyone and anyone with an interest. Finally, we held a large rally at Westminster Central Hall which attracted over 2500 people and was addressed by the Leader of the Labour Party, Neil Kinnock MP, ex European Environment Commissioner Stanley Clinton Davis and Andrew Lees from Friends of the Earth, amongst many others.

The campaign was not based on propaganda, i.e. public sector good, private sector bad. To provide substance and weight to our arguments we commissioned our own studies, assisted other individuals and groups researching into the subject, and encouraged others to use our resources. This involved experts in fields such as environment and finance, experts whose independence would command respect and would not be tarnished as abetting a political propaganda campaign. In time we accumulated quite a library of published reports, books and other information, and went out of our way to make them available to anyone interested. It was clear from quite early on that openness and candour were in our interests – secrecy fed the aims of the government and supporters of privatization.

The experts in the various fields soon became known and established, and in fact were used by different groups representing different interests, including ourselves. Quite often these people gave their time and effort freely, because they felt strongly about the issue – whether financial or environmental. This did not jeopardize their professional or academic integrity, as their arguments were subject to, and withstood, full public and expert scrutiny. As is often the case, however, although they won the argument, privatization went ahead anyway for political reasons. At one stage producing reports and studies on water privatization became quite a growth industry, not restricted to stockbrokers and the City. A wealth of information and comment was gathered which if nothing else should contribute to the future efficient running and organization of the industry.

One of the major problems we encountered was that environmentalists did not have financial expertise, and financiers did not have environmental expertise. Both were sympathetic to the concerns of the other, but when it came down to fundamentals they did not talk the same language. Within the industry itself this same difference occurs, where environment is only one aspect of 'the business'. In fact one of the arguments against privatization was that it would give profit and dividends priority over the environment. This was illustrated when in the summer of 1988 we received anonymously through the post a leaked copy of the draft Water Bill. An early clause in the Bill, setting its general philosophy, qualified the industry's environmental responsibilities by making them subject to and conditional upon 'profitability, economy and efficiency'. This created something of a furore, and in the published Bill this particular clause was suitably reworded so as not to cause offence, though the sentiment remained.

When the industry was in the public sector there was, amongst its employees and our members, a sense of providing a service to the public rather than merely supplying a product. The campaign against privatization was popular amongst our members because of this. They genuinely felt that an industry like water should remain in the public domain for the public interest.

They acknowledged the environmental concerns of the public, and whilst receiving a good deal of criticism about the state of the industry throughout the campaign against privatization, they recognized that this was inevitable. They could not pretend the industry was perfect – the shortcomings were too obvious – therefore there was a recognition that to improve things they had to be subject to public scrutiny. Prior to privatization the water industry received little public attention. It was privatization that raised the profile of the industry and its environmental impact and shortcomings.

We deliberately did not try to defend the status quo, but went on the attack over the state of the industry, the argument being that privatization was not the answer, but the solution was in improving standards and providing adequate investment with the industry in the public sector. This was summed up by one of our campaign slogans – 'Keep Water Safe, Clean and Public'. Information about the environmental and financial state of industry was therefore crucial to this tactic. The industry has always been under a duty to provide information, especially relating to the environment. For example, Acts of Parliament such as the Control of Pollution Act, set out the kind of information the industry had to provide. However, prior to the privatization debate the industry generally received little attention or scrutiny.

It was our aim to encourage such attention and scrutiny. Our members were well aware of their duty to the public and the importance of providing information in order to encourage a full debate about the industry and the possible shortcomings of privatization. Our members were in a unique position: they ran the industry and were well aware of the shortcuts and economies with the truth. They were also in a position to expose the problems!

This posed something of a dilemma for some of our members and NALGO as a union, concerning the position of employees releasing information vital to the public interest (i.e. a pollution incident) which was being withheld by the water authority. Our members wanted the information in the public domain but risked dismissal if they released it and it was traced back to them. Our advice, first, was that if they were members of a professional institute with a professional code of conduct where possible that code could be called in support of their action. Secondly, they should confront their seniors with the problem and try to force the issue out into the open. If all that failed we suggested they send the information to us in a plain brown envelope! Fortunately none of our members suffered as a result of releasing information, and there did appear to be a 'condoning' of such action whilst strictly speaking it was a sackable offence. I did get the impression that whilst in the public sector there was a genuine feeling in the industry that employees were public servants with a duty to provide information. However, this situation has changed for the worse now the industry is in the private sector.

Because of privatization and the wider concern about the environment, the public (and media) suddenly became interested in scientific data relating to water which, though obscure, was of major interest and concern. For example, information on river classification, biological oxygen demand, sewage discharge consent conditions and European water quality Directives suddenly became much sought after. Our members not only were able to provide detail not normally available, they were also capable of interpreting it. If there was a pollution incident we were in a position to provide information and explanations which the industry and government were anxious to conceal!

One example of this was information concerning sewage works discharge consent conditions. A consent condition sets the standard for the quality of treated sewage which can be discharged from sewage works into rivers. The concept is straightforward but the science complex. We discovered that many sewage works were failing their consent conditions, and discharging sewage into rivers that had not been properly treated. To bring these works up to standard would require massive capital investment, and as far as the flotation of the industry was concerned this would result in prohibitive financial burdens. We came across information passing between the industry and government indicating that they intended to resolve this dilemma by temporarily relaxing these standards, and 'temporarily' meant for some years! Therefore to ensure a successful flotation the public was to continue to be subject to inadequately treated sewage discharged into our rivers. We had the correspondence and technical information, and knew some dubious practice was afoot.

However, we were not well placed to use the information – we needed an authoritative environmental organization to give this issue full exposure. We passed the information to Friends of the Earth who made full use of it. Unfortunately this did not result in the withdrawal of the industry and government's 'solution' to the problem. It did, however, illustrate and provide weight to our argument against privatization – that the industry required massive investment that could only take place in the public sector, and in the private sector financial considerations would take precedence over those of the environment.

The use of information was not restricted to the environment. We managed to unearth a large amount of financial information damaging to the government's case, for example, when the statutory water companies tried (and in some cases succeeded) to raise their prices higher than was justifiable, prior to the 'K-setting' (price setting) formula being implemented. Documents passed via ourselves to the Labour Party came at a particularly sensitive time for the government, when the Water Bill was in its Committee Stage in the House of Commons. The documents revealed not only an attempt to raise prices higher than was necessary, they also revealed a political row between the government and the statutory water companies, where the government was putting political pressure on these companies because their action was discrediting privatization.

As this whole process of dissemination of information gathered pace, a fascinating situation developed. We became known to certain people and groups as a reliable source on the industry. We were in something of a dilemma, as trade unions are not usually taken seriously as authoritative commentators or experts on such things as river and water quality. We needed to get the information to the right people who could make optimum use of it at the right time. We never withheld information, and in the early stages when environmental groups were making the running, we sent the information to them. When the Water Bill entered Parliament, that became the focus of attention. When we came across a valuable piece of information we had to decide who would make best use of it. This was, of course, amongst other things, conditioned by the nature of the information. If we passed it to politicians, the environmentalists would complain, and vice versa. Some unseemly squabbles developed. There was some criticism within NALGO, mainly from our press and publicity people, that we undersold ourselves and that the environmentalists and politicians were receiving publicity and attention we could have attracted ourselves. Whether or not this was correct, the course of action we took was effective.

We also exploited the financial information that came our way. As flotation approached the environmental aspects of the campaign took second place to the financial aspects of flotation. This is not to say that environmental concerns diminished in importance or seriousness, but that the government was well into the privatization timetable and was entering the hard-sell stage. In the spring and summer of 1989 the government and industry began a multi-million pound public relations and advertising campaign to promote the industry, flotation and sale of shares. By this stage the argument really got down to money, mainly the cost. It was here that the European Community's water related standards (Directives) had a major impact. However, for the flotation to succeed the government had to convince the City that this was a worthwhile investment, for despite 'popular capitalism' it is still the big financial institutions that buy the vast majority of shares in a major flotation such as this.

City and financial analysts descended on the industry with a vengeance, with a voracious appetite for information. They were interested in the environment, but solely in terms of its impact on the industry as a financial investment (with a very few honourable exceptions). By this time the government's initial proposals had been subject to major rubbishing and consequent amendment, but in our view these changes were only aimed at making the industry an attractive investment. It did not take a brilliant City analyst to discover that in pure financial terms the industry was a very good investment, not least because of the government's decision to write off the industry's capital debt and set an initial share price equivalent to giving the industry away.

The government did introduce a further novel way of guaranteeing the industry's future financial success – cost pass-through. The industry is not free to set prices as it sees fit – even this government was not prepared (in theory at least) to afford this facility to a monopoly supplier of water. The industry's prices are set via a procedure of negotiation called 'K-setting', involving the industry, government and the Office of Water Services. In theory at least this is a guarantee that the industry does not abuse its monopoly, and once all factors are taken into account, including capital investment, prices are fixed and cannot be increased, other than by specified amounts, for a five- to ten-year period. However, the industry can pass on to the consumer unforeseen costs that could not have been predicted at the time of the 'K-setting' negotiations. This rather loose concept of cost pass-through, though not yet tested, provides some comfort for the industry.

Up till about six months before the actual flotation, December 1989, information was relatively easy to come by, but as flotation loomed a clamp-down came into effect. This was under the guise of the 1986 Financial Services Act (and others), which seeks to protect potential investors from misleading information that might affect their investment decisions – and eventually the flotation.

The clampdown on information was quite dramatic. Water authorities and the Department of the Environment set up 'Documentation Clearance Groups', involving employees, government officials, banks, stockbrokers, tax accountants and many more. Whilst the Financial Services Act was probably applied quite properly in this context, there was no doubt that the water authorities were zealous, and quite relieved to have a pretext to clamp down on the leaking of information that up till then had been extremely damaging to their image, privatization and the flotation. Employees were issued with detailed and strict instructions as to whom they could speak to, the information they could release, who could clear it and so on. Ridiculous lengths were reached – for example, when there was a controversy in North West Water over the content of the publicity display in their reception area! Employees were instructed not to respond immediately to telephone enquiries in case they released sensitive information or contravened the Financial Services Act. Instead they were instructed to note the enquiry and call back when the response had been vetted. On one occasion a water authority would not read out to me the content of a press release issued the previous day, even though it had appeared in some newspapers! They took note of the call and rang back.

There was even the question that in their zealousness the authorities may themselves have been acting illegally, in not complying with the Control of Pollution Act, i.e. in making available information on river quality and sewage discharge standards. This we could never establish, but in the final six months prior to flotation the Financial Services Act became the water authorities bible and text.

Our members were quite rightly concerned about these developments, so NALGO took legal advice on whether the Financial Services Act was being correctly interpreted and implemented. The advice we received, and issued to members, was that the Act was being improperly used in this context, and should one of our members have been disciplined for contravening the Act, we were prepared to defend our position and the member in court. In our view the Act was being used to restrict information which was potentially 'embarrassing' to the industry and government, or 'politically' sensitive, which quite clearly was not the intention of the Act.

AFTER PRIVATIZATION: THE NEW BUSINESS ETHIC AND ITS EFFECT ON INFORMATION PROVISION

Now the industry is in the private sector there is very little information coming our way. No doubt this is partly due to the industry no longer being under the public and press scrutiny it was prior to flotation. However, the business ethic is taking over and information which once was regarded as public property is now jealously guarded. Information suddenly began to be described as 'commercially sensitive', and information falling within this category is increasing.

As privatization loomed the business ethic of the private sector emerged in a number of small and large ways. For example, instead of 'consumers' the water industry now has 'customers'. In Southern Water it was decided that any reference to 'sewage' or 'sewerage' was offensive to the public. These words have now been eliminated from their vocabulary, and the substance(s) is now called 'waste water'. This caused some hilarity and confusion, as most consumers did not know what they were paying for when they received their bills! No doubt this scheme was thought up by some ambitious PR person.

Water plc Annual Reports and Accounts are of limited value. For one thing, to the non-expert they are obscure – you have to have the expertise to be able to interpret them. For example, what is the difference between directors' 'salaries' and 'emoluments'? Whilst there is usually some passing reference to their environmental commitment, water plc Annual Reports and Accounts provide hard information solely on their financial performance. One thing

I have discovered is that company accounts can be presented to mean anything the company wants them to mean.

Although the water industry has been in the private sector only since December 1989, the business ethic is having its impact on the philosophy of providing a public service. One manifestation of this is the way the new companies are structured. Instead of having an all embracing water authority, we now have a water plc holding company with several subsidiary companies covering such things as property services, laboratories, engineering, design, plumbing, 'enterprise', etc. (though it should be noted that the directors of the holding and subsidiary companies are usually the same). Each subsidiary is now a 'profit centre' and capable of being sold off. Employees will more and more come to identify with their immediate employer, potentially putting one subsidiary at odds with others. This is even more graphically illustrated by the creation of the National Rivers Authority (NRA). Prior to privatization all environmental responsibility was under the one umbrella, the water authority. This itself caused conflicts, where the industry was responsible for policing itself (the poacher turned gamekeeper conflict).

The water plcs are now responsible for providing clean water and disposing of sewage, all within the business and profit imperative. The NRA has powers which potentially can severely inhibit the business and profit imperative, i.e. setting costly river quality and environmental standards, and monitoring the industry to ensure it complies with existing set standards. Consequently in many areas the two organizations – and employees in them – see themselves pursuing different, often conflicting, ends.

In the campaign against water privatization some of the information we used, both environmental and financial, was in the public domain. However, the most telling information we used was not normally available or accessible to the public, and came to us via unofficial channels from within the industry and others. This will probably remain the case with the industry in the private sector. The difficulty with both types of information is comprehending and interpreting it, and we were fortunate to work with people who could do both.

The industry has only been in the private sector since December 1989, therefore it is too early to draw definite conclusions. However, information does now appear to be less easy to come by. This may be because the industry is no longer in the public eye to the extent it was during the campaign against privatization, therefore people (and the media) are not as assiduous or vigilant in obtaining it as they were previously. In addition, the mechanism and structure to exploit this information, the campaign against water privatization, no longer exists in the form it did. It could be that the business ethic is taking hold and the new plcs are clamping down for reasons of commercial confidentiality, finance and business.

As already mentioned, certain types of information have to be made publicly available whether the industry is in the public or private sector, but it is the information not normally made available, irrespective of the ownership of the industry, that matters.

GREEN NEGOTIATING: THE MSF APPROACH

Hilary Benn

RAISING AWARENESS OF THE NEED FOR CHANGE

The need to protect our environment, and so hand on a sustainable planet to our children and their descendants, is our greatest challenge. As a trade union, MSF strongly supports measures being introduced to protect the environment, and recognizes that environmental concerns will play an increasingly important part in decision-making, both nationally and internationally, as we move into the next century.

In the long term, the protection of the environment will be of direct benefit to all employees and their families. Indeed, we have found that our members are only too aware of the need for change, not least because most of them live in the communities that are affected by pollution and environmental damage. However, in the short term the introduction of more stringent environmental protection policies (e.g. energy taxes, and transport and pollution controls) could have an adverse effect on job security. This needs to be tackled, therefore, by planning ahead.

To adapt to these new circumstances, companies will need to alter their operations, invest in new product development, identify new markets, clean up their processes and retrain their employees. Firms that do not respond will find themselves either caught by new legislation, overtaken by their competitors or the subject of damaging adverse publicity. We have a very large number of members in industries that will be directly affected, including oil and chemicals, metal manufacturing, engineering, power engineering, motor vehicles, electronics, electricity supply, and paper and packaging. Above all, the way foward for these firms will lie in the development and adoption of 'clean technologies', i.e. technology or techniques that will reduce or eliminate *at source* the production of any nuisance, pollution or harmful waste, and help save energy, natural resources and raw

materials. Change *is* needed – in the way we live and the way companies
work.

MSF's approach has been founded on raising members' awareness of the
issues. We have taken a number of steps, including:

- the publication of a leaflet and strategy document, which have been widely
  circulated within the union and publicized externally (including taking a
  stand at the 1990 Green Show at the NEC Centre, Birmingham);
- holding the first ever trade union conference on the subject of clean
  technology at Imperial College. Speakers included Dr Hans Dielman from
  Erasmus University, Bryan Gould MP (Shadow Environment Secretary),
  and experts from the Imperial College Centre for Environmental
  Technology;
- circulating a questionnaire on environmental awareness to our members
  in the chemicals industry;
- the publication of an Environmental Action Checklist focusing on the office
  environment.

We have also been closely involved in the work the TUC is doing on
environmental matters, including the work of the TUC Environment Action
Group.

Our starting point was *MSF and the Environment: A Policy Strategy Document*. It outlined the following policy objectives.

Overall policy

MSF is campaigning for:

- recognition that protecting the environment is an international responsibility
  which requires collective action by public and private sectors – the 'free
  market' offers no solution;
- the establishment of a UK Environmental Protection Executive to oversee
  all aspects of the environment and directed primarily at the *prevention*
  of pollution, with an effective system of penalties for breaches of legislation;
- improved dialogue between trade unions, employers and environmental
  groups.

In the workplace

MSF is campaigning for:

- the environment to be put on the bargaining agenda at every company/plant;

- employers to be encouraged to respond to environmental concerns, set higher standards, tackle pollution/hazards at source, and become more aware of their responsibilities. All companies should have a written statement of their environmental policy (which should be consistent with their written health and safety policy). This policy statement should clearly state:

- who in the company is charged with implementing the policy, and what their exact responsibilities are,
- what the arrangements are (i.e. procedures and systems) for implementing the policy;
- agreements with employers to carry out an environmental impact audit of the company, looking at both products and the production process.
- the negotiation of Environment Agreements, and the establishment of joint management/trade union committees (using the model of health and safety committees) to review and monitor company policy and practice. Safety representatives already have considerable powers to investigate potential hazards and receive information;
- a legal obligation on all employers and employees not to take actions which would seriously damage the environment;
- all employers to audit their health and safety performance, with independent inspection being the responsibility of a strengthened health and safety executive;
- a statutory right of access to information for employees and the community on matters relating to a workplace and the environment (e.g. information about pollution levels, hazardous wastes, etc.);
- the promotion of 'clean technologies', i.e. production processes that significantly reduce or eliminate harmful pollution.

In the community

MSF is campaigning for:

- members to raise awareness of environmental issues, and to use their influence to promote conservation, waste recycling and energy efficiency;
- improved public transport;
- strengthened regulations to improve significantly the insulation and energy efficiency of new buildings, and incentives to improve the existing housing/building stock;
- food policies that discourage, and where possible prevent, the use of pesticides, harmful additives, and nitrates.

Global warming and pollution

MSF is campaigning for:

- implementation of the Toronto Conference targets for a global 20% reduction in CO_2 emissions by 2005;
- the phasing out of all CFCs by the earliest possible date, and no later than 1995;
- a transport policy aimed at reducing harmful vehicle emissions, energy consumption and damage to natural habitats;
- increased R&D funding for work on acid rain, flue gas desulphurization and the Grimethorpe PFBC project;
- improved water standards, including full compliance with EC directives;
- a ban on the importation or export by the UK of nuclear, domestic and toxic waste, including a ban on all toxic and nuclear waste dumping at sea.

Energy policy

MSF is campaigning for:

- greater emphasis on, and investment in, energy conservation;
- a national system of energy labelling, including information on the pollution produced;
- a preference in the longer term for capital investment in conservation rather than generating capacity (e.g. comparing the cost of a new power station with the effect of investing the same amount of money in energy conservation measures). In the short term, any new generating capacity ordered should use the most up-to-date clean technologies;
- continuing research, with a substantial increase in funding, into renewable energy sources (such as wind, solar and wave technology);
- a phased run-down of existing nuclear plants, while maintaining research into nuclear power technology (including safety, decommissioning and waste disposal).

Information

MSF is campaigning for:

- full public access to information on the environment, including the results of pollution monitoring;
- an EC system of environmental labelling (i.e. information on the environmental impact of products and processes);
- support for environmental and health education in schools.

PUTTING THE ENVIRONMENT ON THE BARGAINING AGENDA

Once awareness has been raised, the next stage is to try and generate discussion within the workplace and with management. All companies will be affected by the development of environmental awareness and the new, tougher regulatory framework. Firms will have to consider changes in public attitudes towards their products and processes. Concern about pollution is already at a high level, and there is evidence that consumers are willing to choose what they see as environmentally friendly products, and are prepared to pay a premium in doing so.

Our members are being affected by these developments. The most effective step we can take is to react positively to these changes by anticipating them and working with employers. To do this, the environment must be put on the bargaining agenda of every workplace. The best way to start is to ask questions, and we have prepared the following checklist to help our members do this. It focuses specifically on the office workplace, although we also offer specific advice relevant to industrial plants and factories.

THE OFFICE ENVIRONMENT: AN ACTION CHECKLIST
FOR MSF MEMBERS

General principles

As a general rule, try to avoid products, processes or actions which:

- cause harm to the environment, in its broadest sense;
- endanger your health or the health of other people;
- involve unnecessary waste (e.g. built-in obsolesence or over-packaging) or the consumption of an excessive amount of energy;
- use materials from threatened environments or endangered species.

This action checklist is intended to help you assess your company and your workplace from an environmentally friendly standpoint. Some of the information will be readily available; the rest you will need to find out.

Energy efficiency

- What steps have been taken to maximise energy efficiency? Are there any incentives to minimize use? Is energy efficiency taken into account when buying new machines/appliances (e.g. are energy efficient light bulbs used)?
- Is information available showing energy use in your building so that the least efficient areas can be tackled first?

- Is energy conservation taken into account when buildings are constructed or refurbished? What insulation standards are used (e.g. loft spaces, double-glazing, and draught excluders)?

Purchasing and recycling

- Does the company purchase environmentally friendly products? This could cover, for example, recycled and non-bleached paper products, low fuel consumption vehicles, no tropical hardwoods, biodegradable and phosphate-free cleaning materials, and recycled building materials.
- Are there any arrangements at your workplace for recycling materials, e.g. waste paper, and possibly glass?
- Is recycled paper used in offices for stationery and printing? Are other paper products (e.g. towels and lavatory paper) made from recycled paper? Are envelopes recycled (e.g. by using over-stickers or internal mail envelopes that can be used again)? Have you assessed mailing/circulation lists to minimize duplication?

Health and safety

- Does the company have a written safety policy, and is it consistent with its written environment policy (if there is one)?
- Has the company carried out assessments under the Control of Substances Hazardous to Health Regulations 1988 (COSHH) of all hazardous substances in the workplace (e.g. photocopier chemicals, printing materials, adhesive sprays, glues and cleaning solvents)?
- As the first line of prevention of exposure under COSHH, has the company eliminated as many hazardous substances as possible or substituted less hazardous alternatives?
- Is exposure to remaining hazardous substances (i.e. ones that have not been eliminated) controlled at source (e.g. by local extract ventilation) as far as is reasonably practicable? Is hazardous waste disposed of safely?
- Has the company identified all asbestos in its buildings? What is the company's policy for dealing with asbestos?
- Has the company carried out noise assessments under the Noise at Work Regulations 1989? Is noise controlled at source as far as is reasonably practicable?
- Are the air conditioning systems regularly cleaned and checked for harmful micro-organisms, e.g. legionella bacteria?
- Are microwave ovens regularly checked for radiation leaks?
- Does the company have a policy on smoking in the workplace?

- Is there a workplace canteen, does it promote healthy eating? Does it have re-usable crockery and cutlery?

Dealing with pollution

- Are any CFCs used? Has a decision been taken to phase out their use, and if so by what date?
- Do company vehicles run on lead-free petrol? Are there plans to fit catalytic converters to cars in advance of legislation?
- Has consideration been given to encouraging use of transport other than cars, e.g. public transport or bicycles? Is there a car pool arrangement?
- Will Integrated Pollution Control (IPC) affect your workplace? Is any pollution monitored, with information available to you and to the local community?
- Are any airborne or water pollutants produced (this could include illegally pouring substances down the public drainage system)? What steps have been taken/are being taken to reduce their emission?

Company policy

- Does the company have a policy statement on the environment? Is there a board member with responsibility for environmental issues?
- Has the investment policy of the company pension fund been considered? Within the constraints of legislation, does it avoid investing in companies that damage the environment?

What next?

Having discussed these questions, approach management with the following suggestions:

- Ask them to provide information in response to the checklist. This could then provide an agreed statement of what has been done as a basis for further discussion.
- Ask them to consider carrying out an environmental impact audit, either internally or by calling in outside consultants. Point out that tackling some of the issues identified could save the company money as well as helping to save the environment.
- Ask them if they are prepared to set up a joint union/management working group on environmental issues. Suggest that an Environment Agreement

be prepared for joint signature setting out what steps the company and its workforce are taking to address environmental issues.

Don't forget that you will also need to raise members' awareness of these issues and develop a sense of shared responsibility for tackling problems.

Other things you can do

There is also a great deal we can do as individuals to promote environmental awareness and help tackle some of the problems we have identified. There are practical steps that all of us can take at home and in the workplace; for example saving electricity, recycling paper and other materials, pressing local authorities to take action, buying environmentally friendly products, campaigning for better public transport, and joining organizations concerned about the environment. By playing our part in this way, we can help create a better climate for ourselves, our fellow human beings, and the planet.

THE WAY FORWARD

The above gives only a very brief account of how one trade union has approached the environmental question. Much remains to be done. Environmental auditing must involve those in the workplace, both because their livelihoods could be affected and because they have knowledge and expertise that can be tapped. Employees must be given a seat at the green negotiating table. It is sad therefore that the government White Paper *This Common Inheritance* contains not a single reference to the role that workers and their trade unions can play in this process. It is a view which reflects the present government's attitude to trade unions generally and that of many employers. It is not a view that is sustainable in the long term if we are to meet the environmental challenge that now faces us.

Chapter Four

THE ACCOUNTING PROFESSION

Why is the environmental debate of interest to
accountants and accountancy bodies?
*Roger Adams, The Chartered Association
of Certified Accountants*

A questioning approach to the environment
*Anthony Carey, The Institute of Chartered Accountants
in England and Wales*

The contribution of management accounting to the
environmental debate
*Lesley Phillips, The Chartered Institute
of Management Accountants*

WHY IS THE ENVIRONMENTAL DEBATE OF INTEREST TO ACCOUNTANTS AND ACCOUNTANCY BODIES?*

Roger Adams

WHY SHOULD WE BE INTERESTED?

In June 1990 the Chartered Association of Certified Accountants (ACCA) held a seminar to launch a research study called *The Greening of Accountancy: The Profession After Pearce* (Gray, 1990). We had invited guests from across the spectrum of interested organizations and the discussion after the main presentation promised to be lively and stimulating.

---

* The views expressed in this paper are solely those of the author and should not be attributed to the Council or Technical Committee of the ACCA.

In response to a question from the chair one of the representatives (from the ethical trust industry) replied that he had indeed found the paper interesting but that his initial reaction to our invitation to the seminar had been 'why is the environmental debate of interest to accountants and accountancy bodies – what's their angle?' In this short article I will attempt to present some personal answers to that not altogether unexpected question.

First there is the obvious response that accountants as individuals should have a natural and legitimate personal concern for the future of our planet.

Secondly it is important to point to the practical skills which accountants have developed over the years as managers, processors, originators and verifiers of information. Quantitative data concerning the environment within which accountants work is little different in principle from other organizational data which accountants deal with on a regular basis.

Thirdly it is necessary to recognize that 'environmental auditing' derives much of its methodology (and terminology) from longer established auditing processes such as operational auditing (internal auditing) and external compliance auditing. In order for credible environmental audits to take place the process must borrow wholesale from the experience and expertise which accountants and the accounting/auditing profession have developed over the years.

For the accountancy profession to contribute in a meaningful way to the environmental debate there should be:

- agreed definitions of what is to be measured and why (e.g. emissions of pollutant to be checked against statutory compliance levels);
- the technology to measure and capture the required data;
- systems to record it and controls to ensure that corrective actions are taken when required;
- reporting systems to convey performance measurement data to those requiring it (senior management, external regulators, etc.);
- an audit which can attest to the reliability of the data reported;
- a willingness to accept estimates when precise cost apportionment is not possible (e.g. the environmental improvement aspect of the cost of a new piece of plant may be difficult to ascertain exactly).

(Note that far more is required for fully effective environmental audits to take place – in particular senior management must have publicly demonstrated their willingness to commit their organization and its resources to the audit process. Such a commitment also involves accepting the responsibility to implement necessary changes: see Elkington, 1990; CBI, 1990.)

THE ACCOUNTING PROFESSION AS A BROAD CHURCH

Before exploring each of the above points in more depth it might be useful to examine the range of environments where accountants – *qua* accountants – operate.

Within commercial and non-commercial organizations there will be accountants acting as management accountants, financial accountants and internal auditors. In addition accountants operate within the treasury function and, increasingly, there are accountants on the board of management. Outside the organization accountants will act as statutory auditors. There are also likely to be accountants on such regulatory bodies as OFTEL and OFWAT. Similarly there are accountants within local government, central government and the European Commission.

It could be argued that accountants, perhaps even more than environmental scientists, will hold a pivotal role once the environmental debate is operationalized at organizational levels due to their ever-present involvement in the resource allocation/decision-making process.

ENVIRONMENTAL REPORTING REQUIREMENTS

It is unlikely (though not impossible) that accountants will be involved in agreeing *definitions of what should be measured* or why. This is a sensitive policy area requiring high levels of scientific knowledge and the makers of future industrial environmental policy will probably reside in Brussels or the Department of the Environment, not in the accounting department.

Similarly, it is unlikely that accountants will be able to help much on the *recording technology* side. That said it should be remembered that management accountants are good at recognizing the potential of technology. Hopwood and Loft (1990) have examined the impact of time recording technology on management accounting and point out that the increasing sophistication of management accounting systems in the latter part of the nineteenth century could not have happened without a technological revolution at the entry-gate to the factory and on the shop-floor.

Technology of all descriptions affects both the accountant's role and the approach to the accounting itself. Thus the increasing level of automation on the production line coupled with new resource management techniques such as just-in-time methodology have revolutionized data collection for internal accounting purposes.

First indications from within the EC are that Brussels will soon be demanding comprehensive statistical and environmental data from companies as well as requiring tougher environmental impact assessments (EIAs). It is inconceivable that the finance function within a corporation could divorce itself from the implications of non-compliance with external standards or the cost-significance of EIAs. The recording technology (above) will be linked into formal management information systems to ensure a rapid flow-through of data. If, or when, economic instruments (charges or taxes) are introduced then the link between product manufacturing process design, environmental monitoring and financial accountability will be further strengthened.

Systems and controls are the accountants bread and butter. Involvement at this level is inevitable since accountants are widely employed both as consultants and as internal (operational) auditors. They will thus be involved in the design and monitoring of internal environmental reporting systems. Each of the major accounting firms ('the big 6') already employs a team of environmental consultants.

Accountants are also good at dealing with the output of systems – the *performance measurement data*. Whilst it does not follow automatically that accountants will be responsible for performance reports on emission type issues (an independent department may deal with this type of compliance reporting), they will be involved in the prior evaluation and subsequent assessment of capital projects where an environmental cost factor has been incorporated.

Accountants both professional and academic will also be heavily concerned with the *theoretical development of investment appraisal methodologies* – the choice of discount rates (cost of capital), estimation of decommissioning costs and the allocation of environmental improvement costs. Each of these factors has yet to be fully explored at the theoretical level and much work needs to be carried out at the empirical level in order to ascertain what it is possible to do given the resources and the willingness to experiment.

The ACCA is to continue its initial research sponsorship in this area (Gray, 1990) with a further long-term project examining in detail the activities of environmentally conscious companies.

It is also probable that companies will choose to make public increasing quantities of environmental performance data. A natural vehicle for this data is the *annual financial report*, traditionally the province of the financial accountant. Companies already make some 'social reporting' disclosures – charitable donations, community project work, ethnic and gender personnel data – but the extent and the quality of disclosure varies widely from company to company and from country to country.

The ACCA has recently issued a survey on the social responsibility disclosures of 200 of the largest companies in the world (Roberts, 1990).

It is often argued that corporate environmental disclosures will not be credible to the user unless the data is *externally audited*. This task will require the development of an appropriate auditing methodology. As yet there has been little or no discussion concerning the form of an auditor's environmental report but it is certainly within the capabilities of the accounting profession to assist in the development of both the methodology and the reporting framework.

Early indications are that the European Commission will be pressing for an *independent environment audit*. As noted above, much of the methodology and terminology of this process appears to be borrowed from more mainstream auditing activities. Once again, the involvement of accountants as advisors (or consultants) seems pretty inevitable.

Estimation of environmental improvement costs should not pose a major problem for accountants in industry. The allocation of gross capital expenditure between normal capital expenditure and environmental improvement expenditure should not prove difficult provided that the same technical experts who advised on the original choice of asset are also asked to provide a reasoned allocation of costs. This cost breakdown need not affect the statutory balance sheet but can be provided, with suitable caveats if thought necessary, in the notes to the accounts, or even outside the formal statutory financial statements altogether.

Legislation on any of these topics from a UK source looks unlikely. The recent White Paper *This Common Inheritance* (DoE, 1990) explicitly ruled out green taxes and did not propose any amendments to company law in respect of environmental disclosure requirements. A more likely source of legislation looks set to be Brussels where (as noted) EC environmental auditing directives are in the pipeline. The United Nations is also preparing guidance on corporate environmental disclosure.

THE ROLE OF THE ACCOUNTANCY PROFESSION

The role of the accounting profession is thus as follows:

- To conduct research into all aspects of the environmental interface with business finance and corporate accountability. This process has started but it is not coordinated in any way. Thus there is a risk that some (perhaps unnecessary) work will be duplicated whilst other (essential work) falls between the cracks. A list of potential research topics is provided in the appendix to this section on p. 86.
- To expand on the ethical responsibilities of accountants so that environmentally destructive activities are recognized as such and affected (or implicated) individuals receive clear guidance on how to act.
- To assist in the development of environmental auditing methodologies. This is an area where professional accountants excel – the major problem is to define what it is that needs to be audited. Once the objective of the exercise is settled the appropriate methodology will not be long in coming.
- To monitor compliance with environmental reporting standards. This may be as a result of legislation or simply at the request of the enterprise.
- To incorporate environmental awareness into the educational process. This is likely to be quite difficult since professional accountancy curricula are planned anything up to a decade ahead. The most obvious areas where environmental issues could be inserted into a syllabus would seem to be:

- *financial management*: in investment appraisal problems where the problems connected with the ascertainment of environmental cost factors could be examined;
- *advanced auditing*: where environmental auditing could sit alongside other specialized forms of auditing as an examinable topic;
- *regulatory framework of accounting*: where environmentally related disclosure requirements could be included in normal disclosure based questions.

A SHARED TERMINOLOGY FOR FINANCIAL AND ENVIRONMENTAL REPORTING?

Few companies provide any significant environmental disclosures via their annual financial statements (Roberts, 1990). Fewer still publish a separate annual environmental report. The likelihood is that both financial statement disclosures and environmental (audit) reports are set to become more common. If so, we should consider how to ensure that such disclosures are both *relevant* and *objective*.

Words such as 'accountability' and 'transparency' and phrases such as 'economic reality' and 'substance over form' exercise powerful influence over the direction of research effort and regulator intention in the accountancy field. They can be adapted to the environmental reporting arena with minimal difficulty. The use of the words 'relevant' and 'objective' in the previous paragraph shows just how easily the terminology can be transferred. Disclosure may turn out to be a 'bandwagon' effect – companies will jump onto the bandwagon as they discover that in particular circumstances it pays to make environmental activities 'transparent'. Particular examples here might include:

- to ensure that local authorities engaging in compulsory competitive tendering exercises do not use the absence of environmental disclosure(s) as a pretext for awarding contracts to the internal DLO;
- to ensure that such potential shareholders as the ethical investment trust movement are not 'frozen out' or alienated by inadequate environmental disclosure.

At present financial statements contain little or no environmental reporting data – the environmental activities of companies are certainly not 'transparent' and there is little evidence that there is a concerted move to increase voluntary disclosures. Such encouragement as there is comes from the accountants, the greens and the ethical investment industry, not from the CBI or the preparers of accounts.

Whilst accountants are struggling to make financial statements portray 'economic reality' it is clear that that 'economic reality' is one-dimensional since it largely ignores both environmental and employee factors. Increased attention to these areas will not be at the expense of financial reporting but will be additional and (one hopes) complementary. A barrier to increasing the reality of corporate financial and/or environmental reports is cost. It would seem logical for future legislation in the environment area to follow the same pattern as is currently adopted in the financial reporting area: all companies are obliged to comply with the law to maintain proper books and records and to produce accounts which show a true and fair view, but small and medium sized companies are exempted from certain (onerous) disclosure requirements. Whether this would satisfy the environmental lobby is open to question.

'Substance over form' takes on new meaning in an environmental context: it is easy to see that companies will comply with environmental regulations when there is a penalty attached. Thus an environmental audit can report compliance with specific regulations and the existence of the penalty should ensure a high level of compliance.

However, not all aspects of the entity/environment interface are (or ever will be) covered by regulations. Thus environmental (audit) reports should also consider the voluntary (or discretionary) activities of organizations – activities which go beyond mere compliance with external regulation (legal form). Information concerning the real 'substance' (or scope) of their environmental protection policies is probably likely to be much more informative than a bland statement reporting statutory compliance. Publication of a top management 'environment charter' (or policy) will also assist in enabling outsiders to assess the extent of the organization's commitment to significant environmental improvement.

SHOULD THE ACCOUNTING PROFESSION ATTEMPT TO 'GO IT ALONE'?

There has been much criticism of the accounting profession's alleged monopoly of standard setting both in the accounting and auditing fields. The absence of 'users' at the focal point where decisions are made is usually cited as the crime. Can the accounting profession go it alone in developing environmentally acceptable accounting techniques and defining the limits of environmental auditing?

The simple answer is 'no'. The accounting profession has always been reactive rather than proactive and the reason was exclusivity: dominance by the profession. It is only now, with the abolition of the ASC and the inauguration of its successor body the ASB, that some non-accounting interests are represented in the debating chamber. But trade unions and green activists are still excluded, and probably will be forever so long as accounting and auditing standards continue to be set independently of statute.

In one sense that's acceptable. The types of technical accounting and auditing issues which are currently being debated are, and should always remain, within the jurisdiction of accountants and other finance parties. It's wholly unreasonable (not to say unrealistic) to expect the accounting profession to try to represent in standard form the entire spectrum of opinion (in addition to its current constituents) which makes up the green movement, the trade union movement and the political activists of the far left.

But the environment is just too big and too complex an issue to be left to the major league teams like the accounting profession and the International Stock Exchange. It seems inevitable that government departments, industry groups and an increasingly environmentally aware business community will force the development of an entirely new profession – the environmental auditor. The role of the accounting profession may well be peripheral except to the extent that many of the first environmental auditors may be consultants (but not necessarily accountants) from the major auditing firms.

Really this shouldn't be such a bad thing. The lobbyists will get the assurance (though I'm not sure that they would agree) that independent experts have verified and delivered an opinion on the degree of compliance with environmental legislation. The environmental auditors (or consultants), of course, will get the money.

However, I suspect that environmentalists will see this as an unfair bargain. Consultants and accountants always get the money – and all they get is more pollution.

This is where relativity comes in. In reality it might take only a day to confirm that a company is complying with an environmentally protective law. It may take a decade, maybe a century, to perceive the beneficial consequences of that compliance.

Much the same arguments about the increasingly peripheral role of traditional accountants apply to environmental accounting research.

In researching many accounting and auditing issues it is most often the case that the researcher has a closer affinity with the mainstream of the accountancy profession than any other intellectual pursuit. In the environmental accounting area, however, this appears not to be the case. Mainstream accounting researchers simply do not know how to approach the problem.

There does exist, however, a small core of individuals who have backgrounds embracing accounting, economics and environmental science. I suspect that most of the successful initiatives will be stimulated by these people rather than by standard accounting researchers. It is also reassuring to know that similar people exist as officials of, or advisors to, the Department of the Environment. 'Green credentials' are as important in the environmental accounting research field as quantitative ability is in the area of market-based accounting research.

WHAT WILL THE ACCA AND THE REST OF THE ACCOUNTING PROFESSION BE DOING?

I have already mentioned our existing research publications and plans.

A personal view is that on this issue – the environmental accounting/auditing issue – we should combine forces with the research arms of the other accounting bodies, and possibly with the DoE, the CBI and the Green movement as well, to form a really effective research unit: a unit which has the power most coveted by researchers in all fields – unrestricted access to field operations. Whether or not such cooperation is possible remains to be seen – it may turn out to be an honourable but unrealistic ambition.

CONCLUSION AND POSTSCRIPT

I hope that the foregoing has demonstrated clearly my belief that the accounting profession does have a role to play in the environmental debate. The role will vary depending on the part of the profession under scrutiny.

If environmental auditing takes off in a big way and is enslaved by statute then I see a possibility of a new profession emerging – a profession which shares some of the terminology and methodology associated with more orthodox forms of auditing, but little of the training. As I have noted, however, I see this as being additional to (and hopefully complementary to) the traditional external financial audit.

Accountants within companies will have to learn to grapple with the spin-off effects of the increased environmental consciousness of their organizations. Companies will wish to disclose environmental activities in the non-statutory part of their financial statements. Companies will need to consider the environmental cost aspect of new projects and of new capital equipment acquisitions. Management will want to know the cost-benefit relationship inherent in any discretionary environmental expenditure. Auditors will need to consider the issue of contingent liabilities (clean-up costs etc.) in a great deal more depth and financiers will consider their liability *vis-à-vis* securities accepted for loans lest they inherit significant liabilities in respect of previous unchecked pollution.

So there is much still to be done – in particular the merging of the concept of sustainable development into our modern business/accounting decision-making rationale. As the following extracts from *The Accountant* (4 December 1896) show, we might all be a lot better off today had the accounting profession of 100 years ago had the foresight to develop the revolutionary ideas presented to the Liverpool Chartered Accountants' Students' Association. Let Mr M. Wade FCA bring this piece to a suitable close.

Addressing the theme 'What is Income?' Mr Wade observed:

This question ['What is Income?'] arises in some form or other in connection with nearly every branch of the profession . . . and it is desirable that at all times an answer should be founded upon sound and well thought out principles.

Income may be likened to the fruit which a tree yields periodically, and which may be gathered and used without injury to the tree itself.

If [however] when the fruit season arrives we not only pluck the fruit, but break off a large portion of the branches as well and use them, our tree is reduced, and next season bears less fruit, and so on until in the course of time there is no tree left at all.

Capital often undergoes a very similar process, and it should be our care that our clients do not gradually exhaust their capital while under the impression that they are living upon their income only.

Suppose a man owns an orchard and depends upon it for his living. Each season he gathers the fruit, sells it and lives upon the proceeds, and thinks he is living strictly within his means. What is the consequence? The trees languish for lack of manure, and the crops grow smaller. The old trees die, and there are no new ones to replace them, and in the end there is no fruit at all to live upon.

It is obvious that if our friend wished truly to live within his means it would imply that out of the proceeds of that fruit he would make ample provision for digging about and manuring his orchard, and for buying and planting young trees in place of old ones, and so maintain the fruitfulness of his orchard, and it was only what was left after making this provision which could truly and safely be treated as income.

Shades of conceptual frameworks, Hicksian theories of well-offness and physical/operating capital maintenance merge here with a telling parable about how mankind treats the environment.[2]

There is little doubt that accounting is heavily implicated in the destruction of the environment. If by some happy chance the accounting profession at long last possesses the skills to assist in decision-making processes which have the slightest possibility of either minimizing future damage or (preferably) reversing past damage, then I suggest that accountants convert this possibility into a personal duty, a duty which should override any environmentally detrimental activities of their employers.

REFERENCES

Adams, R. (1988) '102 years on and none the wiser', *Accountancy*, October.
Confederation of British Industry (1990) *Narrowing the Gap: Environmental Auditing – Guidelines for Business*, CBI.

---

2. See Adams (1988) for a fuller discussion of these issues.

Department of the Environment (1990) *This Common Inheritance*, DoE White Paper, HMSO.

Elkington, J. (1990) *The Environmental Audit – A Green Filter for Company Policies, Plants, Processes and Products*, Worldwide Fund For Nature.

Gray, R.H. (1990) *The Greening of Accountancy: The Profession After Pearce*, Research Report No. 17, Certified Accountant Publications.

Hopwood, A.G. and Loft, A. (1990) *Accounting and Time*, Paper presented to the 1990 European Accounting Association Conference, Budapest.

Pearce, D., Barbier, E.B. and Markyanda, A. (1989) *Blueprint for a Green Economy*, London, EarthScan.

Roberts, C.B. (1990) *International Trends in Social and Employee Reporting*, Chartered Association of Certified Accountants Occasional Research Paper No. 6.

APPENDIX: RESEARCH ISSUES

- How companies comply with current environmental legislation – typical organizational strategies.
- Why companies engage in discretionary environmental expenditure and how they measure the benefits.
- Methods of environmental disclosure: within or without the audited financial statements?
- Attitudes to compulsory disclosure of environmental activity – statistical/performance measures.
- Incorporating environmental cost factors into project appraisal exercises – an empirical study.
- Employee attitudes to the environmental issues relevant to their current employment.
- The auditability of environmental impact predictions.
- Management accounting/information systems and environmental cost issues.
- How the environment can be incorporated into professional examination systems.
- Environmental audit: scope, methodology and reporting issues.
- Environmental audit: industry's willingness to make public disclosures – an empirical survey.
- Green taxes: the impact on management decisions and information systems – accounting issues arising.
- Environmental accounting/employee/social accounting: burdens on business – a rationale for allocating reporting responsibilities.

A QUESTIONING APPROACH TO THE ENVIRONMENT*

Anthony Carey

> I keep six honest serving-men
> (They taught me all I knew);
> Their names are What and Why and When
> And How and Where and Who.
> ('I keep six honest serving-men', Rudyard Kipling)

In order to fulfil its duty to serve the public interest the accountancy profession must at all times be ready to address the main questions facing society and there can hardly be any of greater importance than those related to the future of our planet. Responding to the challenges posed by the environment is likely to lead to changes in all the main subject areas of the profession including financial reporting, audit, management and taxation. This chapter reviews the key environmental issues from an accountancy perspective and in doing so calls on the services of all of Kipling's serving-men. *What* are the main issues? *Why* will our current practices need to change? *When* should that process of change begin? *How* should changes be implemented? *Where* do we start? *Who* should be involved?

CORPORATE GOVERNANCE

For most companies the days when their valuable assets were mainly in the form of bricks and mortar and plant and machinery, 'things which you could see and kick', are gone. Consequently, if the business community and the economy in general are to continue to enjoy sustainable growth we must pay far greater attention in the future to maintaining and developing our stock of human and natural assets than has traditionally been the case. If we are to be successful it is essential that environmental problems should not be seen in isolation but placed in the context of a wider debate on corporate governance. In particular, careful thought needs to be given to how best to foster the relationship between enterprises and their employees and the wider community. The increased rate of change facing modern business caused by technological progress and

---

* The views expressed in this paper are the author's own and not necessarily those of the ICAEW.

the globalization of markets means, for example, that the quality of an enterprise's workforce is a crucial determinant of the degree of its success. Increasingly, the most able employees will not wish to work for companies with a poor environmental record.

In the first Michael Shanks Memorial Lecture at the Royal Society for the Encouragement of Arts, Manufactures and Commerce, Professor Charles Handy addressed the question 'What is a company for?' He challenged what he saw as the myths that the principle purpose of a company is just to make profits and that companies, in effect, consist of transferable property rights in the form of shares. He accepted that good profits are essential but argued that they are a means to an end and not an end in themselves. In Professor Handy's vision the company 'operated in a bounded space, a sort of hexagonal ring, surrounded by competing pressures from financiers, the employees, the customers, the suppliers, the environment and the community – the so called stake-holders'. Within that ring of forces he wanted to see the development of an existential corporation. Such a corporation would aim 'to fulfil itself, to grow and develop to the best that it can be . . . it owes something to each of the ring holders but is owned by no-one . . . it is not a piece of property, inhabited by humans, it is a community, which itself has property.' In a wealth-creating corporate sector based on this vision far more companies would be likely to initiate action of their own accord to improve the environment. In many instances there would be greater pressures to eliminate any adverse impacts that a company's manufacturing processes had on the local environment and to ensure that goods produced by it did not cause environmental damage.

A PROACTIVE RESPONSE

In discussing the benefits of a change in our approach to corporate governance we should, however, be careful not to overlook the environmental improvements which can be achieved within our current system or the efforts being made in this direction by a number of companies, business organizations and professional bodies. As the largest professional body in Europe whose members are finance directors of most of the UK's leading companies and are in leadership positions in the global accounting practices, the Institute of Chartered Accountants in England and Wales has unrivalled contacts in the business community and has recognized that it can play an important part in persuading enterprises to equate good environmental practice with good business practice. Mr Michael Lickiss, the President of the Institute, has exhorted managements to 'see environmental pressures as primarily providing opportunities for business rather than placing constraints on it. There will be scope for developing new products and, in many cases, for improving efficiency and achieving cost savings, for example, through waste management and energy efficiency schemes.'[1]

The rising of environmental issues towards the top of the political agenda calls for a response from the business community. A number of leading companies have already shown a strong commitment to reducing any adverse effects that their business has on the environment but unfortunately others are moving forward at a much slower pace. The time for corporate action is now. It is far better for managements to be proactive in identifying the changes required than to wait until action is forced on them. Whenever change occurs there will be winners and losers. The winners are likely to be those who anticipate changes in consumer and investor attitudes and in legislation. This will allow them to gain a competitive edge and to minimize any unavoidable costs such as those arising from changing product specifications, from moving from declining product markets into new areas and from changing production processes. It will also enable companies to have greater control over their cash flow requirements since they will be better able to plan their capital expenditure programme. The self-selecting losers on the other hand are likely to be those who react late to developments and may as a result face fines, claims for damages or additional taxation which in extreme cases could drive them out of business. In the coming years a company's attitude to the environment is likely to be seen as a benchmark of its commitment to innovation and good management. Companies setting the pace on environmental issues will be seen as the leaders of the corporate sector.

PERSUASION AND LEGISLATION

In developing environmental programmes intergovernmental organizations, national governments, professional organizations, representative bodies from the corporate sector and individual companies should work closely together in order that each can maximize the effectiveness of their contribution to improving environmental performance. This will also require governments, in consultation with the above groups and other interested parties, to decide on the optimum balance between persuasion and legislation. A dogmatic preference for one or the other is unlikely to best serve the needs of the environment. An excessive amount of early legislation would probably lead to the corporate sector feeling that environmental changes were being imposed on it without due regard to the practicalities of implementation. This would be likely to create a negative attitude towards environmental improvement and as a result companies, instead of striving for environmental excellence,

---

1. Lickiss, M. (1991) 'Measuring up to the environmental challenge', *Accountancy*, January, p. 6.

may make little effort to achieve more than the minimum required standards. On the other hand, an entirely voluntary approach could put environmentally conscious companies at a disadvantage compared to their less responsible counterparts who were taking little or no action to reduce the costs they were imposing upon society. In time the more progressive companies might come under pressure to improve results by reducing environmental expenditure.

Striking the appropriate balance between legislation and persuasion will involve applying a cost-benefit test to see which is most likely to achieve a particular policy objective. Sometimes an element of both may be the most appropriate with the legislation, for example, sketching out the framework for compliance and a voluntary code providing implementation guidance. Another way of combining legislation and persuasion is to indicate that improvements will initially be sought by voluntary means but that if they are not forthcoming or if the rate of improvement is too slow legislation will have to be considered. Care does need to be taken, however, to ensure that in a rapidly changing area legislation encourages rather than stifles innovatory policies and, secondly, that it is sensitive enough to take account of the very different impacts that individual companies have on the environment.

PUBLIC SECTOR

In addition to regulating the corporate sector, the government has direct responsibility for promoting good environmental practice by the public sector. Indeed, David Dewar, the Assistant Auditor General at the National Audit Office, has persuasively argued that there are a number of reasons why the widest range of environmental issues may be encountered in this part of the economy. First, many public sector operations and activities have a direct impact on the environment, for example in areas such as road building, public transport, nuclear installations and environmental health. Secondly, the public sector has responsibility for national environmental policies and for passing and enforcing environmental legislation. Thirdly, the public sector is responsible for determining taxation, duties and levies and other measures which directly and indirectly influence decisions by organizations, thereby having an impact on their treatment of environmental issues. Fourthly, the public sector has the main role in initiating and responding to national and international developments on environmental issues. Fifthly, the use of public funds brings with it additional requirements for accountability to Parliament and the public. Chartered accountants who are ministers in HM government, members of Parliament, senior civil servants or employed in institutions such as the National Audit Office, of which there will be an increasing number now that it has become the first organization outside public practice to train students for membership of the Institute of Chartered Accountants in England and Wales, will therefore have at least as many opportunities as their colleagues in public practice or in commerce and industry to play their part in creating a better environment.

Traditionally, chartered accountants do not seem to have taken a major interest in the preparation of our national accounts which has often seemed more the preserve of the economists, but there are some signs that this is starting to change. One way in which we could contribute in this area would be to assist in the development of information systems for the provision of environmental accounting data at the national and international level. Dewar has suggested there is a need 'to build up and maintain, by regular scrutiny and update, a national databank of key environmental information. Though planned as an integrated whole, this need not be totally centralized and could be compiled in separate sections and at different levels, for example, by industrial sectors, main activity areas, regionally and nationally'. While Professor David Pearce *et al.* in *Blueprint for a Green Economy*[2] are not in favour of following the French and Norwegian governments in seeking to develop a full system of national accounting which takes account of environmental factors, on the grounds that the cost of such an undertaking is likely to be very large and the returns are still unclear, they do support expanding the existing environmental database and seeking to measure sustainable income at the national and global levels.

ENVIRONMENTAL POLICIES

For organizations developing environmental policies, whether they be private sector enterprises, private non-profit-making organizations or public entities, e.g. nationalized industries, local authorities and government departments, it is important that the policy permeate the whole organization and be a seamless whole rather than a series of fragmented initiatives treating management, auditing and reporting aspects separately. Drawing on the experience of companies that have already developed environmental policies, Tom Burke and Julie Hill in *Ethics, Environment and the Company*[3] have identified key elements that might be expected to appear in any successful corporate environmental policy. The criteria, which appear worthy of support, are as follows:

---

2. Pearce, D., Markandya, A. and Barbier, E.B. (1989) *Blueprint for a Green Economy*, London, Earthscan Publications.
3. Institute of Business Ethics (1990) *Ethics, Environment and the Company: A Guide to Effective Action*, London, IBE.

- *Comprehensive*. The policy should deal with all aspects of a company's impact on the environment, its use of resources as well as its emissions, product and process impacts and the short- and long-term effects of its actions.
- *Measurable*. The policy should include programmes to implement and goals which can be measured.
- *Communicated*. The policy should be available in a convenient and comprehensible form and as much as possible of the goals, targets, procedures and information generated should be made publicly available.
- *Implemented*. Responsibilities should be allocated to different functions and the necessary machinery to manage implementation put in place. Progress should be monitored frequently and the policy reviewed regularly.
- *Results of a process*. The workforce and management at all levels should be involved in the preparation and implementation of the company's policy.
- *Led*. There should be a single clear focus in the company to report to and to provide inspiration and motivation.

How can the accountancy profession help ensure that as many companies as possible implement policies which meet the above criteria? In addition to bringing environmental issues to members' attention through articles and speeches it may be worthwhile exploring the benefits of developing codes of good practice, perhaps in partnership with other interested organizations, on disclosures to be included in annual reports and on guidelines for environmental auditing. Companies adopting the codes could disclose the fact in their annual reports and hopefully analysts and journalists, through links with institutional investors and comments in circulars and the press, would encourage as many companies as possible to comply with them. A Coopers & Lybrand survey[4] of finance directors in September 1990 showed an increasing trend towards business taking account of environmental issues but significant scope for further progress remains. Whilst 41% of the companies surveyed had environmental policies only 16% had conducted environmental audits covering the whole business and many of these were probably subsidiaries of US companies. A further 21% had carried out an environmental audit covering certain aspects of the business but 60% had not done so. On the financial reporting side, only 29% had included details of a company's environmental policy and/or performance in their annual report compared to 65% that had remained silent, although 44% did expect to devote at least one paragraph to the environment in their next annual report.

---

4. Coopers & Lybrand Deloitte (1990) *Environment and the Finance Function: A Survey of Finance Directors*, London, Coopers & Lybrand Deloitte.

FINANCIAL REPORTING

The 1991 report on Accounting for Environmental Protection Measures by the Secretary-General to the UN Commission on Transnational Corporations could provide a useful starting point for a more systematic approach to disclosures on the environment and on environmental protection measures. The Commission's Intergovernmental Working Group of Experts on International Standards of Accounting and Reporting concluded that environmental protection measures are an important matter and that enterprises should at least provide a description of their environmental policy, programmes and achievements in the directors' report. It was noted that some enterprises already included details of capital and current environmental expenditures in that report suggesting that calculation of such figures was feasible. It was therefore recommended that the following disclosures should be included in the management discussion and analysis section of the annual report:

- the type of environmental issues pertinent to the enterprise and its industry;
- policy and programmes adopted with respect to environmental protection measures;
- improvements in key areas since the introduction of the policy or over the last five years, whichever is shorter;
- the environmental emissions targets the enterprise has set for itself and its performance relative to those targets;
- the extent to which environmental protection measures have been undertaken due to government legislation and the extent to which government targets are being achieved;
- any material proceedings under environmental laws;
- the financial or operational effects of environmental protection measures on the capital expenditure and earnings of the enterprise for the current period and any specific impact on future periods;
- when material, the actual amount charged to operations in the current period together with a description of the environmental measures to which they relate;
- when material, amounts capitalized cumulatively and in the current period together with amounts written off in respect of environmental measures and a description of those measures.

The UN report proposed disclosure in the notes to the financial statements of the policies adopted in accounting for environmental protection measures in, for example, recording liabilities and provisions, in setting up catastrophe reserves and in disclosure of contingent liabilities. It also recommended disclosure, when material, of details of contingent liabilities and liabilities, provisions and reserves that have been set aside for the current period as well as amounts accumulated to date in respect of these items.

THE ENVIRONMENT RESEARCH GROUP

If enterprises' environmental policies are to move forward in the direction tentatively discussed in this paper there is a need for a comprehensive research programme embracing accounting, auditing, management and finance issues. Developing such a programme is the key task of the multidisciplinary Environment Research Group which has been established by the Research Board of the Institute of Chartered Accountants in England and Wales. The members of the group are:

- Professor Richard Macve (Chairman), Professor of Accounting at the University College of Wales, Aberystwyth, and member of the ICAEW Council;
- Dr David Cope, Director, The UK Centre for Economic and Environmental Development;
- Mr David Dewar, Assistant Auditor General, National Audit Office
- Mr Richard Freeman, Corporate Chief Economist, ICI;
- Dr David Owen, Financial Analyst;
- Mr David Owen, Senior Lecturer, School of Business and Economic Studies, University of Leeds;
- Mr David Pimm, Senior Technical Manager, Coopers & Lybrand Deloitte.

The decision to establish the Environment Research Group was taken by the Research Board following a research seminar on 'Chartered Accountants and the Environment' held at the Institute in September 1990 at which the participants included senior representatives of government, industry, practice, academe and environmental groups. The seminar considered recent initiatives by the government on the environment, the role of the market, financial reporting and auditing issues and highlighted a number of areas in which further research, of a both pure and applied nature, was required.

The Research Board is the largest private sector sponsor of accountancy research in the United Kingdom and its commitment to support accountancy-based research on the environment is evidenced by its decision to make funds of up to £60 000 available for projects in this area in the coming year.

RESEARCH ISSUES

In examining international trends in accountancy-based regulations and practice on the environment, and in particular the nature and speed at which developments are occurring, one of the major issues to be addressed is the identification of the key determinants of the rate of diffusion of new ideas in areas such as inclusion of information on new topics in financial statements. This issue, of course, extends beyond environmental issues to those such as the provision of value-based information. Other financial reporting issues include the nature of information that the users of financial statements want on the environment and whether all of the principal categories of users have the same information needs. In Professor Solomons' *Guidelines for Financial Reporting Standards*[5] the four main categories of user identified were:

- present and potential investors;
- present and potential creditors (including suppliers);
- present and potential employees, and those who may act for them in bargaining situations, such as trade unions; and
- present and potential customers who are or may be tied to an enterprise by long-term supply contracts.

Professor Solomons considered that the four primary groups of users of general purpose reports did not have identical interests but all shared a common interest in the profitability and viability of the enterprise concerned. He recognized that the social behaviour of an enterprise is an important determinant of its viability and pointed out that if an enterprise was seen to be lacking in its concern for the environment it may run the risk of political action being taken against it, with possible implications for its survival. Even if we accept Solomons' conclusion that while each of the main interest groups may attach different weights to profitability and viability, but that these interests nevertheless have enough in common to allow a single set of reports to serve their needs reasonably well, we are still left with the question as to what information should be provided. Should it be similar to that proposed in the UN report or a different set of data?

If, as the United Nations suggests, financial statements should disclose details of environmental expenditures further studies will be needed on the types of items that should be included within this heading. There is probably a good measure of agreement that it should include expenditures to limit emissions to acceptable levels during normal production operations. But should it also take account of the cost of developing more environmentally-friendly products, and even more difficult, the costs of rectifying damage to the environment caused by accidents which take place?

Attempts to determine the amount of environmental liabilities will have to take account of the difficulties of establishing 'reasonable estimates' of the amount at which they should be recognized due to technological, legal and regulatory uncertainties. The long-term nature of many such liabilities poses additional problems. In particular, when does a liability meet the

---

5. London, ICAEW, 1989.

criteria for recognition, that is at what stage does it pass the critical point at which a 'reasonable estimate' becomes possible? In disclosing both liabilities and contingent liabilities how should the uncertainties involved be dealt with in the financial statements? Conventionally, liabilities are stated at their most likely amount but should an indication of the range of possible estimates also be given?

To enable environmental auditing to develop we will need to consider the definition of what constitutes an environmental audit and how such audits should be distinguished from initial assessments undertaken prior to an environmental policy being adopted. Sir Trevor Holdsworth, a past President of the Confederation of British Industry, has described the environmental audit as a management tool comprising a systematic, documented, periodic and objective evaluation of how well management systems and structures and equipment are performing. But should it be carried out by a team reporting to management, by external reviewers or a combination of both? If the auditors are to be drawn from outside the organization should the environmental audit, like the financial audit, be the prerogative of accountants or should it be a multidisciplinary process? Can certain high-level controls be identified which feature in all systems of control, be they financial, production or environmental in nature? Moreover, in considering environmental audits we should not lose sight of the need for the consideration of how environmental factors should be taken into account in the audit of the financial statements carried out in accordance with the requirements of existing companies legislation.

Another key area for research is how to measure environmental costs. Until now, as often happens with new management issues, most companies have concentrated on qualitative performance indicators. But many argue that until we can measure environmental costs, a far wider concept than environmental expenditures, we will not be able to manage them properly. Among the management issues to be addressed are which costs should be measured. Should it just be those associated with a company's production or should account also be taken of any costs attributable to products sold by the company? The difficulty with the latter notion is that these costs may be outside the company's control and may depend on whether the product is properly used or not. Allocating joint costs where, for example, more than one company is discharging waste into a river can also be very difficult. In addition, views differ on whether attempts should be made to measure a company's overall environmental performance. Aggregation of the various effects of a company on the environment, if appropriate measurement techniques could be developed, would enable an overall assessment to be made of whether or not its performance had improved, if it were better in some respects but had deteriorated in others. It might fail to achieve its objective though if, like the earnings per share figure in financial statements, it led to excessive concentration on a single figure rather than a balanced assessment of an enterprise's overall performance.

Further fruitful areas for research include ways of structuring management performance systems to encourage greater concern for the organization's impact on the environment, the effectiveness of alternative forms of market-based incentives and procedures used for identifying eligible securities for environmental trusts. Lastly, but by no means least, case studies on the implementation of environmental programmes in both the public and private sector are likely to yield much useful information on the practical problems that inevitably arise when major changes are introduced within organizations.

CONCLUSION

At present there are many more questions than answers on environmental issues and this state of affairs will continue for as long as the planet exists. Throughout the Institute's 111 year history, however, chartered accountants have always thrived on responding to challenges and on striking out in pioneering directions. In measuring up to the environmental challenge we will help to bridge the gap between questions and answers by developing solutions based on research and innovation in practice.

THE CONTRIBUTION OF MANAGEMENT ACCOUNTING TO THE ENVIRONMENTAL DEBATE

Lesley Phillips

INTRODUCTION

The Chartered Institute of Management Accountants (CIMA) is one of the six leading accountancy bodies in the United Kingdom which together makes up the Consultative Committee of Accountancy Bodies. Its membership is now in excess of 30 000, most of this number being employed within organizations, although about eight per cent are currently involved in consultancy work. There is also a significant element of overseas membership ensuring an international approach to issues affecting the accountancy profession. The environment debate is just one such consideration.

It is clear that the concerns for the environment which are being embraced by the world at large are now coming to the attention of the accountancy profession. With much centring on costs, CIMA has a clear contribution to make. In 1990, CIMA was involved in a number of initiatives of varying shades of green. These included:

- a research study;
- a 'green' business management competition for sixth form schoolchildren;
- a report on current corporate reporting practices; and
- the establishment of an environment accounting working party.

These will be discussed below. Courses on energy conservation schemes are also being planned and the library is building up its stock of publications on environment issues. Each initiative has contributed, in its own way, to the green debate and will act as a catalyst for further discussion on the future of green reporting. CIMA is constantly considering and developing new initiatives.

THE COSTS TO INDUSTRY OF ADOPTING ENVIRONMENTALLY FRIENDLY PRACTICES

A CIMA research study

CIMA's Research and Technical Department, aware that the environment issue was one which could not be ignored, commissioned David Burkitt of the Industrial Research Bureau to investigate the costs to industry of adopting environmentally friendly practices. The study looked into three areas of practice where 'environmentally friendly' policies were commonly adopted in order to assess whether there were any cost savings to be made. These were:

- the introduction of catalytic convertors and the use of unleaded petrol;
- the use and collection of recycled materials; and
- the adoption of energy efficient schemes.

The report also touched briefly on the increasing use of environmental audits.

The report found that by taking positive action, not necessarily at great cost, all companies could achieve some degree of 'greenness'. Table 4.1 illustrates the list of recommended action points for companies to pursue. The key message of the report was that the cost effects of becoming environmentally friendly would work through the balance sheet to the advantage of those doing so.

This report acted as a starting point for further investigation, raising awareness of basic environmental issues. Further, more in-depth studies are currently being planned.

Table 4.1 Recommended action points

A management accountant, or indeed any other executive in a company, reading this report will quickly register possible action points. A checklist is set out below in the form of questions to be asked about any company. Some of them will not apply. For others, a positive response will be indicative of action already in hand. It is recommended that everyone should go through the questions after reading the report. There will be few cases where no possibilities to take positive steps emerge. Where action is indicated, it is vital that it is initiated.

In the context of your company, ask the following questions; and ensure answers are forthcoming

- Do we consistently monitor company practices and performance in terms of effects on the environment?
- Do we systematically check that all public references to the company are picked up, particularly those with environmental dimensions?
- Do we have a positive, proactive policy in respect of publicizing positive environmental actions and policies?
- Are all our company vehicles currently run on lead-free fuel?
- For any that are not, can they be adjusted? If not, replacement should be considered
- Is the presence of catalytic converters taken into account when setting our policy for purchase/leasing of company cars; is it possible to retro-fit catalytic converters to any cars already in the fleet?
- How large is our electricity bill and how is it built up? What is the largest constituent?
- What would savings of 10%, 20% or 30% on fuel bills mean to us in cash terms?
- How can we make the use of lighting and heating more efficient without losses in its effectiveness?
- Is a combined heat and power scheme feasible for our factory or office block?
- Where and how soon can we set up schemes to recycle paper?
- What other materials do we use in quantities that are sufficient to initiate collection schemes? How about cans or glass?
- Do we already use recycled stationery or paper products? If so, what scope is there to extend the range. If recycled stationery is not in use, why not? Are we aware of the range and quality of such recycled products that are available?
- Do we know what environmental audits are about? If not, how soon can we obtain information, particularly copies of two basic publications? If we are familiar with such audits, when will we be undertaking one?

Source: Chartered Institute of Management Accountants (1990) *The Costs to Industry of Adopting Environmentally Friendly Practices*, CIMA Research Study.

WHAT ON EARTH IS INDUSTRY DOING?

In order to stimulate a sharper awareness of the effect that industry has on the environment, CIMA launched a business management competition for Midlands sixth formers towards the end of 1990. With the financial backing of a number of large organizations, the competiton took the form of a case study, focusing on industry and its effect on the environment. Case study teams were required to research and prepare a report on an environmental issue and its effect, particularly financial, on industry. The intention was to demonstrate the effect that consumer demand and legislation has on the financial management, planning, control and decision-making of business. It was also hoped that by highlighting the connection between accounting and the environment, accountants in the making would be aware of the benefits which would ensue from becoming more environmentally aware.

CORPORATE REPORTING: THE MANAGEMENT INTERFACE

The past fifteen years have seen some important debate on corporate reporting practices, including elements of social reporting. Believing that CIMA as a professional body and, as a corollary, management accounting as a science, have a contribution to make on the corporate reporting debate, a working party was set up to look at current practice and develop recommendations on best future practice. A report of its findings, *Corporate Reporting: The Management Interface)*, was made in October 1990.

The report made a number of recommendations on how corporate reports might be dynamized. As part of its findings, it suggested that more information should be disclosed by companies in their Annual Report on, amongst other things, the environment. Initial investigation of over 100 large companies had shown that incidence of such reporting was minimal. Any mention that was made tended to be in the narrative form, used largely for PR purposes and having negligible effect on the balance sheet.

Recognizing the increasing importance of the subject, the working party recommended that there should be increased disclosure of environmental practices. It realized, however, that just as accounting for goodwill, brands and other intangibles was not a simple task, accounting for assets such as the sea, the air and other natural resources was not a straightforward matter either, and recommended that a specialist group should be set up to make further investigation.

ACCOUNTING FOR THE ENVIRONMENT

As a direct response to the recommendation made by the Corporate Working Party that further investigation of environment issues should be made, an environment accounting working party was established under the aegis of CIMA's Law and Parliamentary Committee. Its constitution was geared to reflect those sectors currently concerned with environmental issues and included representatives from Nuclear Electric plc, Severn Trent Water plc, Sainsbury's and KPMG Peat Marwick McLintock. Professor Rob Gray, Mathew Professor of Accounting at Dundee University and author of a report by the ACCA

'The Greening of Accountancy', served on the working party as a representative of the academic world.

The working party investigated the role of accountants in organizations adopting environmentally sound practices. Since it worked on the basis that the environment debate was likely to be at the fore of discussion for some time, its ultimate aim was to provide practical guidance not only to CIMA members, but to all interested in sustaining and improving the state of the environment.

Given that many changes are occurring at a regulatory level, the working party took into account both UK and EC legislation, including the Department of the Environment's 'green' White Paper. It also considered the Pearce Report on sustainable development.

The results of a members survey which was conducted in the summer of 1990 highlighted the need to inform members of both the legislative position within which they found themselves and of possible actions which could make their practices more environmentally friendly. These will form the basis of a report to be published in due course.

THE FUTURE OF GREEN REPORTING

It is expected that the initiatives undertaken by CIMA will enable all organizations in some way to be better equipped to respond to the need for more environmentally sensitive processes and products. This will in turn contribute to the wider debate of sustaining an environment fit for future generations.

Chapter Five

GREEN PRESSURE GROUPS

Business and the environmental movement
Clive Wicks, World Wide Fund for Nature
Green reporting and the consumer movement
Richard Adams, New Consumer

BUSINESS AND THE ENVIRONMENTAL MOVEMENT

Clive Wicks

The World Wide Fund for Nature (WWF) raises funds from industry and commerce for its conservation programme and it works with industry to help develop sound environmental policies. While recognizing that industry is one of the main causes of environmental decline, WWF believes that industry can be a major force for change once the environmental problems created by industry are recognized.

The major problem facing our civilization has now been widely recognized as the threat to the natural systems that sustain life on our planet. Pollution and wasteful use of energy and resources contribute to the degradation of the planet's ecological systems through exploitative demands: (1) on renewable natural resources such as timber, (2) on finite resources which have to be extracted, such as materials for road building or the construction industry, (3) from the disposal of waste. Climatic change, caused mainly by the excessive amounts of carbon dioxide (CO_2) we produce, will affect the lives of billions of people. Although much blame has been attached to rain forest destruction, only 10–20% of the CO_2 emitted annually can be attributed to such activity. Some 75% of the CO_2 is caused by us in the industrialized countries through the use of fossil fuels as our main source of fuel for energy and transportation. Acid rain is another by-product of our fossil fuel consumption. Many waterways and waterbodies in the UK are acidified as a result. Over 60% of all the trees in UK are affected by acid rain.

WWF's objective is to encourage a management culture in industry that promotes responsibility for the environment. Industry should prevent problems rather than pay for the cure.

Fortunately, the enthusiasm shown by some UK industrial leaders for understanding and incorporating environmental thinking into their corporate planning strategies has grown in the past few years. This is explained partly by the reaction of certain industries to major international disasters, such as Bhopal, Chernobyl, the Sandoz Rhine spill and the *Exxon Valdez*, and their cost implications, but industry's response is more than simply self-interest. No doubt, industry is responding to the general awakening of public interest in environmental issues, both at home and overseas, which has taken place in the last decade. Industry is also faced with a steadily increasing number of environmental regulations and directives emanating from the European Community which are subsequently incorporated into UK legislation. The directive on Environmental Impact Assessment which came into force in the twelve member states of the EC in July 1988 is a case in point.

The attitudes held by industry towards environmental issues formed an important chapter of the UK's response to the World Conservation Strategy in 1983. The report offered 24 recommendations for encouraging patterns of investment and protection, which pay greater respect to the natural environment and the sustainable use of natural resources. This message has received powerful, official endorsement in the report of the World Commission on Environment and Development (the Brundtland Report) published in 1987.[1] This is bearing further examples in the latest edition of the World Conservation Strategy which recommends that industries, trade associations and labour unions should establish industry-wide and company policies on resource and environmental management, including compliance with environmental laws. This should include cleaner and more efficient technologies and processes and joint use of waste treatment plants.

In order to reduce the trend in the destruction of the natural environment through pollution and waste, it is essential to address the main economic activities, or industrial sectors, that create the problems.

WWFN has looked at a number of sectors and would like to see industry set objectives for these as follows:

- *Manufacturing*: Prevent the generation of pollution through better resource use and changes in manufacturing design, processes and distribution. Establish by 1993 technology transfer programmes for process technology,

---

1. The World Commission on Environment and Development (1987) *Our Common Future*, Oxford, Oxford University Press.

product redesign, audit systems and well trained staff to ensure that pollution prevention strategies are incorporated as early as possible in manufacturing development.

- *Waste*: Establish measurable goals and implementation strategies for reducing total wastes generated. Reduce use of packing materials and ensure that these are either biodegradable or can be recycled. Set up shared recycling facilities and ensure that 50% of all waste is recycled by the year 2000. Established reduction goals for use of designated heavy metals, such as lead and cadmium, in products and packaging by the year 1995.
- *Energy*: Produce and use energy resources with maximum efficiency and minimum environmental damage. Adopt by 1993 policies requiring incorporation of efficiency and conservation strategies to meet projected energy supply needs prior to investment in generating facilities. Industry should invest in renewable energy sources such as wind, wave and sun which are environmentally sound.
- *Transportation*: Adopt transportation and fuel alternatives that prevent pollution and minimize impacts on the environment. Increase overall fuel efficiency of vehicles by 50% by the year 2000. Increase investment in energy efficient public transport systems. Reduce both sulphur dioxide and nitrogen oxide emissions to critical load levels. Where necessary set up company transport schemes to supplement public transport and help employes get to work at low cost and with minimum use of fuel and low pollution.
- *Agriculture, grazing, and forest operations*: Adopt sustainable practices that maintain resource productivity while minimizing chemical and unsustainable energy inputs. Pesticides should not be used outside integrated pest management systems. Government should help industry by providing incentives for sustainable farming, environmentally sound harvesting and silvicultural practices. The agricultural industry must avoid conversion of endangered prime ecosystems and reduce conversion of potentially fragile lands. They should also reduce the loss of existing cropland from desertification, soil erosion and urban development.
- *Mining*: Employ practices that minimize harm to, and allow restoration of, the environment; avoid any environmentally damaging mining activity in endangered prime ecosystems.
- *Services*: Incorporate pollution prevention and resource efficiency in design, financing, and delivery of services. Banks and other organizations providing financial and technical assistance should adopt policies that make their services conditional on meeting targets for pollution prevention and resource efficiency.
- *Households/lifestyles*: Industry must help to avoid the transfer of unsustainable First World consumer behaviour to developing and recently industrialized nations.

- *Human settlement*: Incorporate environmental considerations in the social strategies when planning land use development. Support organizations concerned with population growth and human poverty.
- *Ecosystems*: Industry should not damage endangered ecosystems in which pollution effects are concentrated and magnified. These include aquatic and terrestrial ecosystems such as coastal zones and tropical rainforests. Terminate the dumping of industrial and municipal waste in all coastal zones by 1995.

The objective of all this is to achieve the concept of sustainable development outlined in the Brundtland Report which is defined as development that meets the needs of the present world, without compromising the ability of future generations to meet their own needs.

The accountancy profession will have a major role to play in achieving sustainable development. Like the legal and insurance professions they work with all industries, large and small. It is going to become increasingly important for the accounting profession to know the right questions to ask their clients about the environmental consequences of their operations.

There will be good professional as well as environmental reasons for this. There will be little point in certifying the accounts of an apparently profitable company if it goes into bankruptcy shortly afterwards due to a failure to insure itself against claims for the environmental damage of its products or processes. The vast majority of companies have so far not carried out an environmental audit to establish the level of risk they should insure against, consequently insurance cover is usually totally inadequate. It will come as a shock to many conpanies to find they are not complying with EC environmental laws and have to make major capital investments in order to meet emission controls and pollution standards. This is particularly true of small and medium size companies, most of whom have not even thought about the environmental problems they are creating.

One of the most important recommendations that the financial adviser could make is to suggest that an environmental audit be carried out. This should establish exactly what environmental problems the company has now, how these impact on the business, and what actions it needs to take. Many businesses have found that the environmental audit has contributed to major savings through waste reduction, increased energy efficiency and improvements in the use of plant, machinery and vehicles.

The audit should be used with an assessment of the economic and business environment to create an integrated business plan. At the same time it will ensure that the company is in full possession of all the facts on the potential risks that it needs to insure effectively. It should also ensure that no member of the company goes to court for failure to comply with the numerous environmental laws.

Environmental auditing should be a continuous proactive process. No company should wait until it is involved in some form of wrong-doing.

There are a number of different types of audit that can be employed.[2] These are outlined below:

- *Compliance audits*. Relatively simple, but nonetheless fairly time-consuming.
- *Site audits*. Spot checks of sites known to have actual or potential problems.
- *Activity audits*. Evaluate implementation of policy in activities that cross business boundaries (e.g. shipping operations throughout the group).
- *Corporate audits*. Typically an audit of an entire business. The aim is to ensure that roles and responsibilities are understood, technical and advisory support is available, and vertical and lateral communications channels are open and operational.
- *Associate audits*. Auditing of associate companies or corporations acting as agents in overseas markets.
- *Issues audits*. These focus on how the group is dealing with specific environmental issues of key concern (e.g. the loss of tropical rainforest habitat, or damage through processes or products). They involve an evaluation of policy, guidelines, operating procedures and actual practice within all businesses.

GREEN REPORTING AND THE CONSUMER MOVEMENT

Richard Adams

THE GROWING INFLUENCE OF THE CONSUMER

In Britain during the last four decades, within a market economy driven by consumer preference and purchasing capacity, greater economic leisure has provided the opportunity to both analyse and reflect on the underlying nature and direction of a demand-led economic system. There is an increasing requirement for information on the social and environmental impact of corporate policy and appraisal of its effects. The movements for healthy eating, ethical investment and, above all, environmental concern have played a big part in awakening the consumer's social awareness. It is perhaps no coincidence that change in Eastern Europe is essentially being driven by consumerist

---

2. For a more in-depth discussion of environmental auditing techniques, together with a wealth of case study material, see Elkington, J. (1990) *The Environmental Audit: A Green Filter for Company Policies, Plants, Processes and Products*, London, Sustainability/World Wide Fund for Nature.

demands, a desire for what the West possesses – democracy but also 'prosperity'. Yet the very process by which the majority in the West have become affluent is increasingly being questioned by some of its beneficiaries. Can we go on like this? Is it sustainable? Is the whole system flawed and ultimately self-destructive? These questions are being asked not just by pressure groups but also by individuals, by business, by governments and global institutions.

The constant factor in market or centralized economies, in the 'Third' World or the 'First', is individual demand. This demand, though in part created by them, is the tune to which our major companies dance. There is now evidence that consumers are realizing the power of their economic votes, votes which can be cast every day. Social reporting enables the public to relate their personal values to their everyday expenditure. In 1990 British consumers spent more than £300 billion on personal goods and services. Of this sum only £30 billion was spent in areas where there was no effective consumer choice or where, through near monopoly, it was severely limited. People in the UK can therefore direct purchasing to the value of £270 billion. With, or because of, the growth in individual spending power has come the rise of green consumerism, the exercise of consumer choice which expresses a preference for less environmentally harmful goods and services.

Green consumerism, like nothing else, has brought home to economists the truism that not all wealth is economic in nature. For two hundred years Adam Smith's model, with land, labour and capital as the three essential factors of production, had prevailed. It was, understandably, heavily revised and criticized in this century, the most significant of these criticisms pointing out the role of social structures in the creation and distribution of wealth. It was also noted that the importance of the natural environment goes far beyond that normally assigned to 'land' and that the process of economic activity can be just as important to people as the product that it yields. Having the opportunity to own and drive a car is generally regarded as one of the benefits of a consumer society, but there is a price to be paid for those living beside a motorway. Green consumerism is beginning to address these issues but it can be taken much further.

The market is well understood as a powerful mechanism for enabling individuals to express their preferences in a decentralized way. It cuts out intermediate bureaucracy, and consumers, however subliminally, understand that not only does their purchasing power secure the product or service of their choice, but they also know that it acts as an economic vote, encouraging producers to provide more of the same. For the market to deliver its benefits it needs to be policed. Contracts have to be enforced, rights protected, producers prevented from undermining consumer choice. Government still has much to do in this area and manufacturing and retailing power continues to consolidate. But although producers have great power, the large following that consumers' associations have in the developed world shows that consumers value, and can still get, independent advice on the traditional virtues of competitive price, safety and reliability. In the UK, the Consumers' Association, the National Consumer Council and a number of consumer 'watchdog' bodies are providing the basic information that enables the consumer to make a valid choice, and, increasingly, environmental information is seen to be part of the required package.

Classic economic theory argues that for a market to work at its most effective there has to be perfect competition. The key to this is extensive and genuine choice in goods and services. But for choice to be exercised in a meaningful way there has also to be perfect information so that customers can truly express their preferences. Until recently the information relevant to economic choice has been understood to comprise those traditional consumer values of price, quality, service and safety. But now, as green consumerism has demonstrated, consumers have additional values beyond the economic sphere. To make the market work effectively they must have information about those values to express their choice.

In Britain, environmental awareness has provided a window of consciousness-raising opportunity. One of the challenges in this field is to strike a balance between whistle-blowing and encouragement. Legislation can enforce, or provide sanctions and incentives, yet one of the striking things about green consumerism is that it has demonstrated how everyday shoppers can, through their own choices, force through change at a rapid pace, well ahead of the proposed opaque legislation on eco-labelling.

There are limits to consumer power but they have yet to be seriously explored. The £320 billion that was spent in 1989 on consumer goods and services contrasts with the £2 billion given directly to charity by individuals in the same year. For every £10 spent on ourselves we give six pence away. The pattern of charitable giving by individuals shows that the poorer one is the higher the proportion of income given away. The opposite is true of the consumer who applies ethical or environmental criteria. It is mainly the affluent who choose to afford the extra cost of environmentally benign products or the inconvenience of finding an alternative to goods produced by a company that also markets tobacco. Green consumerism appeals to the affluent, whether it is conscience, conviction or just a desire to fight the market with the weapons of the market. This is a fact not lost on marketing and sales directors who anticipate that the re-directing of ordinary spending according to social criteria could have a massive impact.

New Consumer, as a public interest research body, is one of the small number of groups which sets out to provide source material which reveals how social and environmental concerns may be practically expressed. These incorporate a wide range of social justice and human development issues upon which the large manufacturing corporation or multiple retailing chain has more influence than is generally recognized.

SOCIAL AND ENVIRONMENTAL DISCLOSURE:
THE NEW CONSUMER SURVEY[1]

New Consumer originally identified more than 70 areas in which corporate activities or involvement had given rise to varying degrees of public interest or concern. The issues ranged from the manufacture of nuclear or chemical weapons to the implementation of thorough-going equal opportunities policies. They could arouse extremes of emotion as in product testing on animals, seem to be relevant only to a minority as in provision for the disabled, or cover a field so wide as to be almost without boundaries as with the environment. From July 1989 to August 1990, New Consumer undertook a detailed survey of 128 companies covering some 35–40% of the consumer goods market. A key issue was the level of disclosure which a company exhibited when reporting key social and environmental facts about its own performance. In a market economy, where competition is a spur to performance, a degree of secrecy in commercially sensitive areas is both necessary and understandable. It must be said, however, that it is still the practice of most corporations to assume that most information is commercially sensitive until proved otherwise.

Successive governments have recognized that companies with the protection of limited liability must be required to inform their shareholders about the financial strengths of their business, but even so such requirements do not prevent unexpected bankruptcies by major corporations. On social issues the legislative requirements are minimal.

It is also clear from an analysis of company literature that a 'minimalists' convention' has been established, even on required disclosure on social issues. It is not an exaggeration to say that the extent of expansion under the statutory requirements in a company's Annual Report is a good guide as to how seriously that corporation treats social responsibility issues.

The New Consumer survey revealed that companies also vary widely in their willingness to provide non-statutory information on environmental and social responsibility issues. Setting aside that small number which, because of impending or recent acquisition or merger, or, in two cases, liquidation, might have had pressing reasons for not responding, the actual number of companies who returned the full questionnaire or part-questionnaire with supporting information was 32 out of 128. When the additional responses on detailed information was taken into account nearly 75% of companies in the survey cooperated to some extent during the research. A notable feature was the comparatively higher response from American-owned companies (32%) and other foreign-owned companies (29%) compared with the response of UK-owned firms (22%).

---

1. The full survey results have been published under the title *Changing Corporate Values*, Kogan Page, 1991.

The vast majority of UK companies surveyed were quoted on the London stock market. These companies all provide annual reports for shareholders which are also made available to the public. These can be an excellent source of information for many categories of social data. However, they do vary. Some companies produce lengthy and detailed reports covering the widest implications of their activities while others provide little more than operational and financially orientated information. Compare, for example, the contrasting reports, both for the year ending 30 September 1989, by Tate & Lyle plc and Berisford International plc. These two companies effectively shared the UK sugar market between them for that period, although Tate & Lyle were the larger company overall. In annual reports of similar size Tate & Lyle's contained extensive information on its community involvement backed up with wide-ranging supplementary publications for staff and the public on the company's affairs such as training and environment issues, together with individual operating unit reports for employees. By contrast Berisford's social information was notable by its absence.

WHY IS SOCIAL DISCLOSURE IMPORTANT?

The 128 companies surveyed had an estimated combined turnover which in 1990 exceeded £1000 billion, world-wide. Their products and services will be purchased or used by nearly every consumer in the UK, often on a daily basis. The traditional view is that a company is accountable to its shareholders but these, by any measure, are a tiny, unrepresentative group. By contrast, the 'stakeholder' concept of corporate responsibility is increasingly being recognized as valid by our major companies. This argues that several groups of people have a right to information about operations and policy – the shareholders, employees, consumers of the goods or services provided, the social community, and the community world-wide, particularly with respect to environmental issues.

To a greater or lesser extent people within all these groups have a genuine interest in how an organization does its business. Their lives, work opportunities, personal development and the surrounding social fabric have all been shown to be affected by the immense resources of manufacturing and retailing groups. In the survey there are outstanding examples of companies whose social reporting is exemplary, such companies often already having a reputation for straightforward financial reporting. By contrast far too many companies operate defensively, providing the minimum required under standard accounting conventions and the Companies Acts.

Some type of response casting light on corporate social responsibility policies was received from 97 companies. Several foreign-based companies consulted extensively with their head offices and several UK companies with overseas subsidiaries went to considerable lengths to verify material with operating units in different parts of the globe. The lack of cooperation by the other companies is therefore all the more disturbing. Any company which admitted that it was unable to exert financial policy direction over its component units or collect relevant financial data would see an immediate slump in share price. The inability to collect social data or determine general social policy guidelines at corporate HQ, either because of lack of resources or because of the decentralized nature of a company's policy formulation processes, was nevertheless given as the most frequent reason for non-cooperation.

A significant part of the New Consumer survey was devoted to environmental analysis which, for the purposes of the study, was narrowed down to the main positive and negative environmental impacts of the companies surveyed. The environmental impact of different industrial sectors varies from the oil companies, the very nature of whose business is environmentally damaging, i.e. extracting a non-renewable resource, to the clothing retailers, whose direct impact on the environment is less apparent. Much confusion still reigns in consumers' minds about what is an environmentally benign product or operation and the 'green' revolution in consumerism has done little to enlighten them. This confusion has, more surprisingly, spread to industry. In mid-1990 ICI was forced to withdraw the 'environmentally friendly' label from its range of cleaning products under the Homecare brand after Friends of the Earth pointed out that the manufacture of the main ingredient, soda ash, is a highly energy-intensive process with intensely polluting discharges. A spokesperson for ICI said that the products were given the label because they were based on sodium bicarbonate, listed in the Green Consumer Guide as 'environment-friendly'.

Substances, which in their final form are environmentally benign, can in their extraction, manufacture and/or disposal have a major impact on the environment. Everything we do has some impact on the environment. Our mere existence takes up resources that would otherwise be unused. The key question is how can individuals minimize their impact on the environment and develop a more sustainable economy.

In industry, science and government there is much debate about the exact extent of humanity's impact on the environment. It is generally accepted that we cannot go on using the world's finite resources and polluting the environment without adverse consequences. Industry must take into account the cost of the effects of its operations on the environment, rather than regarding the planet as a free resource. How companies account for these costs is a matter for debate. Should legislation force them to pay via taxes and should these costs be passed on to the consumer, or should there be some form of market regulation which involves building the true cost into a product? Less consumption and more efficient use of resources are obvious targets and should not conflict too heavily with industry's objectives. Certain materials, such as metals, are already carefully and lucratively recycled. Recycling both materials and energy is good industrial practice. Many of the companies in the survey provided examples of energy conservation and recycling initiatives.

Many of the products now considered to be environmentally hazardous were at the time of their discovery regarded as invaluable solutions to a specific problem. The stability of CFCs was the very reason they were developed for use as propellants and refrigerants in the 1930s. This durability has had unforseen consequences. Predicting a product's long-term impact on the environment has not always been a major consideration in development. This hopefully will change as companies adopt policies of 'cradle-to-grave' management of their products.

One of the problems when assessing companies' environmental records in the UK is the lack of independent information available to the public. Although the government is progressing a number of environmental measures they do little to make company environmental information more freely available and accessible. The statutory bodies with responsibility for monitoring the environmental performance of companies have limited resources and powers. Companies have been shown to be ignorant of current environmental legislation particularly with regard to European Community environmental directives and legislation on issues like water quality, air pollution and waste disposal. A different situation prevails in the US where the Environmental Protection Agency (EPA) is an independent environmental watchdog with teeth.

In the US in 1980 Congress passed the Comprehensive Environmental Response, Compensation and Liability Act (CERCLA), better known as Superfund. Under Superfund generators must report spills and other releases that are greater than a minimum reportable quantity. Violations are criminal offences with penalties of one year in jail and fines up to $10 000. CERCLA also deals with uncontrolled hazardous waste sites. Under Superfund, previous or present owners and operators of a site help pay for removal and remedial actions. If the previous firm is out of business, or bankrupt, the EPA has usually been able to seek and obtain funds from companies that sent the waste for treatment or disposal.

In contrast, in the UK, Her Majesty's Inspectorate of Pollution adopts an approach of constructive engagement with companies rather than fining them for pollution violations. In 1988/89 the number of visits by HMIP inspectors to registered works was less than 500. In 1986/87 there were 3129 contraventions of the Clean Air Act but local authorities only brought 153 prosecutions. More recently the National Rivers Authorities have shown rather more in the way of bite. In the four months from September 1989 they brought 682 successful prosecutions with a further 634 in the pipeline. More recently they have set in motion prosecutions against five of the ten newly privatized water authorities. In future both the HMIP and the NRA records of emissions and discharges will be available for public inspection and such information will be supplied to the public at a reasonable charge.

CORPORATE ENVIRONMENTAL IMPACT DISCLOSURE: ISSUES TO BE ADDRESSED

In the survey the companies were asked a number of questions about both positive and negative aspects of their environmental activities. Because the subject is vast and the companies' activities differ in their environmental impact not all the questions were relevant to all companies. The questions fell into four main categories: renewable resources, non-renewable resources, pollution control and pro-environmental activities. Whether or not a company is involved in the nuclear industry has also been included within the environment section. Other sources of information about companies' environmental activities were gathered from press reports, HMIP reports, and from campaigning organizations such as Greenpeace, Friends of the Earth (FoE), Pesticides Action Network (PAN), Women's Environmental Network (WEN), the environmental management consultancy Sustainability and the Worldwide Fund for Nature (WWF). The issues listed below should be regarded as a relatively modest attempt to assess corporate impact and action and would need to be covered in any serious attempt to implement comprehensive green reporting.

Renewable resources

Sustainable biomass production

This topic encompasses the issues of organic farming and monoculture (single crop) production of both animal and plant crops. A number of companies have direct interests in agriculture; for example, the CWS is Britain's largest farmer, and Unilever has extensive plantation operations mainly growing palm oil. Whether companies involved in biomass production have addressed the issue of sustainable development is the first step as traditional, monocultural, intensive farming techniques are dominant in most operations. When vast areas of land are given over to a single crop – as in monoculture, the farming technique used in this country – pests and diseases can easily and rapidly infect the whole crop so large amounts of pesticides are required. In addition, because farmers have increased the number of repeat crops they can get on a single plot, there is the additional requirement for fertilizers. Organic farming still only accounts for a small proportion of our food production in spite of increased public demand.

Another area of biomass production or use is forestry-linked, both for furniture production and paper manufacturing. Most soft wood forestry is manmade and is managed. For example, in Sweden, more trees are planted than are felled as the result of a policy enshrined in law since 1903 which stipulates that for every tree felled more than one must be planted within three years.

Destruction of the rain forests

This is a pressing current issue, because of the potential loss of diversity and the threat to the indigenous populations. The destruction of rain forests does not necessarily involve multinational companies, though sometimes this is the impression. One of the main reasons for forest destruction in Latin America is the enforced resettlement of slum dwellers in the jungle, a government-led initiative. Slum dwellers are encouraged to slash and burn the forest to grow crops.

Other reasons for destruction of the forests include: mining, particularly for oil, bauxite, tin and gold, for timber and for paper production. In terms of tropical forests destroyed for furniture and/or DIY purposes, in 1988 1.5 million cubic metres were imported into the UK, over 80% of which came from Malaysia, Indonesia, the Philippines, Brazil, Guyana, Ghana, Ivory Coast, Liberia and Cameroon. Britain accounts for between 5–7% of all world tropical timber imports. The timber comes in a variety of forms from raw logs and lumber to plywood and manufactured goods such as door blanks.

On average at least 12.5 million acres of tropical forests are destroyed or damaged each year by commercial loggers. According to the International Tropical Timber Organization (ITTO) less than 0.2% of tropical moist forests are being managed sustainably for commercial production. Encouragingly, however, many timber traders are switching to alternative sources, or introducing new non-tropical products. Concerned members of the trade have formed the Association of Woodusers Against Rainforest Exploitation (AWARE). Habitat (part of Storehouse) announced that it was taking steps to look for alternatives to tropical hardwoods in September 1989, in particular pointing to the replacement of mahogany with stained poplar. B&Q and Sainsbury's Homebase stated that they have policies of only stocking sustainably produced timber doors.

Non-renewable resources

Non-renewable energy sources – coal, oil, natural gas and electricity – all involve some environmental damage, either in their extraction or their use.

In addition coal and oil are major contributors to the greenhouse effect and add to the general levels of air pollution through the production of sulphur and nitrogen oxides. Whether companies have taken steps to reduce their energy consumption and to minimize the pollution effects of such consumption was taken into account as well as any initiatives in the fields of alternative energy sources, i.e. solar, wind and wave power.

Pollution control

Pollution control and emission focused on the manufacture and/or use of ozone damaging chemicals, i.e. CFCs and halons; pesticide manufacture and/or use; use, storage and disposal of hazardous or toxic waste; and steps to reduce air and water pollution, to minimize ground contamination.

Ozone-depleting chemical production and use

This topic has recently attracted urgent international attention. The Montreal Protocol is an international treaty whereby CFC production is to be reduced by 50% between 1989 and 1998. CFCs are one of the major ozone-depleting agents. However, agreement over an earlier date for phasing out of CFCs and other ozone damaging chemicals has not been reached.

An additional proposal to phase out production of the alternative HCFCs by 2040 is a blow to those companies (Du Pont and ICI) which have invested in research and plant to manufacture these. They argue that the lack of an international consensus on which products constitute safe alternatives does little to encourage companies to invest money into research in this area. HCFCs have a small effect on the ozone layer but the chemical companies argue that they should be produced as an interim measure until a more long-term substitute for CFCs can be found.

Pesticide use and manufacture

This topic is a matter of some controversy, not least because, like CFCs, many early problem-solving pesticides have proved to be environmentally questionable (e.g. the chlorinated hydrocarbon pesticides, DDT, Aldrin and Dieldrin, and the organophosphates, Parathion and Malathion, whose long-term effects on the environment and man have been queried). Some pesticides have been shown to induce tumours in laboratory animals, and there is still much controversy over which pesticides are safe.

Legislation governing the use of such chemicals varies from country to country. In the US Heinz required its suppliers to ban the use of a reported twelve common pesticides from its foods in 1986. In the UK Heinz has only banned three of the chemicals, one being Alar (daminozide), a cosmetic pesticide spray used on apples, saying that it accepts UK government advisory service assurances that the residues from the other pesticides are not a cause for concern.

Alar was the target of a campaign led by Parents for Safe Food, the London Food Commission and the Pesticides Trust (the UK arm of the US Pesticides Action Network, PAN), which called for the suspension of use of this chemical after the residues on fruit and in apple products in the UK exceeded the US Federal Government Standards at which it was considered to pose an unacceptably high cancer risk. Although the government has refused to ban the chemical the National Farmers' Union called for a voluntary ban in March 1990 and a number of supermarket chains also imposed a ban, including Tesco and Marks & Spencer.

Alternatives to pesticide use include biological control where natural predators are introduced; mechanical control which literally involves physically removing the pests; ecological control which involves growing plants in areas where the pest/disease cannot survive, and integrated pest management which involves all the alternatives and some limited chemical control.

There is no doubt that some form of pest control is necessary in order to provide the food for an ever-increasing human population but clearly the costs need to be weighed more accurately against the benefits than is at present the case.

Hazardous or toxic waste disposal

This is a difficult area to assess not least because of the secrecy that surrounds the control of such substances.

Companies which are likely to produce such waste are the large chemical companies such as ICI and Du Pont, pharmaceutical companies, and electronics companies through their semiconductor and integrated circuit manufacturing and testing operations. All such operations are ultimately overseen by the Hazardous Waste Inspectorate, part of HMIP, but unlike in the US, where Superfund legislation requires registration of waste disposal, no information about storage or disposal of such chemicals is currently available to the general public, although companies are statutorily required to disclose such information to the relevant governmental authorities.

Only two companies volunteered information on their hazardous/toxic waste, the Body Shop and S.C. Johnson.

Industrial air pollution

This is monitored by HMIP and local authorities and some information is available about companies' performance in the annual district reports which HMIP voluntarily produces. However, the latest available annual reports are only for 1987 – more recent material and major incidents were gleaned from press reports. Information about major air pollution violations in the US was provided by the US based Council on Economic Priorities.

A number of companies stated that they were engaged in efforts to control air pollution above that required by the law but failed to specify exactly what these efforts were. Certain manufacturing works are required to register with HMIP – these include: metal works, such as aluminium, copper and lead; chemical works, such as di-isocyanates, bisulphide and chlorine processes; petroleum, gas and coke works; and mineral and cement works. In all eight companies had at least one works registered with the HMIP in 1987.

Transport

This is a major contributor to air pollution and is an issue which directly effects all the companies in the survey. Although the only specific initial question on transport asked whether or not company cars had been converted to use unleaded petrol some companies volunteered information about other transport policies. The most notable was Mars UK which stated that it aims to increase freight transport by rail to 50%. No other company even mentioned rail transport let alone a policy to increase use of this method of distribution. A few outlined operational transport systems and reduced noise levels of their vehicles. The majority of companies who responded said that all the cars that could be converted to 'lead-free' petrol had been. In addition all the car manufacturers went into great detail about the environmental improvements which had been made to their cars, including fitting of catalytic converters and efforts to develop alternative fuels (mainly electric cars and methanol mixtures), all measures designed to reduce the level of exhaust pollution. New EC regulations on exhaust emissions have also influenced the direction of the major car companies' research and development.

Water pollution

The effects noted in the survey are those of major oil/chemical pollution incidents, industrial and agricultural pollution of waterways, and dumping at sea.

Most manufacturing industries use large quantities of water, with particularly high consumption by paper manufacturers. Phosphates in washing powders have been accused of being major water polluters, causing eutrophication (excessive algal growth) in slow moving waters. In the UK, because rivers tend to be short and relatively fast flowing, phosphates in washing powders are not a major source of pollution at present. They are added to washing powders mainly to soften water. According to the Soap and Detergent Industry Association (SDIA) the phosphates in domestic detergents only account for 20–25% of those introduced into the aquatic environment and can be easily extracted through the existing sewage treatment system. The main causes of eutrophication of waterways are the nitrate and phosphate run-off of fertilizers and slurry dumped from intensive animal farming.

Pro-environmental activities

Pro-environmental activities include: recycling of office stationery, packaging and materials used in the production process; reduced use of packaging and materials; membership of the Industry Council on Environment and Packaging (INCPEN); use of alternative technologies, i.e. use of alternative refrigerants; evidence of reduced energy consumption and/or conservation; use or development of alternative energy sources; involvement in environmental services including oil spill recovery and waste disposal; development of alternative environmentally benign products, such as those which have received the Blue Angel seal of approval in Germany; and the establishment of written environmental policies and a department or section which deals specifically with such matters.

Chapter Six

THE INVESTOR

The environment: a question of profit – the
ordinary investor and environmental issues
in accounting
Gilly Filsner and Malcolm Cooper,
Carnegie International

Green issues and the investor: inadequacies of
current reporting practice and some suggestions
for change
Roger Cowe, The Guardian

THE ENVIRONMENT: A QUESTION OF PROFIT
– THE ORDINARY INVESTOR AND ENVIRONMENTAL
ISSUES IN ACCOUNTING

Gilly Filsner and Malcolm Cooper

When the environmental bandwagon started rolling again during the most
recent period of economic growth it was tempting to dismiss it as a fad. There
are, however, solid economic and financial reasons for believing that green
issues should be considered increasingly important by all investors.

At one level, emotive issues have been translated into general public
awareness of environmental questions and are being enshrined in increasingly
stringent regulations. At another, both visual and scientific evidence have
given irresistible force to the argument that economic survival itself will depend
on careful control of natural resource utilization and toxic waste management.
The costs associated with the environment have assumed tangible form by
way of emission controls, energy consumption and waste disposal regulations. Businesses are finding that they must respond to the environmental

Fig. 6.1 © 1990 Peattie and Taylor. 'Alex' appears originally in *The Independent*.

question – and pay the costs of doing so – whether they care about it or not. The environment, in short, is having a direct impact on profit.

The 'green' investor was identified as a target by the first environmental and ethical unit trusts. The 'ethical' investor must be persuaded that an average or even below-average return for supporting environment-friendly or other ethical causes is preferable to a superior return from other investments. The goal of the 'average' investor in allocating risk capital is to maximize returns. Whereas particular stocks, such as those of tobacco or South African companies, might be avoided, this would principally be because it is believed that enough other people will also avoid them to dampen their attractivenesss as an investment.

AN ISSUE TO BE EXPLOITED

In the pursuit of profit, however, the investment community was quick to recognize the potential associated with environmental issues. Questions such as energy efficiency, waste disposal, recycling and excessive packaging are no longer the province of social rebels. They have been taken on by consumers, the media, politicians, and eventually industry and investors.

The Department of Employment recently estimated the market for environmental goods and services to be worth £4 billion a year in the UK alone. Individual environmental initiatives often have pronounced effects on prices and profits on the supply side. When more stringent automotive emission standards are proposed, for example, the price of platinum (used in catalytic converters) rises.

The question of how the opportunities associated with environmental issues might be exploited has therefore become the concern of the investment community at large. Answering it, however, is not easy.

There is certainly no shortage of information available. A weekly page on Business and the Environment now appears in *The Financial Times*, investment analysts are quick to find the environmental 'angle' on every company imaginable, and the companies themselves are increasingly obliging with statements of policy, colour photos of environmentally sound products, and lists of awards for recycling initiatives.

As these issues come to be more widely appreciated, however, financial logic must take its place in the assessment of candidates for investment, ecolologically sound or otherwise. How do the costs associated with environmental issues affect the bottom line? It is on this question that the shareholder or potential investor is not being satisfied. In the mass of information already required to meet accounting and regulatory requirements, very little can be found that is relevant to environmental questions.

RECOGNITION OF FINANCIAL CONSEQUENCES

Environmental control is not new as a management tool, and will have been conducted by many enterprises without reference to specific terminology or techniques. Compliance with laws, efficient use of raw materials and energy, and adequate provision for the disposal of waste are basic to effective management. Establishment of a formal control process could heighten awareness of the wastage allowed through mundane practices, complacency or ignorance. The evidence from recent annual reports indicates, however, that even if companies are beginning to accept the relevance of environmental data, they have not yet established a means of presenting it.

Perhaps the most comprehensive disclosure of environmental impact from a public company comes from Norsk Hydro, the Norwegian industrial and chemicals group, which produced its first environmental report in 1989. The expanded 1990 edition, published in addition to the annual report and accounts, is 34 pages long. It covers virtually every aspect of the Group's activities, from its philosophy and successes in reducing harmful emissions over the past twenty years to scientific explanations of its chemical processes. It does not, however, satisfy the requirements of a comprehensive environmental analysis, reading more like a public relations exercise, detailing positive achievements, and suggesting that further improvements in minimizing environmental impact are hardly necessary but will be attempted. Statistics are provided, but their content and relevance is not easily comprehensible. Often they relate only to selected plants, and not to all affected operating units.

While a document of this nature makes fascinating reading for those who have the time and inclination, it is of less utility in making an investment decision. Concrete recent developments are buried within a mass of information, and there is little quantification of the financial relevance. Where investments have been made or are planned, no estimate of the costs or potential savings is provided.

On the question of energy utilization, for example, much is made of the low-cost hydroelectric energy which is the mainstay of the Group's production. A commitment is expressed to efficient use of electricity and we are given a breakdown of energy consumption by division and fuel source; but no information is disclosed regarding the costs of energy in either this report or the

1989 profit and loss account except that 'environmental related investments in Norway have been expensed of [sic] NOK 359 million (1988: nil)'.

The green consumer movement has provided a stellar marketing opportunity which the supermarkets were quick to pursue. Their success in capturing this market is therefore one issue which might be of interest to the investor. However, now that initiatives on energy saving, waste recycling, etc., are under way, data on the financial impact of these would be more appreciated by the investor than the self-congratulatory enumeration of the assorted awards which have been won for them. One supermarket chain which has conducted and published an environmental audit is Belgium's Colruyt. According to the 1989/90 accounts, the audit report 'will provide an inventory of all the environmental projects realized in the fiscal year in question, and a survey of all current and future projects'.

Although this may be deficient in the form of the data, the investor is able to assess the savings being pursued and the costs involved in a strongly environmentally aware corporate policy: lower energy costs, more expensive refrigerants, waste disposal, and even computer paper usage are clearly explained and quantified. The cost of complying with new EC regulations on heating installation is also noted, at BFr 40m (£666,000).

By contrast, Argyll Group's report and accounts for 1990 merely seeks to answer the question 'Is Safeway still the "greenest" food retailer?'

A. We have been voted by the Green Consumer Guide as meeting best the needs of environmentally aware shoppers for two consecutive years, but we are certainly not resting on our laurels! Amongst this year's initiatives are a range of recycled paper goods and environmentally safer household cleaning products. Safeway now provides over 100 bottle banks and 34 paper collection points. We opened our first five plastic bag recycling centres in January and now we have 16. We send about 800 tonnes of waste cardboard for recycling weekly and all stores have aluminium can recycling facilities. Also, after much searching, we've sourced a recycled stationery that is of such good quality we will use it for all letters and memos.

This information is virtually useless for the purposes of the investor, though it may gratify other users of the accounts. Similarly, Sainsbury's report notes that new stores employ less harmful refrigeration technology, and that 'an integrated approach to energy efficiency since 1974 has led to substantial energy savings'. Clearly this barely touches on issues which would be of interest to a potential investor in the competitive retail sector.

One of the most useful presentations of environmental information comes from Swiss chemicals group Ciba Geigy. Claiming that 'Protection of the environment is the third pillar of our overall entrepreneurial responsibility, the first two being economic success and social obligations,' the 1989 annual report includes five pages of relevant and quantified environmental information. Not only is the safety and environmental record reviewed, with details of accidental discharges and other incidents, of projects under way to improve environmental performance in production and of products themselves, but the information is easily interpreted and is placed solidly in its financial context. One particularly interesting statistic is related to fuel consumption: 'Consumption of energy per metric ton of output has fallen from 28.9 gigajoules in 1977 to 14 gigajoules in 1989.' The statement is admirable in its simplicity and could easily be developed into a standard.

The most useful data in the Ciba Geigy report is a table giving a breakdown of capital and current expenditure on product safety, process safety, and environmental protection in production. This totalled SF 1.33 billion (£530m), or over 6% of revenues. Even here, however, it may be worrying that while several chemical plant accidents are noted, no specific provision is made for possible environmental liabilities.

The UK chemical giant ICI devoted a half page to 'The Environment' in its 1989 Annual Report, and is one of the few companies to mention the financial aspects of the issue in the audited accounts *per se*.

> ICI continues to incur substantial expenditure on minimizing the discharge of materials into the environment and to comply with laws and regulations relating to protection of the environment . . . Wherever possible, ICI continues to provide for anticipated future costs where these can be reasonably estimated . . . ICI believes that its financial position and competitiveness will not be materially affected by the fulfilment of its environmental responsibilities.

The above statement is augmented by a balance sheet item, 'Rationalisation, environmental and other provisions', which increased by £42m to £220m in the year. This is obviously a material sum, and, having been noticed in one company's accounts, it may then occur to investors that this information is missing from others!

THE ENVIRONMENT: A TRUE AND FAIR VIEW

From the investor's point of view, the rationale behind conducting an environmental analysis is that the environmental concerns of any operating business are quantifiable. Publication of assorted psuedo-scientific data is insufficient unless the information offered to investors clarifies the current and future financial situation. On a day-to-day level, this information should include expenditure on energy, materials and waste disposal; more generally we can also look to the costs of complying with legislation and penalties incurred or likely to be incurred for non-compliance, as well as provisions for potential liabilities for previous infractions – which may not have appeared too serious at the time. Exxon, to the dismay of shareholders, had not adequately provided for the possibility of a disaster such as befell the *Exxon Valdez*, while Shell discovered that its insurer would not pay for pollution which could not apparently be classed as accidental. The potential environment-related liabilities of a company may even dwarf the net value of a company.

For the investor the environment is not an issue in itself. Rather, it is another context in which not only products, but also processes and profits must be evaluated. Environmental awareness is simply a framework within which such issues as energy efficiency, waste management, and product design and packaging can be examined. Ironically perhaps, it is likely that the profit motive will be more effective in furthering the green cause than any amount of self-sacrifice or ideology.

Before environmentalism became fashionable, it was generally thought that being ecologically sound meant losing money. Now, not only are 'green chips' a positive drawing card, but information regarding energy and waste management, emissions standards and, probably most of all, potential liabilities is becoming increasingly important to investors.

Unfortunately, very few companies have yet responded to the need for such information. Many must simply be confused. It is not so long since any sign of social awareness was rejected by investors as unnecessary and costly. The sea change regarding the relevance of the environment has developed only very recently. The public, and hence politicians, now accept that it is not only desirable but necessary to limit the damage inflicted on the public domain by waste disposal, harmful emissions and so on. It is increasingly likely that industry will be forced to pay a higher proportion of the costs than has up to now been the case. Thus discussions are already underway regarding a carbon tax, of higher waste disposal charges through landfill pricing and treatment standards, and of companies being forced to take responsibility for the recycling of their products' packaging.

Statements of environmental 'policy' are now sprouting like mushrooms. For the investor to get more than a happy glow from it all, more concrete data will have to be made available. An environmental audit would be a useful starting point. It is necessary to establish the current state of compliance with current or future regulations and the current and capital costs relating to energy, waste, production and distribution. Presentation of the results from such an audit must be carefully managed; the audience for a full-scale report is limited. From the investor's point of view, the environmental audit is useful because it can help identify ways to improve performance and to cut costs.

On the point of prudence, as with a financial audit, it is not necessary to have every detail of what has been examined to reach the conclusion of true and fair. Unlike the existing financial audit report, however, the new version would require sufficient detail of the procedures undertaken to give assurance that environmental questions had been adequately addressed. The financial auditor's report which we accept as standard and necessary in the accounts of a company has only been a statutory requirement since 1900. It is not difficult to imagine that in a few years' time, an environmental audit will be regarded as similarly essential.

Once the extent of environmental costs is recognized, investors will increasingly look for assurances that these questions have been addressed. In certain frontline industries this will be necessary simply to maintain investor confidence that all liabilities have been recognized and, ultimately, certified.

Whether or not the full environmental audit is published, the investor will demand certain information in the annual report. The discussion above analysed some of the existing corporate reporting on green issues, which has to varying degrees been found deficient. It is only fair to add that the market for this information is still in its infancy, and it will be interesting to note how it develops. At this stage it is only possible to say that demand is bound to increase.

It would be fair to expect requirements for environmental reporting to clarify. As the economic rationale for conservation develops in response to the growing evidence of damage, depletion and resource constraints, so the realization should spread that what makes ecological sense also makes economic sense. If individual companies do not understand the folly of destroying their future resource base, governments can be expected to impose that realization on them. Even before that, shareholders will be making some strong suggestions. For the accounting community, this will pose as many challenges as it will opportunities: judgments on the financial implications of environmental questions will often depend on scientific assessments outside the accountant's own expertise. For investors at large, the picture can only become more detailed. The decisions they will make should be less clouded by spurious distinctions between what is green and what is profitable.

GREEN ISSUES AND THE INVESTOR: INADEQUACIES OF CURRENT REPORTING PRACTICE AND SOME SUGGESTIONS FOR CHANGE

Roger Cowe

INTRODUCTION

Accountancy bodies are interested to a surprising degree in the growth of environmental awareness, and its impact on the business world. Other 'social' and political issues have come and gone – for example, industrial democracy, the social audit campaign, racial and sexual equality movements – and have washed over the profession leaving virtually no impression. While individual accountants may have been interested in some or all of these issues, most individuals and all accountancy bodies seem to have regarded them as 'political' rather than professional concerns, and therefore not issues with which the profession should concern itself.

Ecology is different, however. Perhaps they have a sense that this represents a sea change in social attitudes, the like of which occurs at best only once in every generation, and more likely less frequently than that. More prosaically, even if they see the growth of green awareness as merely another in a wearisome wave of fast-changing social issues, they no doubt sniff an opportunity for the profession to grab a piece of whatever business stems from it, if only for as long as the fashion persists. Perhaps also there is an element of fear. The rise of green feelings carries a threat for all businesses, including accounting businesses. But particularly from the company accountants' viewpoint, the enthusiastic adoption of environmental legislation could hit company profits and circumscribe companies' freedom of action in various areas.

For whatever reason, the profession is interested.[1] The major institutes have commissioned research. Their presidents urge members to be interested in green issues, and to grasp the resulting business opportunities – whether as financial directors cutting costs by energy-saving and capitalizing on demand for new products or services, or as auditors providing environmental audits.

However, the question which this contribution will address is the extent to which 'environmental accounting' can be accommodated within current reporting and auditing practice. It will consider inadequacies in current reporting which hamper investors trying to make decisions which include a green perspective, and suggest some changes which could overcome those inadequacies. While these considerations will be concerned primarily with the profit-maximizing investor, the requirements for ethical green investors will also be considered. Finally, I will make some judgments on the profession's ability to implement such changes as seem necessary, and the possible imposition of environmental reporting and auditing requirements.

CURRENT REPORTING INADEQUACIES

Many issues should concern the profit-maximizing investor contemplating

---

1. For example, Professor R. Gray, *The Greening of Accountancy*, published by the Chartered Association of Certified Accountants (June 1990), an Institute of Chartered Accountants in England and Wales seminar *Chartered Accountants and the Environment*, September 1990, and a report on current practice in June 1990 by the Chartered Institute of Management Accountants.

the green revolution, because environmental action and awareness will affect the business world in many ways.

The most obvious business opportunity from the growth of environmental concerns is for waste management companies. The most obvious threat is to chemical companies and similar process operators who face greater controls (and greater costs) on emissions and effluents. But there are many less subtle opportunities and threats. Consider the supermarkets, for example. Initially, they have benefited by introducing 'green' versions of products, usually at premium prices. They would not be delighted, however, if a charge on disposable bottles or consumer reaction against throw-away containers sparked a return to returnable containers. Similarly, an attack on plastic packaging could result in extra costs in both distribution and store-handling. Returnable containers, on the other hand, would be welcomed by the drinks industry, illustrating how environmental measures are often two-sided, the impact depending on the sector concerned.

The motor industry clearly faces both threats and opportunities. Concerns about emissions and fuel efficiency should help to sustain demand for new cars, which can be expected to perform better on those critieria than older models. But a serious attack on car usage, either by pushing up petrol prices, or by further limits on company car benefits, or by restrictions on car usage in cities, could easily offset those potential benefits.

Some impacts will vary from company to company within a sector. It has been suggested,[2] for example, that within the waste management sector the smaller firms will suffer because they will be least able to cope with new regulations on disposal of hazardous wastes. Similarly, some engineering companies should gain from a drive to clean up pollution, whether by devising cleaner manufacturing processes in the first place, or by supplying additional equipment to restrict emissions. Others may be completely unaffected, or might suffer because their products fail to meet new requirements.

These brief examples illustrate that the potential impacts of rising green awareness are many and varied. They also illustrate how difficult it would be for an investor to make informed decisions without full information about a company's operations.

To some extent, the problems such investors face are the same in relation to green issues as in relation to other investment criteria. Investors need to predict the impact of green and other issues on company profits. In simplified terms, to do that they need to know as much as possible about past and current performance of the companies under scrutiny, make judgments about market developments – both product and stock markets – and select investments accordingly.

---

2. County NatWest WoodMac circular, July 1990.

These actions are already hampered by inadequacies in current reporting practice, and those inadequacies become more important when a new and unpredictable dimension such as greenery is introduced into the investment decision process.

The nature and content of current financial reporting is under intense scrutiny from many directions. Company law, under pressure partly from European Community directives, has become more intrusive, determining to a greater extent than ever before the form and content of company accounts. But the basic principles underlying company reporting are under attack in a campaign for reform which has spread throughout the profession.

The campaign, begun by a group of Scottish chartered accountants in 1988, aims to revolutionize reporting, on the grounds that current practice is inadequate for the purpose of providing information to shareholders and others. It is not concerned specifically with environmental issues, but its criticisms, and some of its proposed solutions, are extremely relevant to investors seeking to incorporate environmental issues in their decision-making.

Criticisms of existing reporting were summarized in a submission to the Accounting Standards Board which was known as *The Financial Report*.[3] It said that present financial reporting:

- is based on historical rather than current amounts;
- places too much emphasis on a single earnings number;
- pays too little attention to cash;
- is essentially backward-looking;
- concentrates on legal form rather than economic substance.

The report justifies its criticisms by explaining the needs of users of company accounts, notably the need to know:

- the company's capacity to generate income;
- its present and future solvency;
- performance against corporate objectives;
- evaluation of movement in corporate wealth;
- company plans and the availability of finance to support them.

GENERAL REPORTING CRITICISMS AS THEY AFFECT GREEN INVESTORS

These needs and criticisms can be illustrated for an investor contemplating the

---

3. *Financial Reporting: Looking Forward*, a research paper prepared by John Arnold, Paul Boyle, Malcolm Cooper and Ken Wild for the research board of the Institute of Chartered Accountants in England and Wales, September 1990.

prospects for a chemical company, in the light of growing environmental pressures.

Following the information needs identified above, such an investor must first try to assess the extent to which environmental legislation and consumer pressure will affect the company's income generating potential, then consider its solvency in the light of corporate plans for dealing with environmental legislation and for developing environmentally sensitive products or processes. The investor will also wish to see how the company is progressing towards environmental objectives, and how such developments are affecting corporate wealth.

Present reporting practice is unlikely to be helpful in satisfying such information needs. First, companies do not generally state objectives except in the broadest possible terms. Similarly, they do not reveal specific plans, such as the development of CFC replacements, and report on progress in such a way that performance may be measured against those plans. Conventional reporting measures resources on an arbitrary basis involving a combination of historical costs and valuations, and excluding resources which have not been the subject of transactions. Similarly, reporting focuses on profits and earnings per share, measured by setting transaction costs against revenues on an accruals basis. Cash flows are inadequately reported. Current practice deals inadequately with investments other than conventional capital expenditure, and ignores the impact of the company's operations on environmental resources. Furthermore, the principle of concentrating on the legal form of a company's operations (rather than its actual substance) acts as a barrier to including such environmental considerations, since they are usually legally beyond the scope of the company's assets and liabilities.

But the most important objection of all must be the backward-looking nature of conventional reporting. Ecology is centrally concerned with long-term issues, with consideration of natural resources for future generations. Yet company reporting does not even look to what, by the time a report is published, is the current year. It lives entirely in the past.

Similarly, environmental investors need information on product development for companies hoping to bring new, 'environment-friendly' products or services to market, and on process development for companies seeking to limit pollution by retro-fitting or otherwise adapting manufacturing processes. Yet few companies provide investors with meaningful plans for research and development, and even fewer report on progress in this area in ways which allow investors to make informed decisions.

SPECIFIC REPORTING ISSUES

Conventional reporting also fails the environmental investor because of the inadequacy of segmental reporting. Companies are not required to break down accounting information in sufficient detail for the investor to assess resources being used on environmental projects, or the returns from investing those resources. The investor would therefore have to rely on vague statements of objectives and would have little information to assess how well those objectives were being pursued, or their impact on a company's current and future solvency and wealth.

Finally, the investor is hampered in assessing the wealth of a company not merely by the broad accounting deficiencies already described, but also because of a weak approach to contingent liabilities. This is an area which must figure large in green reporting, because growing environmental awareness is likely to create liabilities where none previously existed – witness environmental protection legislation in the US, for example, which has suddenly required companies to clean up sites they have been operating for years, creating a liability which is often huge.

Each of these criticisms is relevant to the plight of a green investor. But such investors also require environmental information which would not come within the remit of the financial statements under the current approach, even as modified by the extensive proposals outlined above. Under those proposals, company reporting would continue to ignore the environment, concentrating exclusively on the company's financial transactions with suppliers, employees, shareholders and customers.

Useful environmental information can be divided into two types – specific data on the company's formal use of resources, and wider information on the company's impact on the environment which is not captured in conventional accounting systems. This latter aspect is the more difficult, since it addresses the key shortcoming in conventional accounting and economics – the failure to deal with externalities which was identified in the Pearce Report.[4] How these issues may be addressed is dealt with in the next section.

Environmental investors who are purely concerned with profit maximization should be concerned with these issues, because the growth of environmental measures means that a company's relationship with the environment has important financial consequences. Customers are increasingly concerned with manufacturers' green credentials, so that a poor performance on this issue could threaten sales. Direct financial costs could also arise if a company was not prepared for new legislation, and left itself open to financial penalties for failure to comply. Both the impact of environmental awareness on the company, and the company's impact on the environment, should therefore concern environmental investors.

---

4. Pearce, D., Markandya, A. and Barbier, E.B. (1989) *Blueprint for a Green Economy*, London, Earthscan Publications.

PROPOSED CHANGES IN REPORTING PRACTICE

The broad recommendations of *The Financial Report* would be helpful to environmental investors. But other changes to current reporting are also necessary. Following the approach of the previous section, proposals will be considered in three categories – those which address general reporting inadequacies, specific environmental measurements, and an environmental approach to accounting.

The Financial Report recommended a revised reporting package to replace the familiar profit and loss account, balance sheet and source and application of funds statement. This would comprise:

- a statement of objectives and related strategic plan
- a statement of assets and liabilities
- an income statement
- a gains statement
- a cash flow statement
- forecasts of future performance and position.

This package would be helpful in addressing the general weaknesses identified in current reporting practice. For example, it might help to broaden the way in which financial markets assess companies, reducing the attention currently paid to earnings per share as a single crucial measure of performance. And this approach would give investors more information about companies' plans, and more chance of assessing their progress other than in a purely financial fashion. But following the weaknesses identified in the previous section, I would also suggest that environmental investors need companies to report much finer segmental information, and much more comprehensive details of contingent liabilities.

But this package on its own would not be sufficient to allow environmental investors to make informed decisions. They should also look for changes in the way accounting traditionally measures economic activity, and would benefit from an extension of financial reporting to encompass specific measurements of resource use.

Changes in measurement reflect the need, identified in the Pearce Report, to distinguish between man-made capital and environmental capital, and to strive to maintain the level of environmental capital. By and large, conventional accounting is concerned only with the maintenance of financial capital.

Conventional accounting systems do often capture some forms of environmental information, e.g. the volumes of water used in a process. The major problem for environmental investors, however, is that conventional accounting does not consider the diminution of environmental capital caused by clean water inputs being converted into polluted water outputs. Similarly, conventional internal accounting procedures measure the financial impact of waste materials, but this kind of information is never reported to investors, nor does waste measurement attempt to quantify measures such as the volume of waste produced.

AN ENVIRONMENTAL REPORT

It seems clear that environmental requirements cannot be dealt with merely by reorganizing existing financial statements, even to the extent proposed by *The Financial Report*. These issues need the addition first of specific data concerning the company's environmental impact, and secondly, the development of environmental accounting measures. As well as environmental information in the conventional accounting statements, this probably needs an additional special environmental report.

A model for such a report has been developed by a United Nations working group[5] which suggested that this section of an annual report would cover:

- environmental policy
- capitalization of environmental spending
- environmental contingent liabilities
- spending on environmental protection
- anticipated spending in excess of contingent liabilities
- environmental activity and performance.

But this approach is still rooted in conventional accounting measurement. It merely requires the addition of conventional accounting information because of the potential financial impact of environmental legislation. It makes no attempt to deal with the need to recognize the importance of environmental capital and guard against its depletion.

Professor Rob Gray, in his report for the Chartered Association of Certified Accountants,[6] attempts to deal with this deficiency. He adds to the UN list a report on compliance with environmental standards, and a section on environmental assets.

Gray also proposes a refinement to the Pearce distinction between natural and man-made assets. He suggests a further distinction is necessary between what he describes as 'critical capital' and other natural capital. This is based on the concept that depletion of critical capital is much more serious than depletion of other natural capital which can be substituted, e.g. by other natural resources.

---

5. Intergovernmental Working Group of Experts on International Standards of Accounting and Reporting (reported in Gray, 1990).
6. *The Greening of Accountancy*, June 1990 – see note 1.

It seems to me that this distinction is still not sufficiently widely accepted to merit consideration in the context of early moves towards environmental reporting, and is likely to be far too complex for the current level of environmental awareness among companies. It will be difficult enough to develop any generally accepted environmental reporting approaches, without introducing additional refinements at this stage. Sticking rather to the simpler distinction identified by Pearce, the additional environmental report would consist of:

- valuations of man-made and natural assets
- transfers between these categories
- data on the maintenance of assets.

Developing such reporting will not be easy, however, since the concept of natural assets is still new, and it is as yet unclear how to measure a company's impact. But that need not prevent the reporting of whatever environmental measurements are already available within companies' existing information systems.

I can suggest several specific measures which might help to pin down performance on key environmental issues such as energy use, and which should be readily available within most companies. Indeed, all these items have been suggested as key criteria for an environmentally aware company to monitor:[7]

- total energy used in heating, lighting and power
- total fuel used for transport
- total water used
- volume of physical waste materials produced
- volume of waste output into the atmosphere and waterways.

Companies should report statistics for the past year, together with explanations for changes in resource use and plans for cutting these volumes.

These specific measures, added to the previous proposals, result in a comprehensive environmental reporting package. The information included would give environmental investors a useful insight into a company's environmental impact, and its progress in lessening that impact. To summarize the proposals, environmental investors would benefit from four developments:

- general improvements in reporting as envisaged in *The Financial Report*;
- financial reporting of companies' environmental expenditure and liabilities, as envisaged in the UN study;
- the addition of specific measurements of resource use;
- an environmental report indicating the company's broader impact on the environment.

---

7. For example, *Your Business and the Environment*, published by Business in the Environment, 1990.

CAN ACCOUNTANTS IMPLEMENT THESE MEASURES?

The measurement of environmental capital is clearly an area which requires considerable research and debate before a generally accepted approach can be developed. But most of the other proposals in this contribution do not require the development of new measurement principles. Most could be reported tomorrow by companies which are already environmentally sensitive.

The key question is whether there exists the will to add environmental reports to existing company reporting packages. And here there must be considerable doubts, despite the profession's eagerness to climb on the green bandwagon.

The history of company reporting is one of the accountancy profession resisting every new disclosure, usually on grounds of confidentiality. And where the principle of disclosure has been conceded, the profession has generally engaged in long and fruitless debates on how the required information should be prepared and presented.

The current controversy over the inclusion of goodwill (and the subsidiary issue of brand values) in company balance sheets is merely the latest in a long line of accounting standards issues to split the profession. The standard-setting process has a twenty-year history of trying bravely, but largely failing, to standardize reporting practice.

Britain now has a new standard-setting process, under the auspices of the Financial Reporting Council (FRC), with more financial, legal and political clout behind it. This new structure may well end many of the debates and differences within the profession, and result in greater conformity of accounts preparation and presentation.

But the FRC already has a long list of technical accounting subjects to tackle, beginning with the thorny question of goodwill. There seems little prospect of it turning its attention, or financial resources, towards additional (and what may be perceived as peripheral) issues such as environmental reporting for many years.

The goodwill accounting fiasco has considerable significance for environmental reporting, however. The crucial disagreement is over the principle of valuing intangible assets, especially those which have not been subject to recording in transactions. This is precisely the nature of environmental capital. It is largely intangible, in the accounting sense, and has not been acquired by the company in a recordable transaction.

The goodwill experience does not bode well for the development of environmental accounting standards.

AN ALTERNATIVE APPROACH

This collection of proposals encompasses a range of approaches and types of information, and it seems appropriate that implementation would similarly span a range of approaches. Ultimately, perhaps we can look forward to generally accepted environmental accounting standards. But it would be foolish to expect such developments during this century. That does not mean, however, that no progress can be made in the meantime.

There are two other possibilities for developing environmental reporting, which can and should go hand in hand with each other, and with the development of more formal environmental accounting. First, companies could voluntarily begin to report the specific environmental measures suggested above. These could be included in an environmental statement added as a voluntary addition to the conventional reporting package, much as value added statements have been included by some companies for several years. Such a statement could eventually be developed into a formal environmental impact statement incorporating specific measures such as energy usage, but including a statement of transfers between man-made and natural assets.

The other approach, developed in conjunction, could be to include environmental issues in companies' routine non-financial reporting. Thus the chairman's statement would include passages about environmental policy and goals whilst operating reports would include details of environmental achievement. And perhaps the formal directors' report could include some specific environmental measures.

This piecemeal approach could begin immediately. It need not wait on the development of formal, and formally agreed standards. Nor need it wait for agreement around the set of proposals currently being put forward for revamping the whole financial reporting package. When (or if) those agreements are reached, a formal environmental reporting package could be included on an equal status to existing financial statements.

But in the meantime, companies can begin to report their environmental impact. And they can also begin to allow external 'auditors' to pronounce on those reports.

AUDIT OF ENVIRONMENTAL INFORMATION

Here is another problem, however. Conventional auditing is currently immersed in as much controversy as accounting standards. Auditors have resisted pressure to make a fuller report on their clients' accounts, preferring to stick with the brief statement as to whether the company has complied with company law, and whether or not the accounts show a true and fair view.

An environmental audit would need to be much fuller than such a yes/no certificate. It would be useful to have an external check on environmental statements included in the annual report. But an environmental audit should also report on the adequacy of the company's environmental policy, and of systems to ensure the policy is pursued properly. Thus it would be closer to a conventional internal audit, or to the systems aspects of a conventional financial audit. And while there are strong arguments for publication of these elements of a conventional audit, they still seem to be a long way from being accepted by the auditing profession.

Perhaps publication of such elements of an environmental audit would be less controversial. But presumably not, if the audit were critical. And the possibility of critical audits also raises the question of compulsion. Would companies be prepared to keep paying for audits which were critical of their policies and systems? And would the auditor stand much chance of getting the work in the following year?

Perhaps this is another area where legislation is needed to make it compulsory for large companies, at least, to pay for and publish the results of an environmental audit. It may be some time before the government is prepared to pass such legislation, but in the meantime the concept can be developed voluntarily, as with environmental reporting itself.

Part Three

GREEN AWARENESS: CURRENT TRENDS

Chapter Seven

ENVIRONMENTAL DISCLOSURES IN CORPORATE ANNUAL REPORTS IN WESTERN EUROPE

CLARE ROBERTS

INTRODUCTION

This chapter explores the extent to which corporations domiciled in Western Europe disclose in their annual report and accounts information about the environmental impacts of their activities. Although the annual report is designed primarily to report to investors upon the past financial activities of the corporation such reports increasingly include a wide variety of information, both qualitative and quantitative, regarding past activities and future plans. This increase in information disclosure is due to a wide range of factors. The demand for environmental information comes from investors who are interested not only in the short-term financial performance of a corporation but are also interested in its social impacts. In addition, the corporate annual report is one of the major sources of information used by a wide range of users. Thus, it may also be read by employees, the press, both financial and non-financial, and pressure groups such as consumer organizations and environmental groups. Therefore, the annual report is increasingly being employed to disseminate a variety of different types of information.

While corporate annual reports are often extensive in their scope they are not the only reporting vehicle available to corporations. Thus, any examination of such reports, while providing an insight into environmental disclosures, must, by its very nature, be incomplete. Corporations are likely to use a number of media in order to disclose environmental information. These include press releases and advertisements as well as *ad hoc* reports to interested parties and regular reports on specific aspects of their activities. One particularly interesting example of special-interest reports is the environmental report of Norsk Hydro of Norway. This corporation produced a special report in 1989 describing its domestic activities which was increased in 1990 to a 34 page report on its world-wide activities. This report includes not only an environmental policy statement but also describes the environmental impact of its activities, in terms of both products and processes. Of note is the fact that this includes descriptions of the measures, both planned and undertaken, to reduce adverse environmental impacts as well as detailed quantitative emission levels for various pollutants such as the amount of nitrogen, ammonia and mercury discharged into the air and the amount of nitrogen and phosphate discharged into the water. It also includes information on energy usage, health and safety measures and accident rates and descriptions of the measures being undertaken to improve these. While this is one of the most detailed special-interest reports provided, other corporations also produce special reports covering specific aspects of their activities. For examples, DSM of the Netherlands provides social reports for each of its divisions while Degussa of Germany provides a 'Personal und Sozialbericht' covering further information on employee matters such as training and pensions. This is similar to the Bilan Social provided by French corporations which, despite its name, is primarily a detailed employment report covering such matters as the numbers employed, wages, hours worked, health and safety measures, accident rates and training information. Alternatively, Grand Metropolitan of the UK offers interested parties the oportunity to receive a special report detailing the actions undertaken by the corporation and its employees in relation to charitable and community affairs.

There is no readily agreed definition of exactly what types of information should be included under the term environmental disclosures. At the most general level it may be taken to include any information about the impact of a corporation's activities upon the physical environment. It thus encompasses a wide range of information about the product manufactured, the internal activities or industrial processes employed by the corporation and the inputs used in the manufacturing process. In particular, the information that might be disclosed includes the environmental impacts of products, processes and the inputs used, including the emission levels achieved, energy consumption and the use of non-renewable resources. It also includes any measures undertaken to reduce any diverse environmental impacts by undertaking such activities as research and development, capital investment projects, changing the manufacturing methods and managerial actions including environmental audits. In addition, a corporation will also impact upon the internal environment. Of particular relevance here are health and safety measures, illness and accident rates and measures undertaken to reduce the harmful impacts of its activities on employees through such measures as training and safety audits.

Given the very great diversity in the possible information that might be provided this chapter will consider only the more important or the more commonly provided types of information. Therefore, after consideration of the legislative requirements in this area, the issue of employee-related information is considered. In particular, health and safety information including quantitative accident statistics and employment policies, especially with regard to equal employment statements, are examined. The chapter then explores the issue of product information with special emphasis placed upon the information provided by corporations that supply energy and automobile manufacturers. This is followed by consideration of the issue of capital investment projects and the impact on the environment of such investments, and information on the environmental impacts of the production processes employed. Research and development activities are also considered, and the chapter ends by exploring disclosures highlighting corporate perceptions of the importance of environmental impacts and the apparent desire of many corporations to use corporate reports to disseminate their views on the environment and environmental legislation.

It should be noted that this chapter refers only to the English language versions of annual reports. While this limits the discussion to the reporting practices of large corporations, most of the largest European corporations, irrespective of their country of domicile, produce an English-language version of their corporate annual report.

LEGISLATIVE REQUIREMENTS

The only European country with any specific disclosure requirements in the area of environmental impact information is Norway. The Enterprise Act was amended in 1989 to require corporations to include, in the board of directors' report, information on emission levels, contamination and details of measures both planned and actually performed by the corporation with the objective of cleaning up the environment.

With the notable exception of the supplementary statement of Norsk Hydro discussed above, this requirement appears not to have led to the disclosure of detailed quantitative information on such measures as emission levels or expenditures. Rather, it has generally been interpreted as simply calling for a brief statement confirming that all relevant legislation has been met. For example, VARD states simply that 'Applicable regulations regarding working environment and industrial safety were followed', while Bergesen, for example, goes slightly further indicating the measures undertaken when it states that:

> The company's vessels meet all anti-pollution standards. Bergesen's quality assurance program is designed to prevent environmental pollution and limit

the likelihood of and potential damage from collisions and groundings. Our vessels' propulsion systems are always kept in top condition to ensure low fuel consumption and optimal combustion. Low sulphur bunkers are given priority.

Norway not only requires disclosure of the environmental measures undertaken and the outputs achieved but also has related legislation covering the measures that corporations must undertake in relation to the internal or working environment. This is also referred to in some corporate reports, with corporations similarly informing the reader that the law has been complied with, as the example of Norsk Data illustrates:

In accordance with the Norwegian Working Environment Act, Norsk Data has a working environment committee whose members are elected by the employees and management.

If a somewhat wider definition of relevant legislation is taken then other specific pieces of legislation are also of interest. Of particular note is the UK 1985 Companies Act requirement for corporations to disclose the total amount donated in the UK for charitable purposes. This calls for disclosure, in the directors' report, of the amount given without requiring any information regarding the recipients of such donations, as illustrated by the example of AMEC which states that:

Charitable donations for the year amounted to £210,000 including £50,000 to the AMEC Charitable Trust. Charitable donations amounting to £54,500 in the year were made by the AMEC Charitable Trust.

What is interesting about this requirement is that it appears to have encouraged a sizable number of corporations to voluntarily provide additional information on their charitable activities and community involvement. Such disclosures take a variety of different forms, but are often fairly detailed as illustrated by Reed of the UK which provides four pages of information on arts sponsorship, charitable giving and the fund-raising activities of its various publications, Allied Lyons of the UK with two pages detailing support for local enterprise agencies, education, charities and sponsorship, and Tate & Lyle of the UK with a three-page description of support for education, charity giving, sport and arts sponsorship and, interestingly in this context, the environment. While these are examples of corporations that give more information than is usual it is also clear that very many corporations do provide some information in excess of that legally required. This is in contrast to the rest of Europe. Disclosure of charitable giving can be found in a few cases such as EAC of Denmark or Petrofina of Belgium, although they fail to disclose the actual amount donated in the last financial year. Similarly, a few corporations such as Fiat of Italy and Repsol of Spain describe their arts sponsorship. However, any information in this area is very rarely found in corporate annual reports from mainland Europe.

VOLUNTARY INFORMATION DISCLOSURES

Despite the nearly universal lack of disclosure requirements it is noticeable that many corporations have responded to the increasing interest in environmental matters by providing at least some environmental disclosures. While the types of information provided and the amount of detail considered appropriate vary considerably many corporations have either introduced or expanded the amount of information given in the last few years.

EMPLOYEE INFORMATION

The range of employee-related information that might be disclosed is very extensive. It covers not only information about the numbers employed and the related costs, including indirect costs, but also such matters as training, employment policies, trade union recognition and negotiation procedures, hours worked, employee turnover and absenteeism and health and safety matters. From a social perspective it might be argued that matters of particular concern are health and safety, including information on accidents, and employment policies, in particular with respect to equal opportunities policies and the employment of the disabled.

The information provided by corporations varies considerably, from those that report only that which is required by legislation (generally the total number of employees and employee costs) to those that provide extensive employee-related information. However, even given this diversity it is clear that certain disclosure patterns exist so that some generalizations regarding disclosures may be made.

Looking, first, at information on health and safety matters and accident rates it is immediately clear that such information is relatively rare. Some of the lack of disclosure may, of course, be attributed to the relative lack of importance of such matters in certain industries which have a good accident record and generally safe working conditions. However, this is, at best, only a partial reason for the low level of disclosure as many corporations operating in particularly dangerous areas fail to provide any information. The types of information disclosed fall into two main categories. First, corporations disclose either a brief policy statement that tends simply to say that health and safety is important or that measures are being undertaken to minimize accidents or, secondly, they provide fairly detailed descriptions of specific projects undertaken to improve working conditions, often accompanied by details of the related expenditures. Generally, UK corporations fall into the first category and other European corporations either disclose no information or fall into the second category.

Most policy statements are relatively uninformative. Rather than providing any description of the actual measures undertaken that could be used to assess their adequacy, they are instead generally little more than statements of good citizenship, as illustrated by the example of Argyll of the UK which states that:

The health and safety of the group's employees, customers and members of the general public who may be affected by the group's activities is a matter of primary concern. Accordingly, it is the group's policy to manage its activities so as to avoid causing any unnecessary or unacceptable risk to the health and safety of employees and members of the public.

To the extent that information is disclosed only if the subject matter is considered important then such disclosures may be valuable. However, it would be premature to assume that disclosure automatically equates with adequate performance. The information content is generally fairly minimal although a few corporations go somewhat further – for example, Costain describes the use of safety audits, safety advisors and communication exercises.

In contrast, a number of European corporations provide fairly detailed information. While there are instances of information disclosure from corporations from many countries, such information appears to be most commonly provided by corporations from Germany and, to a somewhat lesser extent, France. Once more detailed information is given then what is relevant becomes a function of the specific operations of the corporation. In particular, the measures undertaken and the most relevant ways of reporting these activities depend upon the type of business being conducted. In some cases very extensive information is given, as illustrated by Exhibit 7.1 from Ciba-Geigy of Switzerland, which discloses not only the costs of measures undertaken but also describes the major accidents that have occurred and the measures undertaken to reduce the number of accidents.

Quantification of accident rates is less common than descriptions of health and safety measures. In addition, it is noticeable that when accident rates are provided they are often presented without any explanation of policies or measures undertaken to minimize the number of accidents. Problems of interpretation exist when it is also realized that such information is, in the majority of cases, provided only for one year. In addition, the exact information given and its adequacy varies considerably. Comparability across corporations is impaired as some corporations, such as BMW and Ruhr Gas of Germany, disclose the percentage reduction in accidents, others such as Ruhrkohle and Continental of Germany give the number of accidents per million hours worked, others such as Bayer of Germany instead disclose the number per 1000 employees while yet another alternative is to disclose the number of reportable accidents. In all these cases the corporations have reported various measures of the frequency of accidents without indicating their seriousness. When information on seriousness is disclosed by indicating, for example, the percentage of time off work, this measure generally refers to

Exhibit 7.1 Ciba Geigy. (Source: Ciba Geigy Annual Report 1989.)

| Our responsibility for the environment | Protection of the environment is the third pillar of our overall entrepreneurial responsibility, the first two being economic success and social obligations. This fact is expressed in what we spend on the principal activities: |

Our responsibility for the environment — Protection of the environment is the third pillar of our overall entrepreneurial responsibility, the first two being economic success and social obligations. This fact is expressed in what we spend on the principal activities:

· Product safety
· Process safety
· Environmental protection in production

Current and capital expenditure for safety and environmental protection in 1989

In millions of Swiss francs	Switzerland	Group companies	Total
Current expenditure			
Product safety	130	110	240
Process safety	90	140	230
Environmental protection (production)	200	260	460
Total	420	510	930
Capital expenditure			
Product safety	20	5	25
Process safety	40	70	110
Environmental protection (production)	180	85	265
Total	240	160	400

We also wish to go on making constant qualitative and quantitative progress, in other words to lower the consumption of natural resources and to reduce risks and the emission of wastes. We see in this, too, a contribution to qualitative growth.

Product and process safety and environmental protection form part of the training of everyone at Ciba-Geigy right up to top management. The results are collected and assessed increasingly systematically by material and energy balance-sheets and by audits carried out regularly at all sites by technically qualified internal auditors.

Safety and environmental acceptability of our products

Our concern for safety and the environment does not stop at the boundary fences of our premises but follows our products through to the end-users.

With this in mind, in August 1988, the Executive Committee issued a set of principles on product safety.

Special implementing instructions go to the various operating sectors, which are directly responsible for the safety of their products.

Our efforts to ensure the safety and environmental acceptability of our products are so manifold that we can mention only a few of the most important here:

Reduction in use of organic solvents

· Development of specific pigments and additives for use in the manufacture of water- and powder-based paints
· Photo-initiators for light-hardening solvent-free surface coatings
· Conversion to a water-based tablet-coating process in pharmaceutical manufacturing

Replacement of ecologically problematic substances

· Anti-wear additives to replace chloroparaffins in metalworking (chlorine-free disposal)
· Search for alternatives to substances containing heavy metals (pigments, corrosion-inhibitors, stabilizers)

Reduction of exposure of human beings and the environment

· Introduction of reactive dyes with improved uptake from the dye-bath and hence appreciably reduced waste-water contamination
· Development of specific formulations (free-flowing, low-dust, liquid), packages (water-soluble packaging material) and application appliances (automatic mixing and dispensing of constituents)
· Micro-encapsulation of plant protection products (cf. Agricultural Division section, page 31)
· Introduction of plant protection products effective in smaller concentrations and more readily degradable (see Agricultural Division section, page 32)

Safety in production

For a number of years the accident statistics of all those Group companies with chemical manufacturing facilities have been compiled in a uniform fashion. During the past five years, the accident-rate in the eleven principal Ciba-Geigy manufacturing plants worldwide has continued to decline. The equalizing safety trend has persisted within the Group.

Accidents and incidents

We regret to report that despite all precautions two fatal industrial accidents occurred in Switzerland, both due to mechanical causes.

The principal specifically chemical incidents with effects that spread off-site were the following: decomposition fumes in the Schweizerhalle area on May 22, 1989, leak of heating oil in Trafford Park (U.K.) on November 30, 1989, acid mist in Kleinhüningen on December 21, 1989. Considerable on-site damage was done by a dust explosion in McIntosh (U.S.A.) on April 10, 1989, a fire in a Basle laboratory on August 8, 1989, and a fire in a ventilation duct at Clayton Aniline (Manchester, U.K.) on August 24, 1989.

Improvement of safety

Efforts to improve industrial safety were concentrated on the following fields during 1989:

· Improvement of risk analysis procedures, especially for process control systems in manufacturing-plants and warehouses
· Implementation of the "longstop" principle, which aims to contain escaped chemicals within the site boundary and prevent them from encroaching on the surroundings
· Further extension of our in-house induction and continuation training programmes

Induction and continuation training

Twelve courses and seminars were held during 1989 for 375 development and production chemists and chemical safety planning engineers. There was a basic course on Process Safety, a seminar on Safety of Thermic Processes, another on Electrostatics, and a six-day Safety Workshop in which managers from ten Group companies took part.

Safety Audits

As envisaged by the Executive Committee, Safety Audits were held during 1989 at Pfersee (Dyestuffs and Chemicals Division, W. Germany), St-Fons (Dyestuffs and Chemicals Division, France), Agrate Brianza (Plastics Division, Italy) and Pamplona (multidivisional, Spain), and in the South African Group companies. The results show that safety standards at these sites are on a par with those in the Switzerland Works and that compliance with and application of the worldwide compulsory in-house safety regulations and standards are of a high order. Stipulated improvements chiefly concerned process safety, occupational hygiene and fire precautions. The measures introduced from 1986 onwards to improve warehousing safety have largely been implemented at these sites; in many places they far exceed the precautions laid down by the public authorities.

all illnesses rather than only industrial accidents. Another frequent problem in this area is the tendency to produce figures that apply to the entire corporation and, therefore, are likely to be made up of very different accident rates across the divisions of the corporation. The problem with such corporate-wide reporting may be illustrated by reference to one of the few corporations that provides a sector breakdown of accidents. Thus for Solvay of Belgium the accident frequency rate varies from a low of 4.3 per million hours for administration and research up to a high of 18.1 for the processing sector.

Another area of employee information likely to be of particular interest from a social perspective is the corporation's employment policies, in particular with respect to the employment and promotion of minority groups. It is noteworthy that, as for health and safety information, certain fairly clear patterns emerge. UK corporations are required to disclose their policies with respect to the employment of the disabled. In practice this requirement is generally taken to mean the provision of a non-quantified statement confirming that the corporation endeavours to employ or retrain disabled employees whenever possible, as illustrated by Pilkington:

> The Group continues to meet its obligations to offer employment opportunities to disabled people, with special attention being given to the redeployment of employees becoming disabled in service.

Similar information is very rarely provided by other European corporations although a small number of German corporations report the number of disabled employees reflecting the legislative requirement that large corporations employ at least 6% disabled personnel.

A significant number of the larger UK corporations, such as Unilever, Bass, ICI and BOC, also provide a general statement covering personnel or employment policies. This statement generally describes the corporation's policy of ensuring equal opportunities to all people in respect of employment, training or promotion, as illustrated by Taylor Woodrow:

> Entry into and progression within the group are determined solely on the basis of personal merit, effective performance and the needs of the business. All team members receive equal treatment regardless of sex, marital status, race, national origin, colour or religious belief.

This statement is, again, generally unquantified although there are a few exceptions to this such as Grand Metropolitan which describes specific initiatives to encourage the employment of ethnic minorities in both London and the US along with details of the proportion of African Americans employed by its US subsidiary Burger King. Disclosures in the rest of Europe are both less common and of a rather different nature. Specifically, the majority refer not to all possible groups of employees, but instead refer only to females. Less commonly discussed is the employment of less well qualified recruits as illustrated by Henkel of Germany which runs a Youth Assistance Programme to introduce 'young people with poor educational qualifications into the workforce' or Ahold of the Netherlands which 'subscribes to an employment policy that aims at helping less qualified job applicants find productive work'.

Statements regarding the employment of females are found in the statements of corporations from a number of countries although, again, they are most commonly found in German reports. The information provided generally takes one of two possible forms. One alternative is to provide a general policy statement giving details of any measures undertaken to improve the position of females in the workforce. This is often accompanied by some quantified details of employment, as illustrated by AEG of Germany:

> In implementing personnel and educational policies, AEG emphasises equal professional opportunities for women. In a joint program with the working committees, we are running a pilot program for the professional advancement of women. The proportion of women in the workforce, not including apprentices, has slightly increased to 29% (28% in 1988).

The alternative, also quite common in German reports, is to provide details of what Siemens terms its 'family orientated policy'. This refers specifically to information on the provision of extended parental leave for the care of children and, less commonly, other relatives. This is often accompanied by details of the number of employees benefiting from the policy as illustrated by BASF:

> 182 employees took advantage of BASF's 'Parent and Child' program. Of the total, 114 women and 3 men took temporary long-term leave of absence, 64 women and 1 man chose part-time work.

PRODUCT INFORMATION

The final product manufactured or sold by a corporation may have major environmental impacts not only in terms of the raw materials used and the production processes employed but also in terms of its impact upon the environment once the consumer begins to use the product. One aspect of increasing public interest in the environment is consumers' concern regarding the environmental impacts of the products they purchase. As such, it comes as no surprise to find that a number of corporations are disclosing information about the environmental impacts of the products they sell.

Such information may be found in the reports of corporations from most European countries and there appear to be little in the way of country specific patterns discernible in the disclosures made. However, largely reflecting public concern about a limited number of products and types of environmental issues, very clear industry specific patterns of disclosure exist. In particular environmental impact information is especially common in three industries. First, information is given by those engineeering corporations that provide environmental services whether chemical, mechanical or plant engineers or providers of waste disposal services. The information given is generally limited to descriptions of the major activities carried out and is very similar in style to the information given about any of the activities of these corporations. As such, the fact that the subject matter is environmental services appears to be largely irrelevant to the disclosure decision. Of more interest are the disclosures found in the other two industries, the energy industry and automobile manufacturers. In these cases, specific product information is routinely provided in a manner that appears to be largely designed to alter readers' perceptions and continually to emphasize the message either that the products are environmentally friendly or that the corporation is at the forefront of technology and doing everything possible to minimize adverse environmental impacts. To a large extent the information provided appears to be designed to reassure the reader and may be seen at least partially as a type of product marketing exercise.

Given the increasingly strong concerns expressed both by the general public and governments over the burning of fossil fuels and the consequent environmental impacts of the greenhouse effect it is noticeable that a number of energy producers take the opportunity to reassure readers of the 'environmental friendliness' of the particular type of energy they produce. Such statements appear in a variety of places in the reports rather than in any specific or clearly defined environmental section. In addition, similar sentiments are expressed in the reports of corporations producing a variety of different types of energy. For example, Raab-Karcher of Germany talks of 'environmentally friendly light heating oil' while ASEA of Sweden and ABB of Switzerland make similar claims for nuclear energy. However, such comments are especially prevalent in the reports of gas producers with AGA of Sweden, Wartsila of Finland, Gasunie of the Netherlands and Ruhr Gas of Germany all being keen to be seen to be producing a product that, in the words of Total of France is: 'a reliable, readily available and easy to use energy source producing less carbon dioxide than any other fossil fuel, it is the most environmentally friendly energy source.'

Most of these disclosures are relatively brief and uninformative, in many cases simply being a repetition of the message that the energy source is 'environmentally friendly' with little or no explanation of this claim. One interesting exception to this approach is that of Ruhr Gas of Germany which provides a fairly detailed description of what is meant by the greenhouse effect and what causes it, as illustrated in Exhibit 7.2.

Even more common, and generally more extensive, is information regarding the environmental impacts of the products produced by the automobile manufacturers. The actual information given, the amount of detail provided and the prominence attached to it varies across the corporations. However, virtually all provide at least some information. The more common policy is

Talking about ......

The Greenhouse Effect

Apart from water vapor, carbon dioxide and other trace gases influence the Earth's heat balance. The trace gases are transparent for the short wavelengths of solar radiation, but absorb and reemit toward the Earth the long-wave radiation emitted by the land and water surfaces. This natural greenhouse effect raises the air temperature from – 15 °C, at which it would otherwise be, to the average atmospheric temperature of + 15 °C.

The anthropogenic increase in trace gas concentrations may, as climatologists fear, increase the natural greenhouse effect to a degree which may imply global warming risks. Scientists estimate that the shares by which the various gases contribute to the anthropogenic greenhouse effect are 50% for carbon dioxide, 19% for methane, 17% for chlorofluorocarbons and 14% for other trace gases.

Anthropogenic carbon dioxide emissions are chiefly attributable to the combustion of fossil fuels, such as coal, oil and gas. However, gas releases less carbon dioxide than the other fossil energy sources, as it contains substantially more hydrogen than these fuels. The share of methane in the anthropogenic greenhouse effect associated with the use of fossil fuels totals 4%. The main sources of methane include rice paddies, ruminants and landfills.

Natural gas contributes less to the anthropogenic greenhouse effect than other fossil sources of energy, accounting for all trace gas emissions including carbon dioxide and methane releases.

Exhibit 7.2 Ruhr Gas. (Source: Ruhr Gas Annual Report 1989.)

to provide a description of specific products or examples in the review of operations or, less commonly, in a description of research and development activities. A highlighted environment section giving such information alongside a policy statement or quantified details of actual outputs achieved is far less common.

One area of particular concern is the emission levels achieved and the environmental protection legislation of the EC. Thus, for example, PSA of France produces a diesel engine with 'emissions within EC limits' while DAF of the Netherlands claims for its diesel engine for trucks, emissions 'well ahead of requirements currently being discussed'; Stockman of Finland instead produces a new turbo which meets 'international pollution standards'. Volvo of Sweden is developing a diesel with 'the highest degree of clean exhaust emissions currently available in Western Europe' while Daimler-Benz of Germany manufactures a diesel which fulfils 'EC particulate values planned for 1992, which are compatible with the strict regulations in the USA'. Only slightly less common is information on catalytic converters, normally for petrol engines. However, despite the prevalence of these types of disclosures it is often extremely difficult to interpret the statements and to compare the performance of the various manufacturers. This problem arises for two reasons. First, the information provided generally refers to only a limited number of the products manufactured, so that an overall picture of the corporation's activities is impossible. Secondly, the information provided is generally descriptive. Quantification of the outputs is not only rare, but when provided is often in the form of the reduction in emissions achieved rather than in the form of the actual emission levels achieved. So, for example, BMW of Germany has developed a diesel catalytic converter that 'reduces emissions of noxious substances by up to 50%' while Daimler-Benz of Germany instead states that it has achieved 'particulate emissions reduced by 40%' and DAF has a new engine which achieves 'fuel consumption improved by 6%'.

Quantification of the emission levels achieved is not only very rare, but, when provided, is often incomplete. For example, DAF of the Netherlands quantifies the nitrogen dioxide emission levels from its truck engines. While such a disclosure is clearly superior to that produced by most of the automobile manufacturers it falls short of what could be provided. This general omission of quantified disclosures may be contrasted with one of the most informative examples, that of Saab-Scania of Sweden. This corporation is unusual in providing a two-page statement giving detailed information on the activities undertaken to reduce the environmental impacts of its products. This includes detailed information on the emission levels achieved by its new diesel engines, as illustrated in Exhibit 7.3.

Exhibit 7.3 Saab-Scania. (Source: Saab-Scania Annual Report 1989.)

A s cities continue to grow, traffic also increases – regardless of what means of transportation is used – thereby creating, an environmental problem. Exhaust emissions from passenger cars affect current buildings, nature and the climate. The question of how these effects can be limited has become an increasingly important topic in the international automotive industry.

The Effect of Emissions

The world's fleet of cars is dominated by two types of combustion engines: standard gasoline engines and diesel engines.

Both electric and steam engines existed during the early years of the car. However, these technologies were unable to keep pace with technical development. Today, they are still not competitive alternatives.

All types of combustion, whether based on gasoline or diesel oil, result in emissions. Lead, sulphur dioxide, nitric acid, carbon monoxide and particles can affect people's health. Sulphur dioxide and nitric oxide cause acidification in nature. Hydrocarbons form a chemical reaction with nitric oxides, resulting in a build-up of smog and ozone. Carbon dioxide is a completely safe natural substance found in air. But an increased concentration of carbon dioxide can, through the so-called greenhouse effect, cause an increase in the Earth's mean temperature.

Corrective Measures on the Way

In recent years, greater knowledge about air pollution and its effects has led to a goal-oriented program to reduce harmful emissions from the engine. A considerable portion of Saab-Scania's research and development work in its engine laboratories in Södertälje is focused on this area. In addition, Saab-Scania, together with several other European car manufacturers, is active in the Prometheus Project, an effort to limit environmental pollution by achieving more efficient traffic control.

Gasoline Engines

The introduction of a three-way catalytic converter was a decisive advancement in the cleaning of gasoline engines. The first Saab car with catalytic exhaust cleaning was sold on the American market in 1976. The technology was developed by Robert Bosch GmbH of West Germany. In 1987, Günther Baumann, a pioneer behind the technology, was awarded the Saab-Scania Prize.

Catalytic exhaust cleaning requires totally lead-free gasoline. The catalytic converters reduce the level of hydrocarbons by up to 95 per cent, cut carbon monoxide by 90 per cent and nitric oxide by 85 per cent. These figures are based on a standardized test that simulates congested inner-city traffic. Results are considerably better for ordinary inner-city traffic and rural driving. At year-end 1989,

21 per cent of all passenger cars in Sweden were equipped with catalytic converters. Through a continued renewal of the vehicle fleet, the total emissions from passenger cars can be reduced by two-thirds, compared with current levels.

The remainder of emissions from catalytic converter equipped cars occurs mainly in two phases of driving: immediately after cold-starting of the engine and during acceleration or deceleration. The official test is adapted to the California standard. In a colder climate with shorter average driving distances, it is essential that the maximum effect of catalytic converters be achieved as soon as possible. In 1989, under normal Swedish driving, conditions, Saab was able to achieve a 25–30 per cent reduction in emissions from its engines. This was achieved by connecting a special electrically-heated oxygen sensor and an electronically-controlled adaption of the combustion and ignition system.

Turbocharged power units recover an extra boost from the exhaust. The original turbo concept was to harness this additional power to achieve high performance. But the Saab 9000 model, newly developed for the Nordic market, features a low-pressure turbo. These figures are based on a standardized test that simulates congested inner-city traffic, better for ordinary inner-city traffic and rural driving. Turbo technology utilizes energy from the exhaust and enables lower emissions and noise level without impairing the engine's overall performance.

At the Scania diesel-engine laboratory in Södertälje ... the largest portion of Scania's development work is devoted to reducing emissions from vehicles. Pertti Kimari is an employee at the laboratory. Diesel engines, with their low fuel consumption, are the superior alternative for heavy vehicle traffic. Development work focuses on combining these advantages with lower emissions.

However, the present technologies for energy storage with such engine types are not competitive.

Diesel Engines

Diesel engines are mainly characterized by their dependability, long lifetime and high efficiency, that is, they offer low fuel consumption in relation to work performed. These qualities are particularly important in heavy, long-distance transport. Accordingly, diesel engines are the dominant power source for trucks and buses.

Diesel engines give low emissions of hydrocarbons and carbon monoxide. Nitric oxide and particles, however, are more difficult to deal with. Unlike gasoline engines, diesel engines consume a large surplus of air during combustion. Thus it is impossible to use the same three-way catalytic converters as those employed with gasoline engines.

The lower combustion temperatures reduce the content of nitric oxide in the exhaust. An important measure for cleaning diesel exhaust is therefore the cooling of air supplied to the combustion chamber. Attempts are also being made to minimize the emissions of particles and sharply reduce carbon monoxide and hydrocarbon emissions through post-combustion catalytic treatment. Engines that eliminate hydrocarbons in the exhaust are odorless. Improved combustion quality and lower sulphur and aromatic content are, however, essential conditions for post-treatment in a diesel engine. Reducing the sulphur content of diesel fuel also helps in reducing acidification.

The current focus in reducing emissions of standard cars is on gasoline engines. However, standard car engines can also be modified to accept methanol or ethanol. These substances, however, have a lower energy content than gasoline and are more expensive. More attention should be given to the production of fuels, particularly as regards carbon dioxide levels. There are, however, no technical hindrances to using alcohol in standard engines.

Efforts to limit fuel consumption have a direct impact on the emission of carbon dioxide, which is reduced in proportion to fuel consumption. One possibility is developing smaller and lighter cars, but this option must be weighed against the fact that heavier cars are considerably safer.

A breakthrough could well be achieved for technologies such as electric and hydrogen gas propulsion, sometime in the next century.

Three-way catalytic converters eliminate nearly all emissions of hydrocarbons, carbon monoxide and nitric oxide from highway traffic. Today, slightly more than one-fifth of all cars in Sweden are equipped with catalytic converters. It is estimated that as a result of the successive replacement of older vehicles with new cars, passenger car emissions in Sweden could be cut by two-thirds by the year 2000, compared with current levels.

An alternative method for limiting particle emissions is the so-called particle trap, which collects dirt and other particles that appear in exhausts.

Scania has supplied buses with so-called environmental engines since 1988. These engines have emission levels that already meet the forthcoming Swedish legal requirement, due to take effect in 1994.

An additional step will be taken in early 1990 when a field test is conducted on 70 city buses for adaptation to low emissions requirements. Regular production of the new engines is scheduled for 1991. The tests were conducted on two different engine types – an ethanol-based engine, and one designed to run on a more efficient diesel fuel – 'inner-city fuel'.

For ethanol-based engines, the pressure and injection system have been specially adapted to handle ethanol. The engine produces a much lower content of hydrocarbons and particles. The only drawback is the cost of an ethanol engine, which is twice as much as a diesel engine. However, this cost may be defended when weighed against the emissions of inner-city traffic.

A diesel engine designed to run on 'inner-city fuel' has been developed parallel to the ethanol-based engine. The fuel that should be used is low in sulphur and aromatic properties. However, the emission level is somewhat higher than that of an ethanol engine.

Both new engines are equipped with turbochargers, intercoolers and oxidizing catalytic converters. As a result, they achieve better combustion, an optimization of the intake air and a very low emission of particles that is equivalent to the amount which can be recovered in a so-called 'particle trap'.

Comparison of emissions

Engine	Fuel	NOx	HC	CO	CO2	Particles
Scania DSC9*	Mol. Diesel	11.8	0.3	4.9	199	0.30
Scania DSC9*	City Diesel	11.8	0.3	0.8	199	0.20
Scania DSC9*	Ory Diesel	11.9	0.1	0.1	196	0.06
Scania DSC9* with int. com.	Ory Etan	11.8	0.1	0.1	190	0.11
ECE R49		14.4		13.5		14.0	

Intercooled engine

Scania's environmental engines already have emissions below the forthcoming European requirement EEC R49.

However, if any report reader is looking for the all-round environmentally friendly vehicle perhaps they should consider British Aerospace's Rover which appears to be a clear contender with its lead-free fuel, lean-burn engine, lead-free paint, asbestos-free vehicle with 'one of the lowest levels of CFC use of any vehicle'.

A number of other corporations across a variety of industries disclose some information on the environmental impacts of their products. These disclosures cover a wide variety of products and environmental concerns such that industry specific patterns are far less obvious. However, many of the disclosures clearly mirror public concerns. Thus, especially common is information upon the production for sale of either non-bleached or non-chlorine bleached paper products as disclosed by several of the Scandinavian timber products corporations and chemical corporations such as Sandoz of Switzerland. Information on CFCs is also fairly common. Such information appears in reports from chemical corporations such as Montedison of Italy which are producing alternatives, refrigerator manufacturers such as AEG of Germany which are reducing the use of CFCs in their products, and retailers such as Ahold of the Netherlands or Sainsbury and Marks & Spencer in the UK which have stopped selling aerosols containing CFCs.

CAPITAL INVESTMENT PROJECTS

Given both the increasingly stringent environmental legislation in much of Western Europe and public concern over the environment, corporations are having to consider not just the financial impacts but also the environmental impacts of capital investment projects. Capital investment which improves the environmental impacts of operations may be an integral part of new investments or may be specifically aimed at improving the performance of existing plant. However, irrespective of which type of capital investment project is being undertaken, information upon the types of projects, their costs and environmental impacts are likely to be of interest to many readers of the annual reports.

Various types of information may be given about capital investment projects. At the simplest level is a description of any projects undertaken, perhaps accompanied by a qualitative indication of the effects of the investment. Slightly more information is provided by also including details of the inputs or quantification of the amount spent on environmental protection investments. The most information is given in those cases where corporations also quantify the outputs or the impact of the investments in terms of, for example, the reduction in emissions achieved. While it may be thought that quantification of costs or outputs is clearly more desirable than simply describing the activities undertaken, care must be taken in interpreting such information. Cost information may be difficult to obtain as many capital investment projects are not designed specifically to improve the environmental impacts of operations but such improvements are instead a welcome side-effect of investments carried out to improve the financial returns of corporations. As such, it may be extremely difficult to measure the proportion of the investment that is attributable to improvements in the environmental impacts of operations. Even if this problem of measurement can be satisfactorily resolved problems of interpretation still remain. There is no simple or direct relationship between the amount spent and the outputs achieved. Indeed, it can often be the case that an inverse relationship exists between the amount spent and the results achieved. Likewise, measures of outputs achieved are also often extremely difficult to interpret. Such information is entirely voluntary, and as such, it may often be only partial or incomplete.

Non-quantified descriptions of investment projects are far more common than any quantification of costs or outputs. Such information may be found in reports from most countries and industries although, as would be expected, they are most commonly found in the reports of heavy industries. The types of information, the amount of detail and the prominence attached to it all vary considerably. However, the most common approach is to include such information in the divisional review of operations alongside descriptions of the activities occurring in the previous year. Such disclosures vary in detail with a number of corporations simply highlighting the fact that investments have been made with the objective of protecting the environment, as illustrated by Elkem, Norway:

> . . . particular emphasis placed on measures taken to improve the external and internal environment. This has shown that environmental investments in many instances also have produced improvements in the environment and increased productivity.

Other corporations appear keen to highlight the desirable environmental impacts that arise from investments that, presumably, have been undertaken primarily for financial reasons rather than for environmental reasons, as illustrated by SAS of Sweden:

> One of SAS's most significant environmental contributions is the changeover from DC-9 and DC-10 aircraft to the quieter and more efficient MD-80 and Boeing 767 aircraft.

An alternative approach which is also relatively common is to find information on investments in a specific environmental review section of the corporate report. Such sections typically do not contain any more information than that found scattered across the divisional reviews of other corporations. However, it has the clear advantage of bringing all such information together into a clearly defined and visible section, thus simplifying the task of location for the interested reader, as illustrated by Exhibit 7.4 from British Steel, UK.

Given the problems inherent in ascertaining the amount of investment that may be directly attributable to improvements in environmental impacts a

Environment, Health and Safety

Developments in UK and European Community legislation, including tighter controls on atmospheric discharges and liquid effluents, are evidence of a growing public determination, which we share, to improve the quality of the environment.

British Steel's policy is to manage its activities so as to avoid causing unnecessary or unacceptable risk to employees, contractors, customers, members of the public or to the environment. British Steel aims to comply with relevant health, safety and environmental regulations.

New plant developments incorporate environmental control facilities, which are agreed with and approved by the relevant authorities. The new sinter plant at Scunthorpe, which, following commissioning during the year, is being progressively worked up, incorporates the latest air pollution control equipment.

The Company recognises that, with the advent of progressively higher standards, pollution control equipment associated with some older plants may not be adequate to meet increasingly demanding requirements. To help deal with this situation, programmes to effect improvements are developed annually.

Pollution control plant, of in-house design, is being installed on existing Teesside coke ovens to control coke pushing emissions, and at Llanwern a new gas recovery system at the steelmaking plant has benefits for both the environment and energy conservation.

Trials are under way with a much less energy-intensive fume extraction system for the steelmaking vessels at the Stainless steelworks, also incorporating original equipment developed in the Company. In anticipation of tighter restrictions on the discharge of non-ferrous metals into the environment, a plasma smelting furnace has been developed which will be used to treat all the dust collected from stainless steel production in Sheffield, so as to recover nickel, chromium and molybdenum for recycling.

At Port Talbot Works, a new cold mill effluent treatment plant has come on stream, and a modified biological treatment process is being developed to treat ammoniacal discharges at Orgreave coke works.

The health and safety of employees of the Company and its contractors has continued to receive careful attention and a trend of steady improvement has been maintained, with the number of lost-time injuries falling to 1,304 from 1,369 in 1987/88.

It is very regrettable that one of the Company's employees and one contractor's employee died following accidents in British Steel works.

The Company has continued efforts to raise standards of health and safety performance. Substantial progress has been made in protection against the effects of exposure to hazardous substances and noise.

Exhibit 7.4 British Steel plc. (Source: British Steel plc Annual Report 1989.)

relatively large number of corporations disclose the amount of capital expenditure incurred. Such information may be found in reports from a large number of countries such as Solvay of Belgium, Enso-Gutzeit of Finland, Rhône-Poulenc of France, Montedison of Italy, Perstorp of Sweden and Alusuisse of Switzerland. However, again, it is only in Germany that such disclosures

Exhibit 7.5 Bayer AG. (Source: Bayer AG Annual Report 1989.)

Environmental Protection

A step ahead in environmental protection

Money spent on environmental protection is money invested in the future. Technologies that protect the environment as well as conserve raw materials and energy will ensure our long-term competitiveness. To invest in these technologies is to safeguard tomorrow's markets.

In 1989, we spent DM 305 million for capital improvements in environmental protection and safety and DM 1,189 million for operating expenses. We spent an additional DM 429 million to research ways of protecting the environment from potential risks associated with our products and manufacturing processes.

We can only meet increasing requirements if environmental protection is integrated into every new product and process from the beginning. Essential to this is a corporate philosophy in which comprehensive environmental protection is seen as a management responsibility.

The Committee of the Board for Environmental Protection and Occupational Safety coordinates and monitors the worldwide implementation of Bayer's environmental protection program. A coordinating committee, comprised of members of the Board of Management and the General Managers of the Plant Administration and Central Engineering Divisions, develops company-wide technical approaches to environmental protection.

Training and motivation are provided by an extensive continuing education program, consisting of seminars that employees at all levels are required to attend. In 1989 alone, about 8,000 employees attended some 500 environmental protection seminars.

Less waste water from production plants

The new incineration plant for sewage sludge and concentrated process effluents in Leverkusen, which became operational at the end of 1988, significantly reduces pollution of the North Sea. This facility alone decreased emissions of organic substances by more than 10 percent in 1989.

Disposal at sea of spent acid from our Antwerp plant ceased in the spring of 1989. This means no more spent acid from any Bayer facility is dumped into the North Sea. The expertise we have developed in spent

capital expenditure program to further decrease the discharges of substances containing phosphorus and nitrogen.

We were particularly encouraged by the success in 1989 of

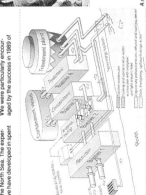

Protecting surface water: Bayer AG's "barrier" system to control discharges into the rivers near its plants.

acid recycling is being made available to other companies.

A second wastewater treatment facility, which utilizes a "Bayer Tower Biology unit, came on stream at our Antwerp site. Our U.S. subsidiary Mobay also has been operating a Tower Biology facility at its Baytown plant since November 1989.

In recent years, we further reduced wastewater discharges through a variety of other measures in our production units and central treatment facilities.

our "integrated environmental protection" program. By this we mean systematically exploiting all the chemical and technical possibilities of interrelated chemical processes to minimize the impact on the environment.

Introducing a new production process may do more to protect the environment than expanding waste management facilities. We therefore place special emphasis on integrated environmental protection in our process research and development.

We have been particularly successful in decreasing the amount of heavy metals in effluents – in some cases by as much as 99 percent. We have also significantly reduced organic loads, and the managements of our plants and Business Groups have drawn up a

Bayer AG
Spending for Environmental Protection and Product Safety

		1989	1988	In the past 10 years
Capital expenditures	DM million	305	388	1,781
Operating expenses	DM million	1,189	1,112	7,919
Research expenses for environmental protection and product safety	DM million	429	424	2,737

On the banks of the Rhine: Prof. Dr. Norbert Caspers (right) and his staff study the aquatic life of the river.

Environmental protection: 8,000 Bayer employees received practical training in this field in 1989

A major contribution to reducing pollution of the North Sea: the new incinerator at the Bürrig waste management center.

"Barriers" to protect surface water

A surface water protection system, in which more than DM 300 million is to be invested, comprises four "barriers" between production plants and

adjacent rivers: in-plant measures to reduce the amount of process effluent, increased analytical controls, the construction of supplementary containment vessels, and treatment in our central waste management facilities.

Leverkusen, Dormagen and Uerdingen, as well as six incineration plants.

In 1989, we completely rebuilt an incineration plant in Leverkusen at a cost of DM 60 million.

Bayer processes for purification of waste air

The catalysts we developed jointly with Siemens for removing nitrogen oxides from the flue gases of power plants are already being used successfully at many locations. A Bayer process for the removal of sulfur dioxide has successfully completed a one-year trial in a pilot facility. The process involves the conversion of sulfur dioxide to sulfuric acid needed for production processes.

Modern incinerators for Bayer's waste

In spite of all these efforts and of our commitment to preventing waste, some disposal and treatment facilities will always be needed.

We own and operate three state-of-the-art landfill sites at

At our production facilities, work is currently under way on some 250 waste air purification projects, for which DM 160 million has been set aside. About DM 1 billion is earmarked for converting power stations and production units to low-emission technologies. Our goal is a 50 percent reduction in emissions of sulfur dioxide, nitrogen oxides, organic substances, and particulates by 1993.

Innovative environmental protection for the 1990s

Environmental protection has a long tradition at Bayer. Never content with what we have achieved, we constantly are developing new technical expertise in response to new scientific findings and to new demands.

We are committed to further reducing environmental risks and burdens. This requires substantial investment. Yet it is not enough just to provide money: solving pressing environmental problems depends ultimately on innovation.

Exhibit 7.5 Bayer AG. (Source: Bayer AG Annual Report 1989.)

are not very much the exception with corporations such as Bayer, Degussa, Hoechst, RWE, Schering and VIAG all disclosing the capital costs of environmental protection measures. In virtually all of these cases such information is contained in a separate environmental protection statement which includes not only the capital costs but also operating costs and often research and development costs alongside fairly detailed descriptions of the activities undertaken. The amount of detail provided varies greatly, so that Hoesch of Germany, for example, provides two paragraphs describing the major measures undertaken and the capital costs incurred 'since the early 1970s'. At the other extreme are corporations such as Bayer of Germany with a two-page statement giving very detailed information including objectives, examples and costs over the last ten years, reproduced in Exhibit 7.5.

Quantification of the outputs achieved is even rarer. When provided it very often tends to be included as a part of the description of specific investment projects. For example, Bayer includes information on the reduction in waste water achieved as a part of its description of capital investment projects. Most of these disclosures are piecemeal concentrating upon one or a limited number of outputs. Information on waste water is especially common, both in terms of the amount of waste water and the contamination load factor. Also fairly common is information on the amount of sulphur dioxide and nitrogen oxide emissions. However, such information is often difficult to interpret as the reductions achieved are often disclosed rather than the actual level. In addition, such measures often cover a number of years so that, for example, BASF of Germany discloses the percentage reduction of waste water contamination load since 1974 while VIAG of Germany discloses the percentage reduction in sulphur dioxide and nitrogen oxide emissions achieved since 1976. Information on the actual emission levels is very rare although it is disclosed by a few corporations such as Thyssen of Germany with a graph of dust emissions per ton of crude steel or Hoechst of Germany with graphs of sulphur dioxide emissions and pollution of waste water, all since 1979.

PRODUCTION INFORMATION

It is often extremely difficult to separate out information on investment activities and production or process information. This problem occurs as capital investment is often carried out to modernize existing production facilities or create new facilities. Thus much of the information about the environmental impacts of production is provided not in the context of describing existing production facilities or the production methods and processes currently employed, but instead is provided in terms of descriptions of the impact on production processes of new capital investment projects. Similarly, it is noticeable that in virtually all cases where information on costs is given it is disclosed alongside capital expenditures. Thus, such information is especially common in German reports, being provided by most of the corporations that disclose capital investments, as illustrated by Exhibit 7.5 from Bayer of Germany.

However, despite these difficulties such a categorization of environmental disclosures is useful as the two categories, whilst overlapping, are not identical. Specifically, environmentally harmful effects of production may be reduced not by heavy capital investment but rather by careful planning and consideration of the possible impacts of operations, as illustrated by Total of France which emphasizes the need to include environmental considerations in all parts of the production process:

> In drilling and production, prevention is key. Environmental impact and safety analysis systematically precedes drilling and construction programs to evaluate in detail operational risks . . .

Often it is also possible to modify existing production processes without recourse to major capital investments, as illustrated by Sandoz of Switzerland:

> Safety improvements in the manufacture and handling of various products were implemented via process modifications. A new production strategy will give further support to our efforts in the area of environmental protection and safety.

Information upon production processes such as descriptions of the actual processes employed and the emission levels from them are very rare. What is far more common is information upon the activities centred around the production process. Thus, information about actions taken to increase the safety of production processes is fairly common. This often includes descriptions of environmental processes or safety audits as illustrated in Exhibit 7.1 (from Ciba Geigy), or Euroc of Sweden which describes the use of environmental audits in the following terms:

> A group wide project was started at year end 1989 to further improve the external and internal environment at Euroc companies. In the initial phase, the project will focus on auditing the current environment and evaluating the desired level of improvements at the Group's production plants in Sweden. Central resources are being made available for the project.

Likewise, there are several instances of corporations describing changes to the inputs used in the production process. Examples include Volvo of Sweden which describes the switch-over to water-based paints which reduces emission levels. Similar to this are descriptions of changes in energy sources by corporations such as provided by BASF of Germany which reduced emissions by switching from heavy fuel oil to natural gas.

The most commonly found types of production related information are descriptions of the treatment of by-products and waste including, in particular,

Protection of the Environment

The period under review was characterized by an extraordinarily high volume of activity on the part of the West German legislative authorities. Existing laws and regulations being updated and new ones brought forward placed our technical departments and production centers under an immense burden. In all, no fewer than 90 new laws and ordinances came into force, necessitating extensive operational measures to ensure compliance.

We effectively and systematically continued in our efforts to recover and recycle the waste and residual material produced by our production processes.

The disposal of special non-recoverable waste from our production plants is becoming ever more difficult. This is due mainly to the lack of suitable disposal sites and inadequate incineration capacities in the various regions. There is also the additional complication that, as residual materials are increasingly recovered or recycled, particularly difficult technical problems arise in the disposal of those substances which finally remain. The substances involved here are not usually of large volume but mostly of small quantities as those e. g. produced by research laboratories and development centers.

In order to avoid the special waste products created by our pharmaceutical agent production plant in Konstanz, which previously could only be disposed of by incineration at sea, the production process has now been converted to a technology which avoids the use of chlorinated hydrocarbons. Even so, the processing of chlorine-bearing products still leaves a certain quantity of chloridic organic waste. Although this could be disposed of without difficulty by special waste incineration methods on land, the lack of incineration plants in Baden-Württemberg has meant that we are still having to rely on incineration at sea or on this waste being accepted for disposal in other regions of West Germany.

At our Wolfgang metal works, our efforts in further improving and supplementing our flue gas cleaning systems have resulted in such a substantial reduction in emissions that the supervisory authorities, which have been recording the immissions in the area around the works over a lengthy period of time, have now stopped this grid-based monitoring operation. At Deutsche Gasrusswerke, our carbon black affiliate in Dortmund, installation of the new residual gas incineration plant means that compliance with the latest and still more stringent limits laid down by the authorities for sulphur dioxide emissions is ensured.

Considerable attention has also been given to combating the problem of soil contamination. This frequently involved taking a firm position in the face of excessive rehabilitation requirements laid down by the authorities and local councils, as for example in the case of our Marquart plant. On the other hand, we have also been able to cooperate successfully with the authorities — for example in the case of our former Brücken works — in the effective rehabilitation of a number of industrial sites. Rehabilitation work at the site of our previous hardening plant in Berlin-Reinickendorf also made good progress, again in close cooperation with the authorities. In order to localize and identify sources of environmental contamination and their pollution potential we have also provided extensive technical and financial assistance in the comprehensive test and analysis work being carried out at our subsidiary Elwenn + Frankenbach GmbH i. L., which only joined the Group in 1984.

Our waste water cleaning and pretreatment facilities underwent further technical improvements. The pollutant levels in the case of treated effluent permitted for discharge into the Rhine have thus been further reduced. The already very low values for chlorine-containing organic substances once again decreased markedly as compared with last year. We also succeeded in reducing the level of organic substances contained in all waste water discharged into the Rhine by a further 20%. The measurement data for our directly discharged purified effluent as compared with the limits set down in the relevant license were so favourable that in most cases we only had to pay half the sewage water rates normally charged.

Investment in environmental protection plant and equipment by the Group as a whole amounted to DM 16 million (1987/88: DM 22 million), including DM 13 million (1987/88: DM 13 million) in West Germany. This represents about 3% of total capital expenditure by the Group.

The running costs of our environmental protection installations amounted to DM 165 million for the Group as a whole (1987/88: DM 145 million). This figure included DM 142 million (1987/88: DM 126 million) spent in West Germany.

As part of the intra-regional system of assistance organized by the chemical industry to cope with incidents and accidents while chemicals are in transit, specialists from our works were called upon several times to assist the local fire brigades by providing expert advice.

Exhibit 7.6 Degussa. (Source: Degussa Annual Report 1989).

the recycling of by-products and the treatment of waste water as illustrated by Exhibit 7.6 from Degussa of Germany.

It is particularly refreshing to find that this is an area where not all corporations simply report upon successful attempts to reduce any adverse environmental impacts. For example, reflecting the disclosure requirements in Norway, Elkem is one of the very few corporations to admit problems with the production process in terms of environmental emissions when it states that:

> Emissions from our plants generally satisfy emission control and licence requirements. The exceptions are Elkem Meraker and Elkem Salten, which have experienced minor breakdowns in their filter equipment, and Elkem Bremanger, which has operated at its capacity limit. These situations are being improved.
>
> Norwegian State Pollution Control Authority (SFT) has commenced proceedings against Elkem Sauda for alleged excess emissions from its water treatment plant during the period 1981–1986. This is now under investigation by the police.

RESEARCH AND DEVELOPMENT INFORMATION

The final type of disclosure to be considered is research and development activities. To an extent this area overlaps with those previously discussed as it covers both the development of new, and the improvement of existing, products and production processes. As found for all areas of disclosure both the types of information given and the prominence attached to them vary considerably. The types of disclosures found are largely dependent upon the type of industry being considered rather than the country of the corporation. Thus, information is more commonly found in reports from corporations operating in heavy industries such as chemicals, metals and other raw materials processing and engineering. In addition to these industry specific differences, the amount of information provided appears to depend upon where in the reports the information is located.

One possibility is to give information in the chairman's statement. In these cases relatively little information is given, either a brief description of a major product development or, more commonly, a policy statement highlighting the fact that research into environmental impacts occurs. Such statements appear to be primarily aimed at reassuring the reader of the corporation's commitment to 'good citizenship' in a fairly general manner as illustrated by Unilever of the UK, which states in the Chairman's Report that:

> Environmental issues are and will continue to be of prime importance and we take them seriously. Research into new production processes, product formulations and packaging which are environmentally sound has been given high priority.

An alternative approach is to locate environmental research and development information in the divisional review of operations. This approach offers the opportunity to provide far more information. However, it does create certain problems for the reader who is interested not in divisional activities taken as a whole but is rather interested either in R&D or in environmental concerns.

Locating such information is often time-consuming and it is difficult to gain an overall impression of the corporation's activities in this field. However, two other approaches are more common and both offer easier access to the information. These are either to provide such information in an Environmental Statement covering all the corporations activities in the area of environmental protection or in a Research and Development Statement covering all R&D activities. To an extent which of these two is employed appears to be a function of the country the corporation comes from. In particular, it is noticeable that virtually all corporations from France and the Netherlands disclose this information in an environmental section while the pattern is less clear cut in other countries. In many cases the location decision is likely to be affected by the corporations' views on why the R&D is carried out: whether it is for specific environmental reasons or is a part of R&D activities aimed mainly at improving the financial position of the corporation. Alternatively, the location decision may be viewed as an intrinsic part of the message being given. If this is so, the location chosen is likely to depend upon the degree to which the corporation wishes to give an environmental concern message or a message that the corporation is research based.

The location decision appears to have little effect upon the amount of information given. In most cases relatively little information is provided. It is also noticeable that cost information is extremely rare although a few corporations such as Hoechst of Germany and Solvay of Belgium disclose the proportion of the R&D expenditures devoted to environmental concerns. Fairly common are policy type statements with little mention of specific projects, as illustrated by Holderbank of Switzerland:

> The task of the technical centre is to support the Group companies in their efforts to utilise the resources and plant necessary for the manufacture of cement both to maximise economic effect and in an ecologically appropriate manner.
> . . . The whole issue of minimising pollution has gained further significance.

When specific items or projects are discussed they tend to reflect common public concerns. Thus, as for product information, the development of CFC substitutes, catalytic converters and environmentally friendly paper bleaching methods are especially common. Other areas that are relatively common are improvements in waste water treatment methods and noise abatement, as illustrated by the environment statement of DSM of the Netherlands:

The Group's environmental policy is also aimed at abatement of noise and odour nuisance to local communities. There are ongoing research efforts to find effective measures in this area. One of the successes achieved here in 1988 was the elimination of an important source of odour nuisance from the effluent treatment plant of the Geleen location.

Despite the generally low level of disclosure there are some instances of fairly extensive disclosures. Often this is accomplished by disclosing a relatively long list of all R&D activities that have some environmental impacts without attempting to prioritize them or describe the significance of the projects, as illustrated by Exhibit 7.7 from Montedison of Italy where the environmental protection statement is mainly concerned with describing R&D activities.

One final type of disclosure policy may be found in certain German reports. This is to describe in detail a limited number of environmental concerns and the R&D carried out by the corporation to solve these problems. In these cases the R&D statements are primarily used to describe environmental matters rather than all R&D activities. Such an approach may be seen in Exhibit 7.8 from Philipp Holzmann of Germany which starts by stating that the main focus of research is environmental protection and carries on to describe the activities undertaken in this area.

A similar approach may also be seen in reports from Ruhr Gas of Germany, where the main research issue is stated to be emissions, and Babcock of Germany, which states that the main concern is the development of new technology to combat the greenhouse effect. Even more noteworthy is the case of Henkel of Germany which starts by describing the main R&D emphasis as being 'to increase environmental compatibility of products'. It then provides four pages of descriptions of the new products developed including chemicals for waste recycling, solvent-free DIY products, environmentally safer industrial cleaners and phosphate-free detergents.

CORPORATE ENVIRONMENTAL CONCERNS

Despite the generally positive tone of most of the examples discussed above, a number of corporations are clearly very conscious of the possible adverse impacts of increasing public interest in the environment and environmental legislation. In particular, a number of corporations appear to have taken the opportunity to use the corporate report to try to influence both the general public and policy-makers.

Such statements take a variety of forms. Some corporations are clearly concerned that either their costs are adversely affected by more stringent local legislation as evidenced by Wintershall, Germany: 'West German refineries

ENVIRONMENTAL ISSUES

Environmental concerns are of ever-increasing importance for industry in general and for the chemical industry in particular. While the chemical industry is in part responsible for the problems of environmental deterioration, it is also the main key to their solution.

Montedison is very aware of these problems and has devoted much of its technology and innovative capability during recent years towards improving the environment.

The primary thrusts of Montedison's efforts are in the development of environmentally compatible materials, in the development of "clean" production processes and in initiatives for industrial waste disposal and for recycling of plastic materials.

The following are among the group's most noteworthy initiatives:

• the development and commercial launching of Retiflex, a polypropylene-based fibrillated netting which is used as an asbestos substitute in cement slabs for covering or panelling and in tubing and piping. Retiflex is a suitable substitute for 70% of the asbestos currently utilized in Italy. This product does not release fibers or microparticles into the atmosphere and eliminates the sanitary problems associated with the use of asbestos. The Retiflex company received one of the E.E.C.'s "European Better Environment Awards for Industry" in 1990 for the eco-compatibility of the Retiflex product;

• the development of chlorofluorocarbon (CFC) substitutes. Alternatives to CFC's for refrigeration applications are now in the industrial production phase, while alternative products for thermal insulation and air conditioning applications are in experimental stages;

• the development of a plastic material composed 75% of natural substances: starch, glycerine and water. This material, which has mechanical properties similar to those of polyethylene and which can be processed using the standard technologies used for most plastic materials, biodegrades at approximately the same rate as paper. Novamont, a new, wholly-owned Montedison subsidiary, was formed to market this material;

• the production of polypropylene using a high-yield process which, in addition to consuming less energy, completely eliminates all liquid and gas effluents, wastes and by-products;

Exhibit 7.7 Montedison. (Source: Montedison Annual Report 1989.)

Research and Development

In 1989, the main focus of our research activities was in the field of environmental protection. We regard our participation in the solution of pressing problems to maintain and purify those media necessary for life – air, water and soil – as one of the most important tasks for Holzmann in both the present and the future.

The cost of cleaning up long-term pollutant deposits and contaminated work sites, currently estimated at 64 billion DM, demands treatment processes which are environmentally compatible. These "historical burdens" represent a serious environmental problem and must be decontaminated, particularly for the purpose of further use. We must be in a position to utilize available engineers to make and keep the environment clean for future generations.

Apart from the thermal processes, which can be restricted to only a few individual cases for cost reasons and low popular acceptance, soil treatment by means of scrubbing and micro-biological processes is gaining in importance. These are the environmentally compatible processes which will prevail in future.

The Kemmer-Harbauer Group, part of Holzmann, has developed a scrubbing process which has demonstrated its effectiveness at the Pintsch site in Berlin. The excavated contaminated soil passes through a stationary unit with several stages, the central component of which is the vibrating screw conveyor. By means of high-frequency oscillations, this device separates the contaminants from the soil particles up to a particle size of 0.015 mm without the use of surfaceactive agents.

The biological water treatment and microbiological soil treatment processes developed by Umweltschutz Nord have achieved much attention in professional circles. These processes are based on the ability of bacteria adapted and cultivated

at the contamination site to use superior hydrocarbons as a feedstuff and convert these into harmless substances. The result is biologically active soil suitable for re-use in agriculture and gardening. The cultivation of suitable bacteria which are found at the contamination sites, and the creation of suitable environmental conditions to reduce decomposition times are major factors in the Terraferm process developed by Umweltschutz Nord. The process is ex-

tremely environmentally compatible and economical in use.

Holzmann has further developed the on-site scrubbing process for heavily contaminated soil. This is of particular significance in cases where soil directly bordering built-up areas is to be treated and on- and off-site processes cannot be used. The process is based on high-pressure injection and treatment technology developed for specialist deep-level engineering.

Trials were successfully carried out on soil at the area of a former gas works in Bremen, heavily contaminated with creosote. A water jet emerging at a pressure of 500 bar splits off the contaminants from the soil particles in a previously sunk bore hole tube. The resulting soil-water-contaminant mixture is separated in a separation plant. The cleaned soil is then re-filled

in the bore hole, and the heavily contaminated residual slurry will be cleaned biologically. The bore hole tubes are sunk in a pre-planned pattern such that the entire area is cleaned step by step. We also undertook research and development in our traditional fields. As before, design methods, building materials and process engineering received priority.

Exhibit 7.8 Philipp Holzmann. (Source: Philipp Holzmann Annual Report 1989.)

continued to be adversely affected by . . . the considerable expense imposed by strict safety and environmental regulations', or that the costs outweigh the advantages, as argued by Marquard and Bohls of Germany:

> Populist measures, their success not commensurate with expended costs, are to be avoided . . . Subsequent rectifications via newly developed and improved methods for the sake of a few additional percentage points of emissions can endanger the involved companies' profitability. Such means will not necessarily promote the goal of providing relief for the environment.

Of equal concern to corporations are public reactions which impact upon the corporation's flexibility in decision-making. Corporations have either called for government actions to mitigate these effects, as illustrated by Veba of Germany:

> The growing difficulties of obtaining approval for waste incineration plants, the necessity for which are not seen by local residents or by municipal authorities or is denied for the individual project, are a source of worry. Clear political decisions are needed here . . .

or have engaged in actions to inform public opinion, as illustrated by Alusuisse of Switzerland:

> . . . derogatory comments about aluminium as a packaging material increased further. It was necessary to launch an intensive educational campaign to counteract emotionally rooted prejudices and implement adequate recycling measures.

In this case this statement was then followed by an eight-page section describing the environmental advantages of using aluminium as a material for cars, lorries and trains.

The most common concern expressed is that over energy policies, or in the case of Sweden, the lack of an energy policy. Thus, many Swedish corporations such as Electrolux, MoDo and Sandvik have used the corporate report to call for a national energy policy, without which Swedish corporations are likely to be increasingly disadvantaged in the international arena. In contrast, EC corporations tend to argue either that energy is too highly taxed in the domestic economy, as argued by Cartiere Burgo of Italy, or, more commonly, inappropriately taxed and regulated. This concern focuses in particular upon policies that fail to consider adequately the environmental impact of alternative energy forms. Thus, Gasunie of the Netherlands and Ruhr Gas of Germany both express concern over national and EC regulations that ignore the greater environmental friendliness of gas while RWE of Germany makes a similar case for nuclear energy. Such concerns are not limited to the energy corporations but are expressed by a number of other corporations such as BMW of Germany which argues that additional taxation of oil-based energy sources is likely to be counterproductive as it would lead to the slower replacement of older vehicles by more efficient and environmentally friendly newer models.

CONCLUSIONS

This review has described a situation of generally increasing levels of disclosure. Although the amount of information provided and the specific topics covered vary considerably it is noticeable that a significant minority of corporations provide quite detailed information. While instances of extensive disclosure exist in reports from most European countries, it is very noticeable that the level of disclosure is generally far higher in Germany than in any other country. However, many corporations from all over Europe are clearly aware of increasing public and governmental concerns about the environment. Many have responded by producing clearly defined environment information sections in the annual report. It is especially noteworthy that disclosures of both the level of expenditure and some quantification of the outputs achieved are becoming increasingly common.

However, the level of disclosure is by no means always adequate. Indeed there are still instances of corporations disclosing no information in this area. Even when disclosures are fairly extensive problems still remain. In particular, the disclosure of environmental information is generally entirely voluntary. This means that corporations have almost complete discretion in deciding what information to provide and the form that the disclosures should take. This gives them the opportunity to present their activities in the best possible light by the judicious choice of what information to disclose and the reporting format used. Thus, while any information is to be welcomed the reader should always consider the possibility that not all corporations follow the policy of Norsk Hydro of Norway which states that:

> We believe, that the public has a right to information, and there is nothing that we want to hide. If we have a problem, it is also in our best interests that it is brought out into full public view.

Chapter Eight

CURRENT TRENDS IN THE REPORTING OF GREEN ISSUES IN THE ANNUAL REPORTS OF UNITED KINGDOM COMPANIES

GEORGE HARTE AND DAVE OWEN

During the latter part of 1990, in addition to the publication of the government White Paper, *This Common Inheritance*, the Environmental Protection Bill finally completed its tortuous passage through Parliament and entered onto the statute book. These major initiatives, together with the ongoing work of the Departments of Environment and Trade and Industry in providing information, advice and support to help business come to grips with the ever evolving green agenda, have undoubtedly begun to foster a climate of greater openness in terms of focusing attention on the environmental impact of corporate activity. However, they have at the same time steered well clear of going on to suggest any specific amendments to external corporate reporting practice.[1]

Within the business community itself, support for environmental initiatives is seemingly often accompanied by a profound reluctance to release *detailed*

---

1. The White Paper suggests it is desirable, and will indeed often be in a company's interest, to publish statements of environmental policy and plans to deal with adverse environmental impacts. However, no guidance is given as to what form the statement should take. Similarly in the section 'Public Use of Data', whilst advice is given to produce environmental statements in the annual report, no stipulations as to the form of these statements are provided.

information into the public domain. Thus, for example, the International Chamber of Commerce has expressed full support for the adoption of environmental auditing programmes by industrial organizations but has also seen fit to stress their role as being one of a purely internal tool whose findings are for the exclusive use of company management (International Chamber of Commerce, 1989). This view is echoed by a leading member of the UK auditing profession, Brian Jenkins, Head of Audit at Coopers & Lybrand Deloitte, who, whilst highlighting the merits of an independent environmental audit report in terms of adding credibility and enhancing reliability, goes on to suggest that:

> The argument for making detailed environmental audit reports available externally is less convincing. An internal report has the advantage that it encourages participation and openness from members of the organisation . . . In many ways the issues are too soft for a proper form of external public reporting. An internal report aimed at management will tend to focus on what management can do to achieve improved performance. An external report will inevitably descend to an unimaginative statement on compliance with rules, rather than genuinely trying to add value.
>
> (Jenkins, 1990, p. 5)

One would not, of course, wish to discount the usefulness of internal reports as an essential input to the managerial decision-making process, nor indeed as a vital means of communication with the workforce. Nevertheless, views such as those outlined above perhaps dismiss too readily the role of external reporting as a vital mechanism of corporate accountability. Admittedly Jenkins is supportive of the notion of a certain degree of public disclosure, namely the publication of a statement of environmental policy within the directors' report. However, as is indicated elsewhere in this book, a major constituency to which the company is legally accountable, namely investors, is increasingly calling for more detailed information than that provided by merely vague policy statements. This desire to be kept fully informed on the environmental, and indeed wider social, impacts of company performance is apparently not confined to the newly emergent 'ethical' investor but is also now being expressed by the more traditional solely profit-seeking investor. Interestingly in this latter context, a number of empirical studies, mainly of American origin, concerned with the relationship between social responsibility disclosures and economic or stock market performance of firms, whilst being less than entirely conclusive, have suggested that disclosing company managements may well reap economic benefits from their policy stance.[2]

---

2. For a review of these studies and discussion concerning their potential usefulness in terms of accounting policy making see the articles by Mathews; Owen, Gray and Maunders; and Booth, Moores and McNamara in the August 1987 edition of the *British Accounting Review* (Vol. 19, No. 2).

Important as investor needs may be in pointing the way towards necessary changes in company reporting practice, it would be, arguably, unduly restrictive to focus sole attention on that particular consistency when considering the issue of corporate accountability for environmental and other social impacts. As Rob Gray (1990) puts it in what has proved to be an influential research report prepared for the Chartered Association of Certified Accountants:

> The environmental debate has raised a long stated concern that the race, the rest of life and future generations have significant rights to information about those things which may well affect their continued existence and will certainly affect the form and quality of that existence. (p. 104)

In a somewhat similar vein it may be recalled that some time ago the authors of *The Corporate Report* (ASSC, 1975) argued strongly for the adoption of the concept of 'public accountability' in company reporting practice, with the responsibility to report publicly being regarded as separate from, and broader than, any mere legal obligation to report. The suggestion was that there is an implicit responsibility incumbent upon economic entities regarded as significant in terms of their scale of command over human and material resources such that their activities have significant economic, and one might add here environmental, implications for the community as a whole.

The essential point is that only by making public not just the positive, but also the negative, environmental and community impacts of corporate activity will management attention be focused on improving these aspects of performance. In accounting theory parlance this has been termed the 'information inductance effect', the observation that the behaviour of reporters is influenced by perceptions of how their reports will be received. Indeed, Gray (1990) suggests that the effect of information doesn't solely operate in one direction and that by reporting reliable environmental information, corporate management may, for example, perhaps begin to persuade the financial markets away from their all pervading frenetic short-term self-interest towards a more measured recognition of organizational realities in an environmental context.

As a personal article of faith we would subscribe to the view that external company reports are extremely important as a means of accountablity in a purportedly democratic society. In particular they have the capability of influencing perceptions of business performance in the widest sense of the term. For far too long it has been largely impossible to arrive at a composite picture of a company's performance as information relating to its impact on the workforce, the consumer and the environment has to be retrieved from scattered locations, if it indeed exists at all. Our purpose in this particular chapter is to ascertain how the more innovative UK domiciled companies are beginning to get to grips with this problem in responding to the emerging green agenda via their reporting practices. In keeping with the theme of the book as a whole our main focus will be on developments in reporting environmental impacts. However, even a cursory glance through the burgeoning 'green' literature indicates that labour issues, the interests of consumers and community impact form an integral feature of a green critique of modern industrial society and we shall therefore not exclude these aspects from our ambit of consideration.

Before, however, turning to our own analysis we shall take the opportunity to review recent survey evidence relating to UK corporate *social* reporting practice, of which environmental reporting is an integral part.

CORPORATE SOCIAL REPORTING PRACTICE: A BRIEF REVIEW OF RECENT SURVEY EVIDENCE

Gray, Owen and Maunders (1987)

For a number of years the annual survey of UK published accounts, *Financial Reporting*, published under the auspices of the Institute of Chartered Accountants in England and Wales (ICAEW), contained a chapter on Social Reporting. Based on a sample of 300 large industrial and commercial companies, an analysis was presented detailing the number voluntarily disclosing information under the following 'social' categories:

- Human resources
- Fair business practices
- Energy
- Community involvement
- Product related
- Environmental
- Other social responsibility disclosures (relating principally to the offer of reports made under Cmnd 7233, *Code of Conduct for Companies with Interests in South Africa*).

Perhaps as a sign of prevailing economic orthodoxy at the time, this particular chapter was discontinued after the 1982–83 edition of *Financial Reporting*. However, Gray, Owen and Maunders (GOM) extended the survey for a further year in Chapter 3 of their book, *Corporate Social Reporting: Accounting and Accountability*, utilizing the same sample of reports as *Financial Reporting 1983–1984*. Interestingly, their analysis highlighted a dramatic fall off in disclosure for this particular year in respect of all information categories with the exception of 'human resources'. This anomaly is most probably explained by an 'anticipation of legislation' effect, in that a number of companies provided statements on arrangements for securing employee involvement (i.e. communication/participation/consultation initiatives) which became a statutory requirement under the Companies Act 1985.

Concerning other categories of information provision, a steep decline was most apparent in the cases of energy, where the GOM analysis showed 27 companies disclosing as against 46 in the 1982–83 survey, community involvement (GOM 25, 1982–83 survey 37), product related (GOM 21, 1982–83 survey 30) and environmental (GOM 16, 1982–83 survey 27). In sum, for all information categories with the exception of human resources, the final year of the *Financial Reporting* survey (1982–83) appeared to represent a peak of disclosure.

Guthrie and Parker (1989)

A major drawback inherent within the approach adopted by the surveys described above lies in the fact that merely indicating whether or not a company has disclosed certain categories of information tells us nothing about either the extent or quality of such disclosure. A somewhat more rigorous approach was adopted by Guthrie and Parker in conducting a comparative analysis of social disclosure practice in the UK, USA and Australia, based on a sample of annual reports relating to the 50 largest companies in the respective countries released in the period ending 1983. Content analysis methodology was employed to examine the material contained within the annual reports, with content being analysed in respect of theme (environment, energy, human resources, products, community involvement and 'other'), evidence (monetary, non-monetary and declarative), amount of disclosure in terms of page measurement and location in the annual report.

Results of the survey indicated that 98% of UK companies sampled disclosed social information, compared to a figure of 85% for the USA and 56% for Australia. For the UK companies, social information was generally disclosed in the directors' report and most commonly displayed a mixture of monetary and non-monetary quantification as opposed to being merely declarative. In terms of space devoted to such disclosure, the weighted average number of pages amounted to 0.89 (USA 1.26, Australia 0.70), with just under 30% of companies providing more than one page of social information within the annual report.

Turning our attention to the type of social data disclosed, only two categories of information score highly for the UK companies in terms of percentage disclosing, these being human resources (98%) and community involvement (96%). For other categories the scores are much more modest being 14% for environment, 10% for products and a mere 2% for energy. The popularity of human resource and community involvement as disclosure categories is, as Guthrie and Parker point out, largely due to the influence of legal requirements. In the case of the former, statute requires, for example, disclosure of information on numbers employed together with a numerical analysis of employees earning over £30 000 per annum, particulars of pension commitments and the provision of policy statements relating to the employment of disabled persons and arrangements for securing employee involvement. As for community involvement, the legal requirement to disclose charitable donations has, as Clare Roberts points out in the previous chapter, provided the spur for companies to present much additional information. Significantly, when re-examining the reports to discover the extent of purely voluntary disclosure, Guthrie and Parker found that only 28 companies (56% of the sample) disclosed information beyond that required by legislation.

A final item of note in the survey relates to the reporting of 'bad news' where, significantly, UK reports display the lowest frequency of disclosure (22%). Breaking down this figure further, 6 companies disclose bad news in the human resources category, 3 community developments and only 1 for environment. This latter statistic in particular perhaps provides food for thought when assessing the degree of public accountability exhibited by UK companies in terms of their environmental impact.

Gray (1990)

Gray's project is particularly ambitious in scope, being essentially concerned with cataloguing the current state of corporate social reporting practice employed by UK companies as well as identifying any major changes in such practice over a ten-year period ending in 1987. Again a content analysis approach is adopted which broadly follows the methodology of the Guthrie and Parker study. The project, which is still in its early stages, will eventually entail an analysis of the published accounts of 500 UK domiciled companies, a sample large enough to encompass different sizes, industrial classifications and other salient corporate characteristics. An initial pilot project, funded by the ICAEW, has been completed based on an analysis of 100 companies drawn from the sample population.

Clearly, given that only a small part of the database for the project as a whole has been utilized in the pilot study, any conclusions drawn from the analysis must at this stage be regarded as extremely tentative. Nevertheless, some interesting pointers as to the present state, and recent trends, of UK corporate social reporting practice emerge. It would appear, for example, that over 60% of the companies studied make voluntary social disclosures of some sort whilst virtually all make some kind of legally mandated disclosure. Additionally, the trend of both total and mandated disclosure seems clearly upwards over the ten-year period. However, it should also be pointed out that the average amount of space devoted to disclosure of social information can hardly be described as generous, only approximating to one full page in the later years of the survey.

Turning to specific topic areas, a number of interesting trends are discernible. In terms of mandated disclosure, the most dramatic growth in coverage, as measured by reference to both percentage of companies disclosing and space allocated in the annual report, is in respect of information on employee consultation and participation (particularly ESOPs). This phenomenon is no doubt particularly reflective of the concept of the employee-capitalist which developed through the 1980s. As far as voluntary disclosure is concerned, a rising trend is discernible in three areas, these being information on product safety and consumer well-being, community involvement and health and safety matters. However, by far the largest incidence of voluntary disclosure over the period as a whole relates to employment information provided over and above that required by legislation.

In addition to completing analysis of the full sample population over the initial ten-year period, Gray's intention is to update the survey beyond the initial cut-off point of 1987. Clearly, this will be necessary in order to capture the effect that the current explosion in green issues is having, if any, on the extent of corporate disclosure in respect of environmental and energy issues. Further work envisaged on the database includes, amongst other things, investigating questions such as whether disclosure is statistically related to factors such as size of company, profitability, number of employees or industrial sector, and what characteristics distinguish the disclosing from the non-disclosing company.

In sum, when completed, Gray's project will provide us with a wealth of fascinating statistical material charting the response of corporate reporting practice towards continually evolving trends in social and green awareness. We can only recommend the reader to follow its progression closely!

More recent trends in the reporting of environmental issues

The survey evidence we have just considered indicates that UK companies have, in general, through the 1980s given a low priority to the voluntary reporting of social information within their annual reports and accounts. Relatively few devote in total more than one page to such disclosure and hardly any are prepared to make public 'bad news'. Only human resource information appears to have been provided with any degree of consistency over the past decade, although Gray's study points additionally to a rising trend in recent years in the provision of consumer orientated and community involvement data. Certainly, none of the studies are able to point to much interest on the part of UK companies in disclosing details of the environmental impact of their activities.

Of course, it must be pointed out that the major explosion of interest in green, and more particularly environmental, issues has only taken place in the past couple of years or so, a period of time not captured in the studies. Three slightly more recent surveys concerned specifically with corporate attitudes to environmental issues rather than social reporting in general are, however, able to shed some light on company responses to new green pressures via the external reporting function.

Touche Ross (1990)

Touche Ross Management Consultants conducted an in-depth survey into attitudes towards environmental issues on the part of 32 major UK companies in the latter part of 1989. On the specific issue of the reporting of environmental issues in the annual report, the survey indicates that whereas more than half the companies studied claimed to devote some coverage, only a few dealt with the issues in any depth. In common with the social reporting studies discussed earlier, it was discovered that environmental issues tend to take a relatively low profile compared to those relating to human resources and community involvement. Whilst the survey points to a rising trend in coverage, a trend confidently expected to continue, at the present time only a handful of companies devote as much as half a page of the annual report specifically to environmental matters. The continued human resource slant to reporting is evident in that the most frequently mentioned issues are health and safety at work and working conditions. However, certain other issues are achieving some prominence, notably control of emissions, conversion of company cars to lead-free petrol, elimination of CFCs from products and product safety.

Institute of Business Ethics (1990)

A survey designed to assess how far individual companies are developing specific policies and programmes to improve environmental performance was carried out by the Green Alliance on behalf of the IBE early in 1990. The survey was based on a questionnaire mailed to the chief executives of 500 of the businesses listed in The Times 1000, from which 82 full responses and a further five partial responses were obtained. In answer to the question, 'Do you set out details of your environmental performance in your annual report and accounts?', only twelve companies (15%) replied in the affirmative, whilst a further sixteen indicated that this was an issue under consideration. Additionally some respondents (numbers not quantified) intimated that the information was made available in other ways. A further question asked whether an external audit of the company's environmental performance had been carried out. Again the positive response rate was low, thirteen replying yes, with a similar number replying that this was under consideration.

Coopers & Lybrand Deloitte (1990)

Coopers & Lybrand Deloitte commissioned Gallup to undertake a telephone survey of finance directors and chief accountants to discover the extent to which environmental matters were considered an issue for business, and more particularly the finance function, and whether commentary from auditors would be welcome. Gallup conducted 108 telephone interviews amongst companies randomly selected from The Times Top 1000 list between the 28 August and 3 September 1990. A large majority of respondents (87%) saw the environment as a significant issue for their business, with 55% believing it raises significant financial concerns. However, only 41% stated that their business had a formal environmental policy. This general lack of practical action to date is reflected in the fact that a mere 29% of the companies surveyed had ever included environmental information in their annual report in the past, although some commitment to a change of policy in this direction is evident in that only 39% expected to ignore environmental matters altogether in the next report. However, this apparent trend towards greater public accountability should not be overstated as very few respondents envisaged including a page or more of information, or providing a separate report. A further issue of some note raised by the survey is that just over half the finance directors intimated that they would value commentary from their auditors on environmental issues. In particular, management information systems and control procedures represented areas where an auditor's assessment would appear valuable.

The overall impression conveyed by these latter three studies is again one of a very limited response in general on the part of UK companies towards the evolving green agenda, at least in terms of making salient information publicly available. However, at the same time there is a clear suggestion that certainly a few companies are beginning to tackle green reporting issues with some degree of rigour. In order to get a flavour of these more innovative approaches we need to move beyond a general overview and look at specific examples of current corporate practice. This then is our task in the remainder of the present chapter. First, we shall look at some recent green reporting initiatives drawn from a sample of companies that have been singled out as 'good' disclosers. We then, more briefly, focus our attention on how companies in a particularly sensitive industrial sector, namely the water industry, are reporting on the environmental impact of their activities.

GREEN REPORTING: SOME ILLUSTRATIONS OF CURRENT BEST PRACTICE

A recent questionnaire survey concerned with the use made of published annual reports by UK-based ethical and environmental unit trusts (Harte, Lewis and Owen, 1991) included a request for respondents to list up to five companies they regarded as being consistently good at disclosing ethical, or social, information. From a total population of fourteen trusts, eleven responded to the questionnaire, from whom we derived a list of 24 companies considered to be good disclosers. Perhaps surprisingly only seven companies received more than one citation, and these are listed in Table 8.1.

Table 8.1 Leading environmental and social disclosers

Company	Sector	Number of mentions
The Body Shop International plc	Stores	5
Caird Group plc	Chemical and plastics	3
Argyll Group plc	Food and catering	2
British Gas plc	Oil and gas	2
Glaxo Holdings plc	Chemical and plastics	2
Halma plc	Engineering: mechanical	2
Tesco plc	Food and catering	2

Based on responses received from eleven ethical and environmental unit trusts (Harte, Lewis and Owen, 1991).

The 24 companies mentioned by the trusts together with a further six companies known to us from previous research as being innovators in green reporting practice form the basis of our subsequent analysis. Clearly, the methodology we have used in obtaining our sample doesn't enable us to claim to have captured an exhaustive list of companies at the forefront of green reporting, although given their relative scarcity, as suggested by the survey evidence cited earlier, we probably do have the vast majority. During the summer of 1990 we obtained the latest available annual report for each company on our list (together with, where possible, the previous year's report for comparative purposes) and it is from these reports, covering in the main year ends between June 1989 and March 1990, that the subsequent illustrations are drawn.

The trend towards greater coverage of green issues

A clear trend towards giving more exposure to green issues, particularly information pertaining to the environmental impact of corporate activity, is apparent when comparing the latest available annual report of companies in our survey with that of the previous year. The overwhelming majority devote more space to coverage of green issues and in a number of cases the increase is significant.

Two examples of innovatory practice are worthy of particular mention. Firstly, Caird Group, a company operating in the waste disposal industry, has broken new ground by publishing an independent environmental audit report prepared by a major engineering and environmental consulting group. An audit certificate, reproduced as Exhibit 8.1, appears in the 1989 published annual report and accounts, with the full consultant's report also being circulated

ENVIRONMENTAL
AUDIT REPORT

TO THE MEMBERS OF CAIRD GROUP PLC

Mott MacDonald have completed an Environmental Quality Audit on the activities of Caird Group Plc (the Company). In total, 21 sites were covered by the audit, these being listed in full in a separate audit report prepared for the Company's shareholders. These sites are in our opinion representative of the operations of the Company. The audit covered matters relating to health and safety on-site and to potential environmental impacts off-site at each of the Company's sites audited.

In general, the environmental aspects of the Company's sites included in the audit were found to be well-managed. The operational staff were mostly aware of and responsive to the stated Company policy for protection of the environment. Certain operations at sites which had in our opinion been less than adequately managed prior to their acquisition by the Company had been markedly improved by the efforts of the new management. This was particularly evident at sites which had been in the ownership of the Company for a longer period.

The audit identified several areas in which improvements might be made to existing Caird practices, although these are mostly not required by the Statutory Authorities at present. The improvements concerned thus relate mostly to the intentions of Caird to afford a high priority to environmental issues and to anticipate forthcoming environmental legislation, rather than to merely maintaining operations within present legislative requirements. A schedule of all recommendations for operational improvements has been submitted to the Company and a summary of these is included in the audit overview prepared for shareholders.

We found the Company to be committed to a policy of attaining a high standard of documentation relating to the operations of its sites. The documentation is being developed to be in accordance with the requirements of British Standard 5750 on Quality Systems (ISO 9000 series) and the basic elements for compliance are being progressively implemented.

Based on the information received and the results of the audit, we believe that the Company is managing the environmental aspects of its business in general accordance with good current practice in this industry.

There are as yet no statutory requirements governing audits of this type. The terms of reference under which this audit has been completed are included in the audit report prepared for the Company's shareholders.

Mott MacDonald
Engineering and Environmental Consultants
31 August 1989

Exhibit 8.1 Caird Group PLC. (Source: Caird Group PLC Annual Report 1989.)

to shareholders. The Chairman's Statement draws particular attention to this demonstration of a commitment to the highest possible environmental standards and stresses that the audit will be a feature of the annual report henceforth.

Our second example of innovation in green reporting comes from an environmental consultancy, RPS Group, which is a relatively small company quoted on the Unlisted Securities Market. Their 1989 annual report features a statement of environmental policy objectives which is reproduced as Exhibit 8.2. The statement is particularly noteworthy in not only listing in general terms the key policy areas and aims of the company but also describing in some detail the methods to be employed in applying the policy to corporate activities. The Chairman's Statement also draws attention to the fact that the company is currently undertaking its own internal environmental audit exercise.

Turning to the other companies appearing in our sample, two disclosure trends are discernible. First we have noted a marked tendency to devote increased coverage to environmental issues in the (unaudited) 'Review of Activities' section of the annual report. British Gas, for example, in an expanded section on 'British Gas and the Environment' in the 1990 annual report seeks to highlight the environmental benefits of gas in terms of impact on acid rain and the greenhouse effect, draws attention to the company's expenditure on energy efficiency programmes over the previous five years and notes the receipt of a Business and Industry Environment Award for the onshore part of the Morecambe Bay Project. A further feature of the report lies in its increased coverage of the customer service issue, particularly highlighting the undertaking of a major survey during the year designed to elicit domestic customers' views on service provision and outlining measures implemented as a result of the exercise.

Another example worthy of mention here is that of BP, a company long recognized as active in the social reporting field. In their 1989 report, BP devotes a full page, approximately doubling the previous year's coverage, to a section entitled 'Health, Safety and the Environment' which describes, largely in qualitative terms, various environmental and safety initiatives undertaken during the year. Mention is made of the establishment of a main board committee to overview health, safety and environment issues for the company, commitment to a continuing programme of environmental audits, participation in scientific projects and continued emphasis on safety training amongst other activities. Additionally, an increased concern with health, safety and environmental issues is evident in the review of a number of specific areas of BP's operations, namely exploration, oil, chemicals, and science and technology. For example, the review of BP Chemicals operations notes that:

In addition to ensuring that we meet all regulatory standards, we are committed to the implementation of policies which improve continuously the health, safety and environmental performance of our operations. We

The RPS Group provides environmental consultancy services to clients in the public and private sector. The range of services encompasses environmental planning, environmental sciences, landscape architecture and architecture.

The Group advises clients whose activities involve or have potential for significant environmental change. In so doing, our aim is to ensure that clients' objectives are realised in an environmentally sympathetic and responsible manner.

In carrying out this work, the Group seeks to ensure that its own performance is conducted in an environmentally sound manner. This is maintained by the adoption of a corporate environmental policy and a commitment to a regular process of auditing company practice and activities.

The policy has two parts:

a) Part I is the policy statement which lists the key policy areas and aims of the Group. The list covers the Group activities which will be subject to environmental control.

b) Part II describes the methods of applying the policy to Group activities. Each policy area identified in Part I has been analysed and the practices to be adopted to achieve the aims are described.

It is important for the successful operation of the Company that the policy is feasible. It must be economically sound and achievable within the Group working practices. The policy will be implemented as rapidly as good management allows.

I. Policy statement

The RPS Group has a comprehensive commitment to ensuring that its activities are carried out in a manner which ensures environmental excellence. This applies to both its own activities and the professional services it offers, thus ensuring that our clients receive advice which is based on the highest principles of environmental awareness. To achieve this, the Group has identified the following main policy areas and aims.

● *Energy*
  – to improve energy efficiency.

● *Waste*
  – to minimise waste and ensure appropriate utilisation of materials.

● *Transport*
  – to introduce greater fuel efficiency, reduce pollution and wasteful use of resources.

● *Communication, education and training*
  – to co-ordinate the dissemination of Group philosophy, policy and practice to all Group personnel.

● *Environmental awareness*
  – to maintain awareness of legislation, trends, research and development, practice and application.

● *Purchasing standards*
  – to ensure the purchase of environmentally acceptable supplies.

● *Environmental audit*
  – to carry out a regular process of auditing Group practice and activities.

II. Policy principles and practice

Energy
The Group recognises that major energy conservation opportunities exist within its offices and buildings. It has a commitment, therefore, to seek to improve energy efficiency wherever practicable by reducing energy loss and energy consumption. This is achieved by ensuring the application of measures such as:

● Energy efficient lighting;
● Use of thermostats in heating and hot water systems; and
● Insulation.

These measures will be adopted in existing offices on the basis of replacement as required and will form the fundamentals of design as new premises are occupied.

Waste
Better waste management will be achieved through appropriate use of materials and a policy of recycling. The main practices involve:

● Use of environmentally acceptable sources of paper;
● Recycling of photocopy rejects and single sided printed paper for internal office use;
● Recycling of waste printed paper and card through appropriate outlets;
● Division of waste to facilitate recycling;
● Reduction of internally generated paper use;
● Efficient use of water.

Transport
The Group policy is to ensure greater fuel efficiency and reduced environmental impact of its transport facilities. This concentrates on ensuring that the Group car fleet will as soon as practicable:

● use lead free petrol or diesel;
● use 3-way catalytic converters;
● meet specified fuel efficiency standards;

The Group will encourage staff to:
● seek car sharing where possible;
● use public transport where practical;

The Group will also:
● limit expenditure on cars to reduce production resource use;
● take into account vehicle safety, reliability, longevity and depreciation;
● provide a list of approved cars.

Communications, education and training
It is Group policy to ensure dissemination of environmental awareness and responsibility to all Group personnel and associates. This is achieved through:

● the development of an appropriate corporate identity;
● training and seminar programmes;
● the Group newsletter;
● the adoption of formal quality assurance principles;
● encouraging staff to make suggestions for environmental improvement.

Environmental awareness
The Group places considerable emphasis on its ability to maintain its awareness of legislation, trends, research and development, best practice and application. To achieve this, the Group:

● maintains a professionally staffed library;
● develops links and dialogue with legal practitioners specialising in environmental law;
● encourages its staff to seek membership of Professional Bodies where appropriate;
● maintains a research commitment in addition to its consultancy activities.

Purchasing standards
The Group policy is to purchase, where practicable, environmentally acceptable suppliers.

Environmental audit
The Group policy is to audit the environmental performance of each office, relative to the above policies and practices. The purpose of this audit is to assess environmental performance against a checklist of questions which will be used to produce a report on each office.

Exhibit 8.2 RPS Group PLC. (Source: RPS Group PLC Report and Financial Statements 1989.)

fully support the Responsible Care initiatives developed by the chemical industries in the UK and USA. We are investing in developments at existing plants to obtain further reductions in discharges and emissions. All our new plants are being designed to meet newly-defined, stricter standards of environmental protection.

The other major disclosure trend we have noted lies in the introduction of specific comment on environmental issues within the chairman's statement. This comment tends to take one of two forms. The first approach is to draw attention to the opportunities for profitable trading presented to the company by increasing levels of green awareness. Two brief examples will suffice to give a flavour of the line being taken. The first comes from Simon Engineering (1989):

> Many parts of the Group will benefit from the increasing concern for the environment. We are well placed with an unmatched range of products and processes that can make significant contributions to the requirements of engineering a better environment.

The second is from Pilkington (1990):

> Increasing concern about the environment can only be of direct benefit to future prospects, with glass fibre able to make an immediate contribution to energy saving.

The alternative, somewhat rarer, approach is to place on record what might be termed a commitment to good citizenship. An example is provided here in a joint statement by the Chairman and Chief Executive of the RTZ Corporation appearing in the 1989 annual report. Under the heading 'Responsibilities of Leadership' it is noted that:

> Our leadership in natural resources carries with it responsibilities which RTZ accepts whole-heartedly. We see our role as a steward of the resources in our hands, so that they can be profitably deployed for the economic benefit not only of our shareholders but also for those countries where we operate and for the world at large which depends on them. RTZ takes the long view, in investment, in planning and in the development of our many resources. Wherever we operate, we involve the local communities in our activities and invest in their well-being. We accept our responsibility to minimize any environmental impact that might result from our activities by endeavouring to ensure that they are conducted in a manner which is balanced and ecologically sensitive.

Finally, in terms of disclosure trends over the two-year period studied, we came across one fascinating example of a company going so far as to change its name in order to emphasize green credentials. The Chairman's Statement

---

Exhibit 8.2 RPS Group PLC. (Source: RPS Group PLC Report and Financial Statements 1989.)

appearing in the 1989 annual report of Creighton Laboratories, a company engaged in the creation and manufacture of toiletries, soaps and fragrances, addresses the issue in the following terms:

> Our reputation as a leading green and environment concerned company could not be higher and I strongly believe that the company's success and future is assured by following this path. Accordingly you will note Resolution No. 8 to change the company's name to Creighton's Naturally plc. We are not a laboratory, we do not harm or use animal materials, but create beautiful natural products. I am sure you will support the Resolution.

Clearly the shareholders were swayed by this appeal as the 1990 annual report appears under the name Creighton's Naturally plc!

The diversity of reporting practice

In addition to noting a trend towards increased disclosure, the other major feature of green reporting practice on the part of companies forming our sample that became apparent during our analysis was the wide variety of techniques employed for disclosing social information. Again, rather than performing any detailed statistical analysis, we will seek to give a flavour of current practice by drawing on a number of specific examples.

A separate social report

We came across only one example of the utilization of a separate report for disclosing information on the social aspect of corporate activities.[3] The company concerned is Body Shop International which, it may be recalled, in terms of 'votes' cast by the ethical and environmental unit trusts appears to be *the* leading environmental and social discloser (see Table 8.1).

Body Shop's endorsement of the principles of 'good corporate citizenship' is forthrightly stated in the following terms within the Chairman's Statement forming part of the main annual report and accounts:

> The company is a leader in many of the issues which directly affects its

---

3. A handful of UK companies, two notable examples being BP and RTZ, have produced what may be termed separate social reports, covering issues other than simply employment, in the past, although not on an annual basis. Additionally, both British Steel and the British subsidiary of Norsk Hydro introduced separate environmental reports in 1990. The only example, however, of the publication of a *regular* annual report of which we are aware is British Nuclear Fuel's Health and Safety Report, a highly detailed document running to some thirty pages.

customers and employees. Our expenditure of £1 million in the building and equipping of a workplace nursery signals the direction we must take. Our environmental concerns and the well focused campaign against Animal Testing have greatly enhanced the reputation of the business and have influenced policy changes in these fields. It is important that we continue these policies which demonstrate our commitment to profits with principles.

This latter commitment is underlined in a series of brief reports from overseas head franchisees contained in the Directors' Report, a number of which make reference to involvement in environmental projects and other social campaigns. For example, the report from Northern Europe mentions the Swedish shops' involvement in a campaign supporting the Children's Rainforest project, whilst from Australasia we are told that, '. . . Body Shop now heads the way in human rights following two successful campaigns: Walk Against Want and Amnesty.' However, the real source of detailed information relating to Body Shop's social commitments is a separate 32 page document entitled 'Another Year Into Our Lives' distributed with the statutory annual report.

Commencing with a statement of the Company's Charter, which outlines a commitment to good employment practices and customer relations, environmental and community awareness together with opposition to animal exploitation, the report goes on to give a number of illustrations of the Charter's practical implementation. Amongst these are:

- The work of the Body Shop Education Department in providing information for schools and colleges.
- Examples of community projects supported by individual shops.
- Information on recent poster campaigns in shop windows.
- Case histories of individual employees.
- The establishment of a day-care centre.
- Criteria employed in developing environmentally friendly products.
- Details of the Soapworks project in Glasgow aimed at promoting the economic regeneration of the depressed Easterhouse district.
- Projects aimed at developing non-exploitative trading links in Brazil and Nepal under the banner of 'Trade Not Aid'.
- Work in progress to ensure that the principle of environmental performance remains a major priority.

Exhibit 8.3 gives an example of the style of reporting employed.

The report, in giving a highly readable and colourful account of the company's central involvement in a myriad of environmental and social concerns, is extremely successful in putting across the message that Body Shop is indeed committed to the concept of 'profits with principles'. Nevertheless, it should be pointed out that there is a danger that the style of

A vulnerable little sliver of land wedged high in the Himalayas between India and China, Nepal has become the most successful expression of The Body Shop's relationship with the Third World.

Nepal

"We are no more nor less than simply traders, and trade – be it in a market stall or a shop kiosk – is simply a place where buyer and seller come together."

– Anita Roddick

TRADE

NOT AID

Trade Not Aid is the key. When The Body Shop sent consultant Mara Amats to Nepal in 1988 to look at possible Trade Not Aid projects, she returned with the idea of revitalising the country's papermaking industry, which had fallen on hard times through over-exploitation of traditional raw ingredients. Instead of the flowering Lokta, whose over-cultivation had caused massive erosion of top soil, Amats recommended the water hyacinth, a river-choking weed that happens to make terrific paper. She also suggested such untraditional materials as bamboo and bananas.

In 1989, The Body Shop initiated its Nepalese paper-making project, reviving the ancient craft of hand-making paper, to be used in gift items and in-store packaging.

The project currently produces paper bags, note books, gift bags, packing paper, calendars and writing pads.

Daily output runs to 1000 sheets of paper, 800 bags, 100 calendars and 50 notebooks.

The project provides work for 23 women and 14 men.

In November, Nepalese Pyramid gift boxes went on sale in Body Shops throughout the country. Made from water hyacinth and banana fibre paper, and lined with delicate Lokta paper, the boxes were filled with pot-pourri or products.

Exhibit 8.3 The Body Shop. (Source: The Body Shop International PLC, *Another Year Into Our Lives*, 1990.)

presentation employed may give rise to the charge of advertising hype. At times one does indeed have the impression that flashy presentation takes precedence over detailed information provision. To give one example, we are told that an environmental audit has been carried out focusing in particular on packaging, waste and trade effluent. However, except for a single reference to problems encountered in using biodegradable bags nothing else in terms of the results of the exercise is disclosed. Perhaps more fundamentally, one could argue that the judicious selection of certain aspects of the company's activities together with the complete absence of critical comment or independent attestation doesn't add up to giving a fully rounded view of Body Shop's environmental and social impact. It is though, of course, all too easy to be over critical. Given the overall paucity of environmental and social disclosure on the part of UK companies one can really only conclude by applauding Body Shop's initiative whilst accepting that it possibly falls somewhat short of perfection.

Statements of corporate objectives

Twelve companies, 40% of our sample, utilized what may be loosely termed a statement of corporate objectives in drawing attention to their commitment to the pursuit of social and environmental, in addition to profitability, goals. Although employing a range of terminology (for example, 'Corporate Statement', 'Mission Statement', Group 'Philosophy' or 'Commitment') what appears in each case at the beginning of the annual report is a statement of general philosophy or policy very much in lines with one of the recommendations of *The Corporate Report* (ASSC, 1975), a particular recommendation incidentally that found little immediate favour in practice. *The Corporate Report*'s suggestion of the publication of a Statement of Corporate Objectives, as one of six additional statements designed to assist understanding of corporate financial statements and reveal more fully how resources have been utilized, also envisaged the inclusion of quantified information concerning medium-term strategic targets. The only example we encountered of this occurring is that of Rentokil whose 'Group Statement' specifies an aim to achieve a growth of a least 20% per annum in profits and earnings per share. However, no quantification is attempted in respect of wider goals, with, for example, reference merely being made to the fact that, 'Services are committed to improving the environment and protecting health and property'. This latter aspect of performance does, though, achieve further recognition elsewhere in the annual report. The Chief Executive's review, for example, draws attention to the fact that a number of services have been relaunched with an emphasis upon optimizing the use of 'green' pest control techniques. Within the Environmental Services section of the Review of Activities additional information concerning these techniques is given in that they, '. . . include the electronic detection of rodents and special services which reduce or completely eliminate the use of toxic materials.'

It is indeed a feature of annual reports containing a statement of corporate objectives that they generally then go on to devote considerable attention, often in the order of at least three or four pages in total, to their pursuit of the environmental and social goals for which commitment has been pledged. ICI provides us with an excellent example of this particular point. The Statement of Group Purpose which prefaces the annual report centres upon a declared aim to be the world's leading chemical company. It is noted that through achieving this aim, '. . . we will enhance the wealth and well-being of our shareholders, our employees, our customers and the communities which we service and in which we operate'. This will be done, it is stated, not only by seeking consistent, profitable growth but also by:

- providing challenge and opportunity for our employees, releasing their skills and creativity;
- achieving a standard of quality and service internationally which our customers recognize as being consistently better than any of our competitors;
- operating safely and in harmony with the global environment.

The annual report then goes on to devote two full pages in total to sections on 'People', 'Safety, Health and the Environment' and 'ICI in the Community'. The former two topics are also dealt with at some length both in the operational review section of the report and a three-page interview with the company chairman, 'Discussing Vital Issues', appearing after the Chairman's Statement.[4] Finally, there is a ten-page feature appearing under the heading 'World Solutions' which comprises five case studies of individuals whose quality of life has purportedly been improved through use of ICI products.

In terms of the general philosophy or policy alluded to in the statement of corporate objectives permeating the annual report as a whole, two companies merit particular mention. First, Caird Group's stated corporate objective is to '. . . provide shareholders with above average growth in earnings and dividends by providing our customers with the highest levels of service while ensuring a strict commitment to environmental compliance.' The strength of this latter commitment is evidenced not only by the publication of an independent environmental audit report, referred to earlier in this chapter, but

---

4. The Argyll Group, whose principal retail identity is Safeway, provides another example of the provision of social information within an interview format. In this case interviews with the Marketing Director and Personnel Director, published within the annual report, are used to focus attention on issues relating to food health and safety and staff training amongst others.

also by particular attention being drawn to this facet of performance in the Chairman's Statement where the financial implications of such a policy are drawn attention to thus:

> We will continue to campaign for higher standards but shareholders should be aware that our policy of operating at the highest environmental standards will not maximize profits in some sections of our business in the short term. We are convinced, however, that this policy will lead to considerable long-term advantages in many different ways.

Finally, and most unusually in our experience, environmental compliance features in an interim report published in April 1990. In view of all this it is perhaps particularly ironic that the company's share price nose-dived in the summer of 1990 following disclosure of relatively poor financial, but certainly not environmental, performance. Clearly investors' purported increased concern with environmental issues referred to elsewhere in this book shouldn't be taken as indicative of a new moral climate within the investment community!

The other company succeeding particularly well in communicating the philosophical stance adopted in a statement of objectives throughout their annual report is National Freight Corporation (NFC). The company's 'Mission Statement' makes particular reference to the seeking of:

- a high level of employee ownership and commitment; and
- a participative and results-orientated style seeking improved employment opportunities.

and an organizational culture is highlighted in which 'people are our most valuable asset'. The annual report then kicks off with a two-page feature on 'NFC People' which highlights, amongst other matters, the activities of the NFC Foundation in securing accommodation for company pensioners and outlines initiatives undertaken designed to minimize redundancy, prepare employees for retirement and provide care for the elderly. The Chairman's Statement and Chief Executive's review continue the human resource theme. The former draws particular attention to the importance attached to employee shareholdings and outlines the work of the Company's Social Responsibilities Council both with pensioner groups and in the community generally, whilst the latter reinforces the employee ownership message and devotes specific coverage to the issue of training. Finally, the statutory obligation to provide information on employee involvement and consultation within the Directors' Report gives rise to two-thirds of a page of detailed information provision in marked contrast to the brief and bland statement with which so many companies content themselves.

Other aspects of disclosure practice

As we noted earlier, the chairman's statement and review of activities sections tend to be the parts of the annual report where information on social and environmental issues is most commonly to be found. The majority of information provided is in a narrative form, with what might be termed 'specific narrative' emerging as an increasingly prevalent disclosure style. This may prove to be an important development as specific narrative, unlike general statements of good intent, is potentially auditable information. The extract from Tesco's 1990 annual report (Exhibit 8.4), whilst being highly selective in terms of data provided, perhaps illustrates this latter point.

The usefulness of specific narrative provision for the purpose of judging a firm's social performance is considerably enhanced when an external reference point is introduced. An excellent illustration of this is provided in the annual report of H.T. Hughes, a waste management, demolition and civil engineering company. The Chairman's Statement contains a section headed 'Hughes and the Environment', from which the following extracts are taken:

> It is our policy to adopt the Best Practicable Environment Option in connection with all our business activities. This standard was first introduced by the Royal Commission on Environmental Pollution in 1985 and is defined as the optimum combination of available methods of operation so as to limit damage to the environment to the greatest extent achievable for a reasonable and practicable cost.

We are further informed that:

> All companies in the Group are working towards achieving the relevant standard set by BS 5750 and this certification will be in place by the late Autumn. Our landfill operations have been ready for assessment by Inspectors from the British Standards Institute since April.

As the recently introduced UK national standard for quality systems, BS 5750 perhaps provides a particularly relevant measuring rod for performance evaluation purposes. In addition to the Caird Group Environmental Audit Report referred to earlier, only one other company in our sample, however, Simon Engineering, specifically reported on compliance with this particular standard, the Chairman's Statement noting that:

> BS 5750 qualification, or its appropriate equivalent, has been, or is being, obtained by all our UK companies with similar standards being applied in overseas companies.

Exhibit 8.4 Tesco. (Source: Tesco PLC Annual Report and Accounts 1990.)

MANY THOUSANDS of our customers are now asking questions about what kind of world we want to bequeath to our children. Very many of them are looking for ways to help solve environmental problems. We are therefore taking initiatives within the company and with our suppliers to bring about improvements and to enable customers to make their own contributions.

During the year, we eliminated CFCs from all products. And we introduced phosphate-free detergents as well as disposable nappies, sanitary products, toilet tissue and kitchen towels which are non-chlorine bleached.

G

Recycling facilities at 135 stores   *Environmentally-friendly products*   *Organic produce is gaining ground*

enuine commitment . . .

VICTOR BENJAMIN
Deputy Chairman

We recognise the widespread demand for the recycling of packaging materials. Facilities for recycling one or more materials are provided at all our new stores. By the end of the year, recycling facilities had been installed at 135 of the 160 stores where there is space for them. Head Office stationery, in-store leaflets and posters are now printed on recycled paper. Toilet tissue and kitchen towels made from recycled paper outsell national brands in our stores.

45% of our petrol sales are now unleaded. The national figure is 25%. All our company cars run on unleaded petrol, and we have decided that from January 1991 we will not buy any car unless it is fitted with a catalytic converter.

Our stores are equipped with energy-efficient systems. And we are increasingly concerned to site new stores appropriately, so that they enhance their neighbourhoods, while protecting road safety and showing proper respect for the local ecology and for the long-term quality of the environment. During the year, we won several important awards for our environmental initiatives, and were pleased to receive a 5-star rating in *The Green Consumer's Supermarket Shopping Guide*.

Such awards, and the many actions we are taking, demonstrate a concern for environmental care which goes right to the heart of our business. We welcome the opportunity to combine sound business principles with a genuine commitment to the environment and its protection in a way that will both satisfy our customers and benefit our business.

An alternative, although perhaps less focused, form of compliance reporting was noted in a handful of other cases. RTZ provides a typical example, with a simple statement in the 'RTZ and the Community' section of their report that, 'in 1989 RTZ Group companies complied with environmental regulations to the satisfaction of the regulatory authorities.'

We also came across a number of instances of companies referring to externally derived standards when discussing specific areas of performance. For example, in reviewing their oil operations, BP disclose that:

> Audits based on the International Safety Rating System (ISRS) were completed and follow up inspections started in our major operations. Four of our refineries achieved particularly high ratings under the demanding ISRS standards.

Turning to R&D work, specific mention is made of the carrying out of successful trials of a solvent extraction process to clean up refinery sludges, and that the process has been selected by the US Environmental Protection Agency as a 'Best Demonstrated Available Technology'. In a similar vein to this latter example, Whatman Group in reviewing the performance of their Speciality Products division note that Whatman quartz and glass microfibre filters used for air pollution monitoring have been adopted as standard by the US Environmental Protection Agency. One final example of the utilization of an external reference point for a specific aspect of performance is provided by Tesco's mention of the introduction of their Nature's Choice range, '. . . the only cosmetic products currently available which satisfy the "Cruelty Free" criteria of the British Union for the Abolition of Vivisection.'

Although, as we have just seen, it is possible to unearth a few examples of what might be termed a 'compliance with standards' approach to social and environmental reporting, these were very much the exception rather than the rule amongst the companies in our survey. An alternative form of external reference point that did, however, prove much more popular was mention of the receipt of awards from outside bodies in recognition of corporate achievements in the fields of environmental protection or health and safety at work. In the former context we have already mentioned the annual report of British Gas earlier in the chapter which provides an example typical of many, whilst in the latter, to note again but one illustration, we have Whatman Group's mention of the receipt by Whatman Paper Limited of a ROSPA gold award for occupational safety in 1989. Finally, in a slightly different vein, Argyll Foods proclaim their green credentials in their annual report in terms of being voted the retailer best meeting the needs of environmentally aware shoppers for two consecutive years by the Green Consumer Guide.

The vast majority of specific narrative disclosure, however, consists of largely qualitative material concerning particular projects undertaken or other initiatives such as the formation of a Board Committee on environmental issues referred to in RTZ's annual report. Occasionally odd pieces of statistical information are provided, as Exhibit 8.4 illustrates, this most frequently occurring though in respect of human resource disclosure. One particular point to note relates to the virtually universal lack of disclosure of 'bad news' except for occasional mention of redundancy issues. A very rare exception here is provided by ICI's coverage of safety issues, where it is noted that:

> . . . the Group regrets to report the deaths of two staff in a plant accident at Billingham, UK, and of a public service fireman at Peterborough, UK, in an incident involving an ICI explosives van. Three staff died in accidents while on company business.

Turning to the provision of financially quantified information, this is most prevalent in the human resource and community involvement areas of reporting. In the latter a fairly routine procedure is to disclose the total amount spent on community activities and then to go on to describe in qualitative terms some of the more notable initiatives undertaken. For example, in the Community Affairs Review section of their annual report Marks & Spencer disclose that they '. . . committed £4.6 million to a programme which touched all areas of the community. Donations and support for over 1400 organizations were determined by three specialist committees: health and care; arts and heritage; community services, education and training.' There then follows approximately one page of further information outlining some major projects supported by the specialist committees. The intrusion of financial data into discussion of environmental impact is a much rarer phenomenon. Again ICI is very much an exception in disclosing the total amount spent on environmental protection whilst also making a specific provision in their accounts for future environmental clean-up costs. Mention is also made of the existence of reporting mechanisms enabling the tracking of environmental performance throughout the Group and the development of improvement plans at each site against which progress is regularly monitored. A mere handful of other companies provide isolated examples of specific environmental expenditures. An illustration is provided here by Glaxo Holdings where it is noted in the Chairman's Statement that:

> We pride ourselves on manufacturing our medicines safely and efficiently to the highest standards of quality under conditions which protect the staff producing them as well as the environment. As a single illustration of this policy, our shareholders will be glad to know that we are spending some £9 million on new treatment facilities at our plants in Montrose, Ulverston and Singapore, expressly in order to maintain and improve our ability to dispose safely of industrial waste.

In similar vein British Gas draw attention to the expenditure of some £100 million over the past five years on energy efficiency programmes, and RTZ specifically mention capital expenditure undertaken at two smelters for the purposes of increased production, improved product quality and environmental enhancement.

WORLD SOLUTIONS

Millions of people around the world benefit every day from products developed by ICI. The following pages focus on five such individuals. Their stories show the variety of ways in which ICI is improving the quality of life – from pharmaceuticals to agrochemicals, from old materials to the very new, and through skilfully adapting its products to the precise needs of its customers.

Like millions of fellow-sufferers, this patient found his work and way of life severely limited by his condition . . . until recently. Now he lives a normal life and holds down an active, outdoor job, thanks to a small tablet developed by ICI.

Under the initial guidance of Sir James Black, who in 1988 received the Nobel Prize for Medicine, ICI revolutionized the treatment of high blood pressure by developing beta-blockers – now one of the commonest treatments in cardiovascular medicine. Subsequent research at ICI has helped millions of people around the world to live more comfortably with heart disease.

At present, nearly one third of ICI Pharmaceuticals' research and development is dedicated to cardiovascular disorders. Of the £2,000 million or more that ICI will spend on pharmaceutical research and development in the 1990s, a large proportion will continue to be spent on cardiovascular research.

The simple and effective treatment of high blood pressure is just one way in which ICI has helped the fight against heart disease. ICI is also developing new treatments for angina, heart-failure and arrhythmias and exploring ways of limiting the damage caused by heart attacks and coronary artery disease.

Looking to the future, ICI is searching out novel medicines to control blood lipids and atheroma development, to prevent heart attacks and to treat peripheral and cerebrovascular disease.

"My problem was high blood pressure, but my previous medication wasn't doing any good. Hard physical work was impossible; I thought I'd get a heart attack."

Pawnee Indian*, Oklahoma, USA.

"The development of innovative treatments for heart disease is a prime example of ICI solutions to worldwide problems."

Michael D. Romack, ICI Pharmaceuticals

The name of the patient is not disclosed for ethical reasons.

A final form of specific narrative worthy of brief mention relates to the provision of detailed information on the type of products or services provided. As might be expected, companies going down this route tend to be those providing socially desirable products and services. Thus, to give but one example, the pharmaceutical group Glaxo Holdings devotes several pages of their annual report to discussing manufacturing and research and development activity in five major therapeutic areas – cephalosporins, anti-peptic ulcerants, anti-asthmatics, beta-blockers (plain) and topical steroids.[5] An interesting, somewhat novel, alternative approach adopted by a couple of companies, Cable and Wireless, the telecommunications operator, and ICI is to include a number of case studies detailing particularly beneficial aspects of their activities in the annual report. Exhibit 8.5 provides an illustration of this approach.

Our concluding, perhaps trivial, comment concerning the survey carried out relates to the actual production of the annual report itself. Here we noted that six companies printed their reports on recycled paper, whilst Pilkington draws attention to the fact that:

> This document has been produced on Consort Royal Silk from the Donside Paper Company Limited. The pulp is brought from North America, Spain, Portugal and Scandinavia where for every tree felled three or four are planted. The Donside Factory also recycles the water, off cuts and rejects from the paper-making process, ensuring that any negative environmental effects are kept to an absolute minimum.

Could this be, perhaps, the ultimate in socially responsible 'reporting'?

THE RESPONSE OF A SENSITIVE SECTOR TOWARDS THE EMERGING GREEN AGENDA: THE WATER INDUSTRY

Some of the attention given to the water industry recently has been due to the privatization of the ten English and Welsh water authorities in 1989. However, as we will see, the industry has also attracted attention due to the nature of its business, and in particular what may be considered to be green or environmental aspects of its product, the production process, and the use of its assets.

---

5. Other notable examples of companies in our survey providing detailed information on 'socially desirable' productive activities are Halma (safety and health and environmental control), Portals (protection and control products for environmental and industrial safety), Rentokil (environmental services) and Whatman (specialist products for filtration and purification).

Exhibit 8.5 ICI. (Source: ICI Annual Report 1989.)

The water industry in England and Wales is now dominated by ten newly privatized water companies, which were previously regional water authorities. These new companies are listed in Table 8.2, and serve approximately 75% of the population of England and Wales, the remainder being served by 29 smaller, local water companies.

Table 8.2 The newly privatized water companies

Anglian	Southern
North West	Thames
Northumbrian	Welsh
Severn Trent	Wessex
South West	Yorkshire

This review concentrates on the reporting practices of these newly privatized ten water companies as shown by their 1988/89 and 1989/90 annual reports and accounts (being the last report before privatization and the first report after). Each of the ten companies was contacted and requested to supply a copy of the relevant accounts, together with other publicly available reports prepared by the company to illustrate the environmental impact of their business. Eight of the ten companies replied, six providing the 1988/89 report, eight providing the 1989/90 report and five enclosing other environmental documents.

The environmental impact of the water industry

Before reviewing the annual reports received it is worth identifying some of the main issues being debated and discussed in respect of the environmental impact of the water industry. The four main areas of interest identified here are:

- the quality of drinking water;
- the quality of rivers;
- the quality of bathing waters, including the issue of sewage;
- the use of water assets.

This identification of issues is not intended to be exhaustive – rather it is meant to be a tentative framework against which we can organize and compare reporting practice as seen in the annual report and accounts.

The water industry, perhaps more than most other industries, deals directly with the public and industry. Its product may, until recently, be one which was largely taken for granted. However, it is clear that due to various factors, including increasing public pressure and legislation developed in the European Community, both the quality of the product and the consequences of its production are matters of growing interest (and in some cases concern).

The environmental impact of the industry has been competing with the financial affairs of the industry as matters demanding attention in recent years. And as we will see the two are not always unconnected.

The quality of drinking water

An EC Directive (80/778/EEC) defines the quality of drinking water in terms of 66 matters. These have been classified under six general headings (Bowers *et al.* 1989) as shown in Table 8.3. While most of these matters are generally considered to be of no problem in connection with British water, Bowers *et al.* (1989) have identified eight which are of some concern. These are listed in Table 8.4.

Table 8.3 Classification of parameters relating to water quality in the EC Directive (80/778/EEC)

- Organoleptic (colour, turbidity, odour and taste) (4)
- Physio-chemical (15)
- Substances undesirable in excessive amounts (24)
- Toxic substances (13)
- Microbiological (bacteria) (6)
- Minimum concentrations for softened water (4)

Table 8.4 Parameters of concern

1. Bacteriological (coliforms and *E. coli*)
2. Colour (caused mainly by iron and manganese), odour and taste
3. Aluminium
4. Lead
5. Toxic heavy metals
6. Pesticides
7. PAH (polycyclic aromatic hydrocarbons)
8. Nitrates and nitrites

Interestingly, particularly in light of the results of our review below, a similar classification of concerns has been used by a firm of stockbrokers in their review of the water industry at the time of privatization. While the concerns they addressed concentrate on the financial aspects of the investment opportunity, it is interesting to note the place of environmental matters in such an appraisal. In this case the ten (then) water authorities were appraised in terms of drinking water problems, and classified as having no problems known, some minor/limited problems, significant problems or potentially serious problems, in respect of nine parameters (CL-Alexanders Laing and Cruickshank, 1989).

The quality of rivers

Concern has been expressed that the quality of rivers has deteriorated over the last twenty years, based on a classification which assesses the ability to support fish life and potability (Bowers *et al.*, 1989). Detailed analysis of the kilometres of rivers within each (then) water authority's boundaries is available, with analysis into five classes, ranging from 1a (high quality) to 4 (grossly polluted and likely to cause a nuisance) (CL-Alexanders Laing and Cruickshank, 1989).

Further issues of concern in respect of river water quality include sewage treatment works (where application can be made to have consents relaxed) and pollution incidents. In the case of the latter, it appears that although there may be a large number of incidents reported in any one year, the number which results in prosecution is only a very small percentage (for example 23 000 and 300 respectively in England and Wales in 1987 (Hetherington, 1989)).

The quality of bathing waters

Here the concerns seem to be with the pumping of raw or partly treated sewage direct into the sea. For example, faecal coliforms as a percentage of the total sampled in the period 1980–85 show an increase from 35% to 59% (Bowers *et al.*, 1989). In addition, the issue of sewage sludge disposal at sea has received much publicity.

The use of water assets

The possible environmental damage arising from the commercial exploitation of land and water assets, or the possibility of the disposal of such assets (due to commercial pressures imposed by public quotation) has also been seen as a possible issue of concern.

Company reporting

Having identified these four categories of concern, this section deals with the reporting practices of the respondent water companies under each heading.

The quality of drinking water

Although we identified specific issues in regard to quality, the information disclosed in the company annual reports and accounts was very limited. Disclosure, generally in the review of operations, was concerned more with:

- quantity of water supplied, sometimes referring to sources and treatment;
- length of mains, sometimes referring to renewals;
- number of boreholes;
- number of treatment works;
- number of reservoirs.

Details of water quality, particularly in relation to those matters referred to in Tables 8.3 and 8.4, were rarely provided. Some reports did refer to the EC Directive, mentioning levels of investment proposed to meet standards. However, perhaps there is general agreement with the view expressed in one 1989/90 report that 'data collected under this new regime show that our product complied with the great majority of standards but, since this programme has only been in place for a short time, it is too early to give reliable statistics'.

The quality of rivers

In this case reporting was more in line with the five part classification of rivers and canals referred to above. However, not all reports referred to the lengths of rivers under each class, and some disclosure was partial or very general, for example referring to quality in comparison to previous years or compared to objectives (neither being specified).

Similarly, information on the number of pollution incidents was disclosed in a number of reports, although this was sometimes restricted to the number of substantial incidents and prosecutions. Little detail was provided concerning the nature of such incidents, although in one case the total number of incidents was classified as due to farm, oil and industrial causes. No financial costing of such incidents was provided.

Other matters referring to water quality included references to fishing quality and the setting up of a specific rivers unit in the water company.

The quality of bathing waters

Although the problems of sewerage and sewage were mentioned initially under rivers above, we will deal here with these matters, although for some companies (which are land-locked in terms of their coverage) bathing waters is less of an issue.

Once again disclosure tended not to focus on the issues raised initially. Instead more detail was reported on the length of sewers, number of sewage pumping stations, number of sewage treatment works and sea and estuary outfalls. In a few cases sludge disposal routes were detailed. However, as before with water quality, greater attention was paid to the planned investment, rather than detailing the condition of bathing waters. Little information was given on the quantity and disposal of sewerage sludge, and only a very few reports dealt, albeit briefly, with the quality of its bathing waters in relation to EC standards.

The use of water assets

Many of the reports reviewed contained a section on the issues of recreation and conservation. Typically this indicated what was being done at specific sites (and referred to links with bodies such as the Nature Conservancy Council). Similarly the range of activities which took place on company sites was described in most reports. Little, however, was said about the possible future use of sites, and in particular the possible commercial exploitation or disposal.

Other matters

Most of what might be described as environmental reporting by the water companies is referred to in the subsections above. Three other matters should also be mentioned. Two matters were frequently mentioned in reports, these being the company's activities in the community, and the second being the setting up of various consultative committees. The third other matter was mentioned on one occasion, this being the energy efficiency of the company in its production, although reporting was limited to some quite general comments and an example of financial savings at one sewage works.

Discussion

This section has revealed some difference between the issues being debated and discussed and the reporting by the water companies in their annual reports and accounts. In general there does seem to be much of interest in the performance of the water companies for investors, consumers and the community. The widespread recognition of the need for massive investment to meet the standards expected nowadays suggests that there may be more to report about present performance than is currently the case. Yet even the water companies themselves may recognize the importance of informed debate. This was illustrated by one Chairperson, who stated in a 1989/90 annual report that:

The current debates on environmental issues touch almost every aspect of the company's affairs. The absence of well-informed comment on these issues, which could lead to inappropriate answers, means that we have a particular duty to play an important role in improving awareness.

It remains to be seen what impact the regulation by the National Rivers Authority (NRA) and the Office of Water Services (OFWAT) will have. The former's concern with discharges from sewerage works, water quality standards, waste water, sewage sludge dumping at sea and the cleaning up of beaches may yet find its way into company annual reports, if not accounts, perhaps in a manner not too dissimilar to the information provided in the 1985/86 Annual Report of one authority reproduced as Exhibit 8.6. Here we see pollution control statistics, including river and canal, and estuary classification, and sewage treatment works performance. Alternatively it may be possible to introduce some of the type of information contained in Yorkshire Water's Water Quality Report, given in Table 8.5.

Table 8.5 Examples of contents of Yorkshire Water's Water Quality Report 1988

- Bacteriological quality of treated water at source, reservoirs and distribution
- Chemical quality of treated water at source
- Treated water at source – percentage samples failing EC standard
- Lead surveys
- Major sewage work discharges to various rivers
- Pollution prosecutions brought during the year, including details of the offence
- Fish mortalities
- Dangerous substances in rivers

CONCLUSIONS

Our purpose in this chapter has been to ascertain how UK companies are responding to the emerging green agenda in terms of providing relevant information within the annual report and accounts.

We commenced with a review of recent survey evidence which suggests that a low priority in general is currently given to the reporting of social, and more particularly environmental, information. Nevertheless we have been able to identify at least a few companies which are beginning to tackle green reporting issues with some degree of rigour and utilized examples drawn from their annual reports in order to give a flavour of what may be considered current best practice.

Within an overall trend on the part of these companies towards a greater coverage of green issues perhaps particularly noteworthy developments relate to the publication of statements of objectives, the increased use of specific narrative and some move towards introducing external reference points in

APPENDIX 8
Pollution control statistics

Table 8A:
Classification of rivers and canals (using national scheme adopted in 1977 – see Fourth Annual Report (1977–78) Appendix 7).

Class	Year	Non-tidal rivers		Non-tidal canals	
		km	%	km	%
1A	1980	2590	51.1	170	28.9
	1984	2579	48.4	131	22.7
	1985	2579	48.4	131	22.7
1B	1980	813	16.1	91	15.5
	1984	664	12.5	106	18.4
	1985	656	12.3	106	18.4
2	1980	798	15.7	299	50.8
	1984	924	17.4	316	54.8
	1985	923	17.3	316	54.8
3	1980	655	16.1	28	4.8
	1984	872	16.4	24	4.1
	1985	897	16.9	24	4.1
4	1980	212	4.2		
	1984	284	5.3		
	1985	268	5.0		
TOTALS	1980	5068		588	
	1984	5323		577	
	1985	5323		577	

Table 8B:
Classification of estuaries (using national scheme adopted in 1980 – see para. 100 of Seventh Annual Report (1980–81)).

Class	Year	Tidal rivers		Tidal canals	
		km	%	km	%
A	1980	220	49.5		
	1984	221	49.7		
	1985	221	49.7		
B	1980	90	20.3		
	1984	101	22.7		
	1985	101	22.7		
C	1980	71	16.0		
	1984	60	13.4		
	1985	60	13.4		
D	1980	63	14.2	6	
	1984	63	14.2	6	
	1985	63	14.2	6	
TOTALS	1980	444		6	
	1984	445		6	
	1985	445		6	

Table 8C: Sewage treatment works performance 1985 in relation to quality criteria of discharge consents.

Design DWF Ml/d	No. of works	Works complying		Works failing to comply		Works where no monitoring samples taken
		within design DWF	in excess of design DWF	within design DWF	in excess of design DWF	
50+	14	8	2	3	1	0
10 – 49.9	29	12	11	4	2	0
2 – 9.99	68	29	23	9	7	0
0.1 – 1.99	136	65	52	9	10	0
<0.1	121	47	65	6	3	0
TOTALS	368	161	153	31	23	0

Table 8D: Trade effluent control – discharge to Authority sewers.

No. of discharges	No. of samples taken	Volume to sewers Ml/year	Settled COD load '000 t/a	Suspended solids load '000 t/a
4,563	31,000	87,700	129	39

Exhibit 8.6 North West Water Authority. (Source: North West Water Authority, 12th Annual Report 1985–86.)

reporting on social performance. However, it must also be pointed out that information provision is generally highly selective and largely public relations driven with a virtually universal reluctance to disclose bad news. Furthermore, in turning our attention to a particularly sensitive industrial sector in the final part of the chapter, there is some suggestion that certain major issues of public concern are not being fully addressed in annual reports and accounts.

In sum, we clearly have a long way to go before we arrive at a recognizable system of formal accounting for corporate social and environmental impact. We can, however, as was pointed out in Chapter 1, confidently expect future moves in this direction as a result of supranational influences, the actions of influential user and pressure groups and, perhaps most fundamentally, simple corporate self-interest.

REFERENCES

Accounting Standards Steering Committee (1975) *The Corporate Report*, London, ASSC.

Booth, P. Moores, K. and McNamara, R. (1987) 'Researching the information content of social responsibility disclosure: a reply', *British Accounting Review*, August, pp. 177–81.

Bowers, J., O'Donnell, K. with Jay, S. and Murphy, L. (1989) *Liquid Costs*, Leeds, Public Policy Unit, University of Leeds.

CL-Alexanders Laing and Cruickshank (1989) *Water: An Explosive Issue*, London, CL-Alexanders Laing and Cruickshank.

Coopers & Lybrand Deloitte (1990) *Environment and Finance Function: Survey of Finance Directors*, London, Coopers & Lybrand Deloitte.

Department of the Environment (1990) *This Common Inheritance*, DoE White Paper, London, HMSO.

Gray, R., Owen, D. and Maunders, K. (1987) *Corporate Social Reporting: Accounting and Accountability*, London, Prentice Hall International.

Gray, R. (1990) *The Greening of Accountancy: The Profession After Pearce*, Certified Research Report No. 17, London, Chartered Association of Certified Accountants.

Gray, R. (1990) *Corporate Social Reporting by UK Companies: A Cross-Sectional and Longitudinal Study*, Paper presented to the annual conference of the British Accounting Association, University of Dundee, April.

Guthrie, J. and Parker, L.D. (1989) 'Corporate social disclosure practice: a comparative international analysis', *Advances in Public Interest Accounting*, Vol. 3.

Harte, G., Lewis, L. and Owen, D. (1991) 'Ethical investment and the corporate reporting function', *Critical Perspectives on Accounting*, Forthcoming.

Hetherington, P. (1989) *Deep Water – Investors Beware*, London, Water Industry Unions Committee.

Institute of Business Ethics (1990) *Ethics, Environment and the Company: A Guide to Effective Action*, London, IBE.

International Chamber of Commerce (1989) *Environmental Auditing*, Paris, ICC.

Jenkins, B.G. (1990) *Environmental Audit: An Auditor's Perspective*, text of a talk given at Glaziers Hall, London, 27 March 1990, Coopers & Lybrand Deloitte.

Mathews, M.R. (1989) 'Social responsibility accounting disclosures and information content for shareholders: a comment', *British Accounting Review*, August, pp. 161–7.

Maunders, K.T. (1983) 'Social reporting and the employment report', in Tonkin, D.J. and Skerratt, L.C.L. (eds), *Financial Reporting 1982–83*, London. Institute of Chartered Accountants in England and Wales.

Owen, D., Gray, R. and Maunders, K. (1987) 'Researching the information content of social responsibility disclosure: a comment', *British Accounting Review*, August, pp. 169–75.

Touche Ross Management Consultants (1990) *Head in the Clouds or Head in the Sand? UK Managers Attitudes to Environmental Issues – A Survey*, London, Touche Ross.

Chapter Nine

ENVIRONMENTAL MANAGEMENT IN PRACTICE

ANDREW J. BLAZA

A number of larger companies have employed a systematic approach to the management of their environmental performance for many years. In doing so they have recognized the benefits which this brings to the business even without the wider interest in environmental issues shown by the general public in recent years.

Other companies in potentially high profile sectors, responding to the concerns of customers, shareholders and employees as well as the general public, have more recently come to address the problems which could be created for their business in a positive rather than a defensive way. Such companies have recognized that by setting and achieving performance objectives way beyond those required by current or pending legislation, they will create for themselves competitive advantage and a more stable basis for long-term business planning.

Examples of the management and reporting systems of a number of successful companies are presented in the following pages. Their inclusion in no way signifies that they are alone in exhibiting a sound approach to environmental issues. They do, however, provide examples of good management systems in practice.

BP

BP was one of the pioneers in establishing environmental management as a clearly defined commercial discipline and has stated that: 'environmental management is a core part of company policy'. Group Chairman Robert Horton stated in the 1989 Annual report:

> Environmental issues are a challenge to which industry must respond – BP accepts this challenge. I am determined that BP should do all in its power to look after the world in which we all live, while helping to provide the world with the resources upon which we all depend. Our shareholders, customers and our staff expect no less.

Formulating a group policy for the environment can be a tough challenge when your operations span the continents and embrace products as different as aviation fuel and animal feeds. Within BP, environmental protection is an integral part of any project. The 1980 policy statement stated:

> It is a primary and continuing policy of the BP group that in the conduct of its activities it will endeavour to protect the health and safety of its employees, customers and others who may be affected by those activities and endeavour to limit adverse effects in the physical environment in which these activities are carried out.

Specific objectives have been developed covering guidelines, standards and auditing programmes. BP has developed a systematic approach to ensure a coordinated response to both existing and emerging environment matters related to its operations. This is termed Environment Protection Management (EPM), and responsibility for implementing EPM policy is devolved to individual operating companies.

EPM consists of three main elements:

1. environment impact assessments (EIA)
2. environment monitoring (EM)
3. environmental reviews (ER).

An Environmental Services Team promotes EPM throughout the group and thereby monitors and coordinates BP's overall environmental performance. The process is extended to all acquisitions, investments, abandonments, continuing operations and new projects and products.

SOUTH WEST WATER

South West Water produced its environmental policy statement in September 1990, at the time of the first Annual General Meeting of the newly privatized company.

The company's mission statement stems from its strong self-interest in protecting water and a clear commitment to sound environmental management. It sets three key goals:

1. enhancing the environment
2. satisfying customers
3. adding value for shareholders, employees and the community.

The policy statement identifies eleven areas of responsibility:

1. The uninterrupted provision to customers of potable water which meets the Water Supply (Water Quality) Regulations 1989.
2. The management of inland sewage treatment works and the sewerage network so that discharges comply with current consents and licences, consistent with the attainment of River Quality Objectives.
3. The construction and use of sea outfalls to enable South West Water to fulfil its requirements and so assist compliance with EC bathing water standards, other relevant EC directives and environmental quality objectives.
4. The disposal or destruction of sewage sludge in a manner consistent with the attainment of EC standards and in compliance with the Sludge (Use in Agriculture) Regulations 1989.
5. The removal and disposal or destruction of screenings from sewage in a manner consistent with the relevant EC directives.
6. The management of water abstraction in a manner consistent with the attainment of environmental objectives and River Quality Objectives.
7. The design and landscaping of facilities to minimize their intrusive visual impact.
8. The sound management and, where appropriate, the sensitive exploitation of landholdings in possession of South West Water consistent with the requirements of the DoE/MAFF Code of Practice on Conservation, Access and Recreation.
9. The promotion of the study of, and the preservation of artefacts from, sites of archaeological interest in possession of South West Water consistent with the requirements of the DoE/MAFF Code of Practice on Conservation, Access and Recreation.
10. The careful organization of works in the highway or areas of public access to demonstrate care of the environment.
11. Conservation of energy and resources.

VOLVO

Volvo corporate literature contains the following statement:

> OUR PRODUCTS CREATE POLLUTION, NOISE AND WASTE. This is a time for action – not excuses. Where satisfactory alternatives exist, we must not tolerate products which will damage the environment.
>
> We shall apply a total view regarding the adverse impact of our products on the environment.

We shall opt for manufacturing processes that have the least possible impact on the environment.

Although the environmental impact of motoring and transport compared with other sources of pollution is now the subject of intense debate, it is enough for us at Volvo to be aware that our products and production methods alike may be injurious to the environment.

This is the basis on which we are working to solve the problems involved.

Volvo's environmental policy is more than just an action programme for dealing with the problems in the short and long term. It also spells out how monitoring procedures will be improved to ensure that all possible corrective measures are actually implemented – and that the overall results are fully effective. In the 1989 environmental policy statement, Peter Gallagher, Chairman, wrote

The basis of the policy statement is:

- to develop and market products with superior environmental properties and which meet the highest possible efficiency requirements;
- to opt for manufacturing processes that have the least possible impact on the environment;
- to actively participate in and conduct in-house research and development in the environmental field;
- to select environmentally compatible and recyclable material in connection with the development and manufacture of products, and when components are purchased from suppliers;
- to apply a total view regarding the adverse impact of company products on the environment;
- to strive to attain a uniform, worldwide environmental standard for processes and products.

In 1988 a corporate Environmental Task Force of six senior directors was established under the direction of the CEO. This Task Force was complemented by a working group of ten senior managers representing the operating companies.

At the beginning of 1989, three- and five-year action programmes were developed for each company and individual 'Environmental boards' formed. The group's three-year programme included the implementation of its environmental policy and the introduction of an environmental audit.

Prior to making any decision concerning major process or production changes which result in pollutant emissions or other environmentally adverse effects, measures are taken to enable such decisions to be based on the utilization of the best technology from an environmental viewpoint.

From 1990 environmental measures became an integral part of the Company's planning process and an item on the agenda of group planning meetings.

Every year each company is required to report to the Group's Management Committee all developments on environmental matters.

SHANKS & McEWAN

Shanks & McEwan is the leading waste management company in the UK, collecting, transferring and disposing of waste, directly or from other contractors and local authorities at its landfill sites and transfer stations.

The company ensures optimum environmental performance by a management system based on a four-part strategy:

1. the principles and objectives of a corporate environmental policy (CEP)
2. quality assurance, based on BS 5750
3. an 'independent' Environmental Advisory Board
4. regular audits and assessments.

Corporate environment policy

The elements of the group's CEP are:

- To carry out the business of waste collection, transfer and disposal in a manner which has no adverse effects upon the environment or public health.
- To improve the landscape by healing the scars left by former mineral workings and industrial dereliction using waste materials creatively to restore the land.
- To ensure that all elements of the environment affected by the Company's activities undergo the minimum amount of interference and in any event do not suffer any material or lasting damage.
- To protect and enhance the environment of people in the vicinity of the Company's activities.
- To conserve resources by maximizing the recovery of energy and materials from waste when economically viable.
- To ensure that all Company facilities are constructed to the highest appropriate standards, that they function efficiently and are visually attractive.
- To operate to standards higher than those required by law, regulations and professional codes of practice, and thus to go beyond minimum legal requirements.

Although the director of Planning and Environment Policy has overall responsibility for protecting the environment, there is no separate environmental department. The environmental management structure is therefore totally integrated throughout the organization with every employee having a duty to ensure environmental performance according to company objectives.

Quality assurance

All areas of the waste management business are covered by procedures based on BS 5750 and set out in manuals for use by staff at all levels. Shanks & McEwan were the first waste management company to be accredited under BS 5750.

All employees and subcontractors are required to follow these procedures and the company conducts frequent reviews to ensure that the procedures are being followed. The reviews are also used to update and improve procedures as well as to demonstrate to all interested parties the Company's real commitment to long-term environmental protection.

Environmental Advisory Board

With the main board directors (including the Director, Planning and Environment Policy) and five external members, the advisory board operates independently from other group operations. The advisory board has the freedom to comment on any matter of environmental significance and minutes of its meetings are circulated internally by the Group Board.

Environmental audits and assessments

Shanks & McEwan recognizes that its service of collection, disposal and recycling of wastes cannot be accomplished without any environmental impact. However, it is company policy to minimize adverse impacts as far as reasonably possible.

Even before applying for planning permission and site licence for a new facility, a full environmental assessment is made of the site which provides details of the working plan and the predicted future environmental impacts.

Regular monitoring of all ground and surface water is conducted within and around landfill sites and discharges are checked to ensure conformity to standards set by the appropriate authority.

Landfill sites are also monitored and controlled for landfill gas with venting or positive extraction of gas as appropriate. Gas monitoring is also undertaken outside the site to ensure that no leakage occurs. This monitoring and control takes place throughout the operating life of the site and for up to 25 years thereafter.

As part of the CEP the accuracy of in-house monitoring of water and landfill gas is subjected to independent environmental audits. An audit report is produced annually for each site and the results made available to community liaison groups and the statutory authorities.

NORSK HYDRO

Although based in Norway, Norsk Hydro's largest market is the UK with sales based on UK manufacturing operations as well as imports from Hydro locations overseas. The company is one of the largest UK manufacturers of fertilizers and PVC polymers. It has a strong position in the UK aluminium market, a new business in the production of large-scale magnesium pressure die castings and it is one of the UK's top salmon farmers.

The common feature of all Hydro's activities is 'putting energy to work' – converting natural energy resources efficiently into products which benefit industry and consumers in a wide range of markets. It is Hydro policy 'to maintain a high level of responsibility to their local UK environment, communities and to their employees'.

In the UK, Hydro's manufacturing operations came into the group during the 1980s largely as a result of acquisitions of already existing companies with their own particular management practices.

Having conducted a thorough corporate review during 1989 of the environmental impact in Norway and overseas of Hydro's individual operations and main products, the UK organization decided to produce an integrated environmental review of the entire organization.

Each of the manufacturing companies was reviewed, first in terms of performance against the appropriate regulations. Both employee health and safety matters and the effects on the external environment were covered. The group's main products were subjected to an 'eco-balance' review – the raw material and energy inputs required to manufacture them, their environmental impact in use, comparisons with alternative products and finally any potential problems after use, including waste disposal and potential for recycling.

The complete report once finished was subjected to review by an authoritative independent consultancy whose remit was to confirm compliance with the environmental, health and safety regulations, to validate individual reports and data, to investigate environmental practices on site and to make recommendations for change as appropriate.

This approach to environmental reviewing is a very typical example of the approach which the CBI has consistently recommended, namely a far-reaching and voluntary review of all operations and products from an internal point of view, backed up or 'validated' where appropriate by an independent body and then published as an authoritative document for internal, as well as external, consumption.

ICI

ICI is one of the world's premier chemical companies, manufacturing in 40 countries and selling 15 000 products to more than 150 countries. Its group environmental policy states that:

> It is ICI policy to manage its activities so as to give benefit to society; this entails ensuring they are acceptable to the community and that any adverse effects on the environment are reduced to a practicable minimum.

The key elements of the policy are:

- To promote the interchange of environmental information and technology among ICI and its subsidiary and related companies.
- To provide information to enable ICI's processes, when used under the licence, to be operated without unacceptable effects on the environment.
- To provide information and assistance to enable the Company's products to be properly used, stored and disposed of in order to avoid unacceptable effects on the environment.
- To encourage its subsidiary and related companies to establish and implement for themselves environmental policies which are in accord with the principles listed.

While increasing the amount invested in environmental protection in the early 1990s by ten times compared to the early 1980s, ICI has introduced a significant change in the way environmental programmes are introduced throughout the group. Because of the semi-autonomous nature of ICI's business, the Group's overall environmental objectives are *implemented* at local level.

But to coordinate the policy throughout the Group, ICI appointed in 1988 Chris Hampson as the main board director responsible for safety and health and the environment. Each operating company has its own EHS director responsible for environmental standards who reports directly to Chris Hampson.

As an example of how the corporate policy is implemented in an operating company, consider ICI Chemicals and Polymers (C&P) formed in 1987 from four divisions of ICI – Agriculture, Mond, Plastics and Petrochemicals.

Action Plan: Improving Environmental Performance

- To establish an environment policy.
- To measure the company's performance with regular reports to the board.
- To define and implement plans for environmental performance.
- To establish comprehensive environmental standards.
- To provide guidance for their achievement.
- To 'audit' environmental performance against these standards.

Measuring environmental performance

Concentrates on monitoring of air and water quality at each manufacturing site. Data collected is collated and submitted to the C&P board each month.

(It is interesting to note that since constant monitoring devices have been installed, there have been fewer variances from standards set.)

Process of data collection:

- Manager appointed to oversee process at each site.
- The number of tests in water and air discharges are reported and their compliance with regulatory consents or *internal targets* recorded.
- Reports on justifiable complaints received from the community and any incidents reported to the regulatory authorities.

Implementing improvement plans

Annual plans are formulated which differ from site to site but with the following common features:

- A target of 100% compliance with all regulatory standards for air and water discharges, waste disposal and noise control.
- support for agreed local environmental quality objectives and standards.
- A community relations programme including a complaints procedure, schemes for improving site appearance and a local information service.
- An ecology management plan.

HEWLETT PACKARD

Company profile:

Fortune magazine rated Hewlett Packard as the 33rd largest company and the 'most admired'. The company is noted for its technological breakthroughs and innovation based on an entrepreneurial culture which is seen in its management approaches.

The company's published environmental policy is:

To be a social and environmental asset to each nation and each community in which the company operates.

Management structures:

The company's approach to environmental management is based on the concept of achieving strategic changes by setting 'breakthrough' goals

The concept involves four basic phrases:

PLAN – DO – CHECK – ACT

In the planning phase, 'breakthrough issues' are identified based on corporate objectives requiring fundamental changes to the way in which the organization operates or produces its products. Breakthrough actions may be driven by:

- changing technologies
- legislation
- concern for the environment
- market needs.

A notable example in recent years is the elimination of CFC's under the Montreal Protocol. Internal research had shown that a change of SMT cleaner and volume increases in printed circuit board production would lead to a greater use of CFCs unless action was taken in advance.

The plan involves setting clear objectives to bring about the required change in a specific timescale, identifying the key players and agreeing performance measures. The plan is then implemented through a series of actions which are coordinated throughout the sectors of the organization which are involved. Periodic checks on progress are made and actions taken on deviations. The final stage is to evaluate the 'goal' to determine if the desired result has been achieved. Again any fine-tuning is done to ensure complete success.

The system is one of total quality management on a continuous basis and totally integrated throughout the organization. Success is achieved in two ways:

1. Executive committee ownership of the 'Hoshin plan' ('top down' planning).
2. Goal cooperation across the organization ('bottom up' reviewing).

Hewlett Packard consider that this system has a major impact on the organization for the following reasons:

- Potential for fundamental breakthrough not just steady-state situations.
- There is full support for and alignment with the *goal*, not just positive agreement.
- Performance measures are defined and variations from the plans are identified at an early stage to enable action to be taken and the process kept 'on track'.

3M

3M is one of the world's most diversified manufacturing companies, specializing in over 100 technologies that have led to the development of some 60 000 products sold in over 100 countries. 3M has been singled out by many commentators, including Chris Hampson of ICI, as an example of a company with an environment policy that is 'promulgated with the firm backing of senior management', and by John Elkington as 'the most impressive environmental success story'.

The elements of the group environmental policy are to recognize and exercise its responsibility to:

- solve its own environmental pollution and conservation problems;
- prevent pollution at the source wherever and whenever possible;
- develop products that will have a minimum effect on the environment;
- conserve natural resources through the use of reclamation and other appropriate methods;
- ensure that its facilities and products meet and sustain the regulations of all federal, state and local environmental agencies;
- assist, wherever possible, governmental agencies and other official organizations engaged in environmental activities.

When the concept of a "Conserver Society" based on 'non-waste technology and production' was first developed at a UN Seminar in 1986, 3M was one of the first to embrace the idea, particularly in the area of waste management.

The waste management strategy is based on a hierarchy of options:

1. elimination or minimalization of waste at source;
2. recycling or re-use of waste materials;
3. treatment of waste by pollution control devices and other methods;
4. landfilling residue.

The first option of waste minimization is the preferred option and forms the basis of the 3M 3PS programme – *Pollution Prevention Pays*. The whole organization is encouraged to minimize 'waste' through *Recovery, Re-use and Recycling*.

Management structures

To ensure the success of the system, responsibility for the environment is given to an operating unit independent from engineering and manufacturing with its head a vice-president reporting to one of the five executive vice-presidents. Thus the environment department has equal status to other operating units. The net effect is that environmental concerns are considered at every step in the development and manufacture of 3M products.

Key objectives of the environmental department are to:

- ensure compliance with legislation;
- minimize potential liabilities;
- maintain and enhance 3M's environmental reputation;
- stay abreast of and develop leading-edge technologies;
- lobby for fair legislation;
- develop new business opportunities.

PROCTER & GAMBLE

Edwin Artzt, Chairman and Chief Executive states:

> The Procter & Gamble Company has a deep sense of commitment to help protect, preserve and enhance the quality of the environment in which we all live. Much lies ahead to be done. Our intent is to be proactive in carrying out our environmental policy.

Environmental policy

The key elements of the corporate environmental policy are:

- To ensure products, packaging and operations are safe for employees, consumers and the environment.
- To reduce or prevent the environmental impact of products and packaging in their design, manufacture, distribution, use and disposal wherever possible.
- To meet or exceed the requirements of all environmental laws and regulations.
- To assess continually environmental technology and programmes and monitor progress towards environmental goals.
- To provide consumers, customers, employees, communities, public interest groups and others with relevant and appropriate factual information about the environmental quality of Procter & Gamble products, packaging and operations.
- To ensure every employee understands and is responsible and accountable for incorporating environmental quality considerations in daily business activities.
- To have operating policies, programmes and resources in place to implement the environment quality policy.

Environmental strategy

Five key elements may be identified:

1. actions will be based on good science;
2. efforts focused on *real* environmental improvements and not false 'greenness';
3. actively oppose misinformation;
4. lifetime environmental impact assessments for all products and services;
5. work together with all partners in society.

Every brand or operation manager in the business is required to review thoroughly the way it impacts on the environment. Areas for improvement are identified and these improvement projects are incorporated into the development plans for the brand or business operations. Objectives are agreed with management and each individual business unit is responsible for executing the projects successfully.

Implementing the strategy

An example of implementing the strategy in a specific area is provided by *Product Supply Organizations*, incorporating buying, manufacturing and distribution. The whole organization is subjected to a continuous 'cradle to grave' environmental review:

Intent: To think of pollution control as avoidance of wastes rather than avoidance of legal prosecution. Designing in good environmental performance rather than end-of-pipe afterthought.

Objective: To aim for zero pollution from the product supply system. As with total quality management, to set ultimate goals which people, by continuous improvement, seek to adhere to.

Strategy: Each plant has an active programme of waste minimization supported by appropriate changes in product and process design. A holistic view including R&D, the *product* formulation, its packaging and the raw materials used in production.

The audit process

Every manufacturing unit is subject to frequent internal and external audits. These involve detailed examinations of both the management structures and the environmental risks. Areas covered include:

Environmental management structures:

- Understanding of environmental regulatory requirements
- Environmental regulatory performance
- Understanding of P&G environmental policies
- P&G environmental policy performance
- Organization and management of environmental systems and equipment
- Plant environmental control capability

- Identification/management of environmental issues
- setting/meeting annual environmental goals.

Environmental risks:

- Direct waste-water discharges to rivers/streams
- Waste-water discharge to publicly-owned treatment works
- Potential sources of groundwater impact
- Process air emissions
- Hazardous waste generation/storage/disposal
- Solid waste generation/storage/disposal
- Toxic chemical sources.

Each of these broad areas is broken down into elements which are checked, analysed and reported on. Further ways to reduce risk of pollution must be identified and improvement plans drawn up and implemented on a continuous basis.

Take as an example the lifetime environmental impact assessment of 'Pampers'. This was a cradle-to-grave assessment of products and processes from raw-materials and production to disposal of the end of product for the 'Pampers' disposable nappy product. In studying the environmental impact of 'Pampers' versus traditional towelling nappies, it was shown that there was nothing to choose between the two types in terms of overall environmental impact, when all factors were taken to account (including the need to sterilize and wash towelling nappies).

Chapter Ten

THE SOCIAL AUDIT MOVEMENT

MIKE GEDDES

INTRODUCTION

The key premise of this book is that environmental and ecological issues will constitute the fundamental challenge for business, and accountants particularly, in the 1990s. Indeed some influential commentators are prepared to hazard that the environmental challenge may come to preoccupy business over the next fifty years in the same way that, since 1945, a key challenge to business has been the issue of social welfare, with the reconstruction, after the inter-war crisis, of a successful private sector within a mixed economy, social-democratic politics, and a welfare state (Cairncross, 1990).

Such a comparison between the social and environmental ramifications of business activity is apposite not just in general terms but in relation to accounting specifically. As the postwar boom came to an end in the 1970s, and the social-democratic consensus came increasingly into question, the increasing prominence of accounting and the new emphasis on financial efficiency and value for money has been met by an alternative theory and practice of auditing – social audit.

The recent explosion of interest in environmental audit and 'green accounting' has thus been paralleled, and indeed preceded somewhat in time, by a growth of interest in social audit and social accounting. This chapter assesses the social audit movement in the UK in the 1980s and draws out some implications for green reporting.

WHAT IS SOCIAL AUDIT?

During the last decade the concept and practice of social audit has become quite widespread in Britain, in contexts ranging from campaigns against industrial closures to community action and the local provision of state services. There appears today to be widespread interest in the potential of social audit, but at the same time considerable confusion as to what a social audit actually is or should be, and some doubts as to both the technical problems involved and the ultimate value of the social audit approach in policy and political terms. This chapter will consider the reasons for the recent upsurge in social accounting and review the main contexts in which social audits and accounts have been produced. Some methodological issues and problems will then be explored, concluding with an evaluation of the future potential of the technique.

First, though, what is social audit? While a precise definition is difficult, social audit is best understood as a reaction against conventional accounting principles and practices. These centre on the financial viability and profitability of the individual economic enterprise, paradigmatically the capitalist firm. By contrast, social audit proposes a broader financial and economic perspective, reaching beyond the individual enterprise for example, to the local economy of which it is a part, or to different types of organization such as state agencies. Relatedly, social audit posits other goals as well as or instead of financial profitability, especially for the state sector. Moreover, social audit attempts to embrace not only economic and monetary variables but also – as its name suggests – social ones, including some which may not be amenable to quantification in monetary terms. (For further discussion of the nature and scope of social audit see Harte, 1986; Harte and Owen, 1987.)

What are some of the broader perspectives with which social audit attempts to grapple? According to Turok (1990) they include:

- The displacement and multiplier effects of individual economic decisions – the positive and negative effects of, particularly, economic investments and disinvestments.
- Social and distributional concerns, especially those of groups and interests with limited economic and political power.
- Issues of quality (as opposed to quantity) which may be obscured or undervalued by a preoccupation with financial indicators of performance.
- The longer-term consequences of investments and policy decisions.
- The impact of actions in the formal sectors of the economy (private and state) on the domestic sphere, outside formal paid work, which is usually excluded from conventional economic assessments.

Some of these perspectives challenge social audit to move into territory which techniques such as cost-benefit analysis and environmental impact assessment have ignored. Importantly, many of these concerns are raised more directly for the public sector than the private sector.

The problems raised in attempting to grapple with these broader objectives are threefold:

- Sophisticated indicators are required to 'capture' such broader economic and social concerns. The problem is, as Turok notes, that such indicators have to be robust enough to stand comparison with the simple, quantitative and apparently harder financial efficiency measures.
- A real understanding of such broader issues requires a deeper understanding of economic and social structures, processes and causal mechanisms. Effective social audit will require conceptual as well as empirical rigour.
- Social audit implies a concern with broader notions of social and economic efficiency and effectiveness, rather than narrower criteria of economy and value for money. This in turn suggests a concern with accountability rather than accounting in the narrow sense: if the perspective of social audit is a broad and plural one, this defines a social audit process as a socially and politically open, responsive and democratic one, not (just) a narrow application of technical, professional expertise.

The concept of social audit is therefore a very far-reaching and challenging one, and the problems which its ambitions bring are in one sense very daunting. Certainly the scope of the social audit agenda has meant that the term 'social audit' is used to describe a wide and indeed disparate grouping of activities. Moreover, it will come as no surprise to find that the social audit movement can give no clear and simple answers to the more difficult questions it raises. But then the claim of conventional accountancy to provide conceptual rigour and empirical exactitude is not itself sustainable (Hird, 1983).

THE ORIGINS OF THE SOCIAL AUDIT MOVEMENT

The upsurge of interest in social audit in Britain in the 1980s is particularly remarkable because the well established movements for corporate social responsibility by big private sector firms in the USA (Belkaoui, 1984) and on the continent (Grojer and Stark, 1977; Schreuder, 1979) have had relatively little impact in Britain (Gray, Owen and Maunders, 1987). A notable exception was the work of Social Audit Ltd, closely associated with the Consumers Association (Social Audit Limited, 1976; Medawar, 1978). Social Audit Ltd conducted a number of critical and detailed assessments of the implications of the corporate strategies of big firms across a wide spectrum, including workers' health and safety, training, access to information, the quality and reliability of products, and environmental pollution. However, these studies and other early forerunners of the contemporary interest in social accounting (such as the work of Barratt Brown, 1971), remained isolated phenomena until recently.

So what has changed? Essentially, the current interest in social audit must be linked to the effects of economic crisis in Britain and its manifestation in British politics from the mid-1970s and through the 1980s.

There is a clear relation between the emphasis of dominant political ideology during the 1980s on private enterprise, the market and the cash nexus (an emphasis not confined, of course, to the Conservative party) and social audit. Social audit asserts values in opposition to this tendency – values of economic and social planning, popular involvement in economic decisions, and social need as a primary criterion for resource allocation. Social audit attempts to challenge the hegemony of money over both the productive economy and society, and of accountants – the technicians of money – over economic, social and political decisions.

ANTI-CLOSURE SOCIAL AUDITS

One important way in which the contradiction between private profit and social need affected many localities in the first half of the 1980s was the decimation of manufacturing industry, with the closure of many major industrial plants and the 'rationalization' of state industries. Social audits were grasped at by many local authorities and trade unions attempting to challenge closure decisions by private capital. For example, on Merseyside, one of the areas hardest hit by deindustrialization in the early 1980s, the local county council produced a succession of audit reports exposing the consequences of a wave of industrial closures on the local economy. Employment multipliers were used to estimate the redundancies in the local economy caused by closures, and the direct and indirect costs to central and local government were assessed (Merseyside County Council, 1983a, 1983b, 1983c, 1984; see also Edinburgh District Council/Lothian Regional Council, 1985; CAITS, 1984a). There has been at least as much use of social accounting in opposing state sector closures and rundowns, especially in the nationalized industries in the early 1980s. In industries like coal and steel, the effect of changed government policies was catastrophic for jobs and local communities across the country but particularly in Northern England, Wales and Scotland. The progressive abandonment of commitments to a domestic supply of these basic commodities, the imposition of harsh financial regimes, and the abandonment of corporatist political accommodation with the trade unions produced widespread closures of mills and pits, and a virtual social audit industry attempting to provide support for trade union or other opposition to closure by demonstrating the costs of industrial change (Rowthorn and Ward, 1979; Sedgefield District Council and Durham County

Council, 1983; Hudson, Peck and Sadler, 1984; Levie *et al*, 1984; Glyn, 1985; Barnsley MBC, 1985; Cooper, Bird and Sharp, 1985; Brignall and Fitzgerald, 1989). By comparison, there appear to be only a few examples of social audits related to cutbacks in the state service sector (Lewis, 1986).

The economic upturn of the mid-1980s produced a fall-off in plant closures and rationalizations, and a consequent lessening of social audit activity of this type. This trend was linked to the failure of the NUM to reverse the NCB's (now British Coal's) programme of pit closures, and the consequent rethink of Labour movement strategy which this entailed, and in particular the conditions in which social audit could best play a part in successful action against the closure and rundown of plants, the loss of jobs and the destruction of working-class communities.

In this context it is encouraging that there have been several more recent anti-closure movements in which some new directions for the role of social audit are being mapped out. In 1988, plans for the closure of the British Aerospace works at Hatfield became known. In response to the likely damage to the local economy which such a closure would cause, the local authority, Welwyn Hatfield District Council, commissioned an audit of the impact which closure would have and an evaluation of British Aerospace's corporate plans and strategic options. This enabled the local authority to hold a public consultation to help decide on the most appropriate response (Benington, 1989).

Also, in 1988, British Aerospace announced the closure of their Bishopton (formerly Royal Ordnance) factory, engaged in armaments production. The consequent opposition to this closure proposal was important for a number of reasons. It was based on strong links between the unions and the Labour-led local government authorities, but the strategy which was developed was one which sought and secured the support of a more wide-ranging spectrum of political opinion, locally and nationally. This was done, first, by playing the 'national defence' card, in a campaign with strong nationalistic elements. Secondly, the goals selected were limited: to maintain the factory albeit with a much reduced workforce. This allowed a real scope for putting pressure on, and bargaining with, the company. A social and economic audit was produced as one of several back-up reports to this campaign.

The campaign was indeed successful in achieving limited objectives (Ramsay, 1990). The wider questions raised are those concerning the compromises which had to be made. Effectively, in order to achieve a limited success, the campaign retreated very significantly from the defence of jobs and communities which have been a feature of other campaigns in which anti-closure social audits have played a part. Moreover, it did so by emphasizing values (of defence and of the armaments industry) which cut against the grain with which social audit is more usually associated. The Bishopton campaign did not argue for arms conversion and alternative plans for production of socially useful goods.

These issues have been raised again by the proposed rundown and closure (again by British Aerospace as the parent company) at Rover's Cowley works outside Oxford. Moreover, such arguments between radical and compromise strategies have been argued out in the context of a public enquiry organized by the local authority.

At Cowley, the agreed basis for a united campaign of opposition has been much more difficult to find than Bishopton, and no unified platform has in fact emerged. The Labour local authority, while not welcoming the rundown/closure, has tended in practice to accept its inevitability and search for alternative ways of protecting or regenerating local jobs and the local economy (Oxford City Council, 1990). Active root and branch opposition to the closure has largely been confined to certain elements in the local trade unions, who have found local academic allies and supporters (Oxford Motor Industry Research Project, 1990). Criticism has consequently been addressed as much against the alleged 'sellout' by the local authority as against Rover/BAe. This failure to find common ground is all the more disappointing in that it might be suggested that in some ways the Cowley situation provides at least as good a basis for broadly-based opposition as did Bishopton. In particular, positive arguments about the maintenance of motor vehicle production in the UK could be linked to criticism of BAe's asset-stripping approach to Rover and the company's apparent preference for financial gain through the property-led redevelopment of the Cowley site over reinvestment in its productive use. Such arguments could also perhaps be linked to the embarrassing public disclosures of the government 'sweeteners' paid to BAe for its acquisition of Rover. The more difficult issue is that of employment. The argument crystallizes around the questions of whether the defence of the existing jobs at Cowley was a viable demand (was Cowley a technologically backward and redundant plant?) and the extent to which such a defence was in fact a popular demand in the local community and even among the workforce. Without attempting to judge the correct response to this question, the associated issue is that of demands for alternative forms of employment as opposed to the defence of existing jobs. Such alternatives may be of at least three kinds: new jobs arising from a restructuring of existing products (i.e. at Cowley, new jobs in a modernized car plant, raising questions about how many such jobs there might be and what changes in employment practices might be associated with them); new jobs in different industries involving a re-use of the site (this raises key issues such as whether the new jobs will quickly re-employ those made redundant, and in turn, whether this is a priority demand); and new jobs arising from alternative forms of ownership and control of production (such as envisaged in the famous Lucas plan).

These are key issues for the politics of anti-closure social audit. Moreover they are issues of some urgency. It is fairly clear that a new phase of industrial restructuring, involving a new round of rundowns and closures, will be one result of the closer integration of the Western European economy focused by the single European market of '1992', not to mention further restructuring associated with the opening up of Central and Eastern Europe (Davenport, Benington and Geddes, 1990).

SOCIAL AUDIT AND STATE SERVICES

Alongside the anti-closure social audits, the upsurge in social accounting has been linked to the defence of the state sector against the cuts of the last fifteen years, instituted by both Labour and Conservative governments. Social audit in this context constitutes a reaction against the growing tendency to apply private sector accounting principles to state activities, most notably the 'value for money' approach to state expenditure of the Audit Commission (Audit Commission, 1989) which, by its emphasis on economy rather than effectiveness, on short-term cost savings rather than meeting needs, 'provides a "theory" to justify cuts and privatisation' (Kline and Mallaber, 1986). The 'creative' accounting practices of local authorities, designed to frustrate central government cuts, have eventually served to entrap them, having to be paid for by more packages of cuts. Furthermore, the dominance of financial orthodoxy and the depoliticizing of questions of social need into matters of efficiency has severely limited the ability of left-wing authorities to make alliances with trade unions and community groups (Clarke and Cochrane, 1989).

The need to defend the 'public' sector has involved a greater realization of the way in which traditional approaches to the provision of state services are difficult to defend, and therefore of the need for alternative criteria for assessing state activity. In particular, social audit has been associated with the defence of the local state against centralizing pressures, and especially with the new urban left's version of municipal socialism, which was a major focus of opposition to the Thatcher government's agenda in the early 1980s. The decision by various left local government administrations to expand their economic development functions and to invest in the local economy with objectives radically different from conventional ones generated a need for accounting procedures which are relevant to such objectives (Barratt Brown, 1984).

While the anti-closure social audits are, by their nature, generally concerned with specific economic establishments and reactive in nature, these 'local state' audits tend to refer to more complex socio-economic situations, such as the overall impact of government policies on a locality (Newcastle City Council, 1985; Lichfield, 1987) or the overall economic impact of a local authority on its locality (Labour Research Department *et al.*, 1985). Such audits are increasingly being employed to make a positive case for the state sector not just where it is under threat but more generally in the construction of a better model of state sector operation.

COMMUNITY AUDITS

Another arena in which social audit has become important is community action. Like the local state social audits, many community-based audits are centrally concerned with the provision of local public services, and, again like the local state audits, have often emerged partly from opposition to central government cuts in the resourcing of local public services. The difference is, however, that community social audits often have a critical, or at any rate ambivalent, attitude to the local state as a service provider. One example is the work of the pressure group Birmingham for People, which has conducted a number of critical audit-type studies of local authority services and policies in that city as part of campaigns to change local government priorities. The Leeds Urban Audit is a community-based initiative designed to make information about local state decisions and processes accessible, to enable local people to exercise greater influence and control over local state policies, and to bring the concept of need back into determination of policy priorities and resource allocation (Leeds Urban Audit, 1990). At Kings Cross in inner North London, where private developers are proposing a massive redevelopment which would have enormous impact on local communities, social audit concepts are again being applied to try to strengthen the hand of local community groups and the local state in their dealings with the developers (Geddes, 1991). There have also been a number of parish audits undertaken by inner city churches in the wake of 'Faith in the City'. These have been seen as the first step in church-based action to assess the role of inner city churches and the service they provide to local people.

Closely linked to community audits is the use of social audit techniques in the cooperative and voluntary sector. Here, the objective has been to find forms of accounting for use within such organizations which are more appropriate to their goals and objectives than traditional profit-based accounting. Pioneering attempts have been made to develop and operationalize concepts such as 'returns to labour' or 'social return' (Jefferis and Robinson, 1987).

ENVIRONMENTAL AUDITS

Finally, an important emerging area of social audit practice of particular relevance to this book is that of environmental issues and associated ones of health. The proliferation of environmental auditing by private companies is a key theme of other contributors to this book and will not therefore be dealt with here. But it is not only private – or public – companies which have been advancing environmental audit practice. There is now widespread recognition in local government that the ever-growing prominence of environmental concerns poses both new challenges and new opportunities for local government. Environmental and ecological processes may be global in scale, and national and international action will be crucial to their solution. But for many people environmental issues are most apparent in the immediate environment of their locality. This challenges local government both to put its own house in order, and to play a leading role in environmental action at the local level (FoE, 1989). Putting its own house in order means that local authorities must comprehensively reconsider their practices and policies for environmental effects and to install environmental awareness and priorities throughout the organization (Brooke, 1990). Playing a leading environmental role in the locality offers local government a new opportunity to develop a role, not just as a regulator and enforcer of punitive standards, but as a leading advocate of good environmental practice which other actors in the local economy can emulate. Numerous local authorities have now produced environmental audits and strategies, both individually (e.g. Kirkless MC, 1989; City of Cardiff, 1990) and acting collectively (SEEDS, 1990). In Kirklees an environmental review undertaken in partnership with Friends of the Earth resulted first in a 'State of the Environment' report and then a local Charter for the Environment. This commits the local authority to a series of actions on waste disposal, noise, air and water quality, and in relation to landscape, open space, wildlife and woodland. New working structures and practices have been set up to implement and monitor these commitments. The Green Plan for the South East, produced by a group of local authorities in the South East Economic Development Strategy association, brings together local initiatives within a regional network providing a broader perspective for cooperative action at the local level.

As in the private corporate sector, local government environmental auditing will be a growth sector in the next few years. Three problems in particular need to be foreseen. There will be a danger of local authorities diving headlong into environmental auditing, without adequate consideration of the problems of achieving effective action. A major such problem (particularly in areas where economic growth is slow) will be how to deal with conflicts between environmental protection and economic growth. It will be difficult in many situations to sustain environmental standards when jobs are at stake. One positive approach to this issue will be for local authorities to work with all sectors of the local economy to ensure that it gains the benefits – in terms of new products, more efficient processes and so on – which stricter environmental regulation of the economy is going to bring. The successful local economies will be those whose actors can compete effectively in a more environmentally-conscious market. Finally, will the environmental commitment of the local authority itself be more than skin-deep? If it is to be so, two initial things will be necessary. Local authorities will need to tackle environmental issues at a central, corporate level, not merely departmentally or in a piecemeal fashion. And they will need to act openly and effectively with a range of community interests, not in isolation.

Alongside the concern with environmental issues in local government is an increasing concern with health questions. In the wake of public concern over health issues, from the effects of smoking to those of pesticides in food, some local authorities are now showing awareness of, for example, the inter-related issues of local health and the local economy. Pioneering work has been carried out in the West Midlands, for example, on the role of the tobacco industry in the local economy, demonstrating that concerns about public health can be pursued without significant damage to the local economy through job loss in cigarette production or distribution (Rao *et al.*, 1990).

We noted before that the Consumers' Association was an important early proponent of social audit. Unfortunately, the growth of the CA and its magazine *Which?* was associated with an abandonment of social audit principles and a narrow concentration on questions of product cost and efficiency. The concern with social audit, though, has now been taken up by *The Ethical Consumer* magazine, an 'alternative *Which?*', monitoring products and services against a wide range of criteria. Going beyond simple green consumerism *The Ethical Consumer* looks at the following criteria when assessing companies and products:

- South Africa
- Oppressive regimes
- Trade union relations
- Wages and conditions
- Environment
- Irresponsible marketing
- Nuclear power
- Land rights
- Armaments
- Animal testing

(taken from *The Ethical Consumer* magazine, ECRA Publishing, 1989).

THE METHODOLOGY OF SOCIAL AUDITS

Conventional accounting is concerned with financial performance within formal organizations, and its techniques have developed accordingly. Because social audit is concerned with wider definitions of performance, and with issues such as the external impact of profit-driven organizations, it has had recourse to very different methodologies and techniques.

The multiplier and beyond

Many of the recent wave of social audits have been based on some kind of Keynesian multiplier or, more often, negative multiplier in the case of closures, and one set of methodological issues is concerned with its use and limitations. Most of them used some combination of employment, income and expenditure multipliers, to show categories of economic impact such as direct, indirect and induced effects. Figure 10.1 shows the 'vicious circle' of linkages within a local economy which multiplier-type analysis attempts to capture.

Essential questions which arise once the decision to use multiplier analysis has been taken are: (1) definition of the economic, geographical and temporal boundaries of the 'system', and (2) data issues. What data is available and what needs to be collected? What assumptions are to be made?

In relation to these issues, it is in the first place possible to identify a number of studies which are relatively limited and simple methodologically. Many of the anti-closure audits come into this category. These typically demonstrate the direct and indirect job loss in the locality and the financial costs to central and local government, such as loss of tax income and increased social security spending, which must be counterposed to any savings at the level of the enterprise. Such studies typically: (1) are essentially microeconomic in the sense that the scope of analysis is tightly defined around, for example, the effects of a plant closure; (2) make many assumptions about, for example, the ability of people made unemployed by closure to find new jobs and the effect of unemployment on incomes; and (3) tend to ignore implications which are unquantifiable or difficult to quantify, e.g. the impact of a closure on the health of a local population, or on 'law and order' spending.

This approach has the virtue of being quick and easy to implement – often a crucial consideration in fighting a closure – but is limited in its interpretation of the scope of social accounting. An interesting study which avoids less easily quantified issues but is macroeconomic in dimension is Glyn's (1985) work for the National Union of Mineworkers (NUM) on the economics of pit closures. Glyn's calculations played an important role in the coal industry dispute, questioning the economic case for pit closure by arguing that in current high unemployment conditions there was not one single pit whose closure would benefit government revenue.

A second group of social audits attempts to explore qualitative and less easily quantifiable issues. The most well known example is probably the Sheffield Jobs Audit (Labour Research Department *et al.*, 1985) which in evaluating the role of the local authority in the local economy is concerned not just with numbers of jobs but with wages and conditions of work. Similarly, the Newcastle Social Audit (Newcastle City Council, 1985) focuses particularly on vulnerable sections of the population – the unemployed, the low skilled, the low paid and the old. Studies such as these represent valuable attempts to develop a fuller and more 'social' version of social accounting but in the process they encounter formidable problems of data collection, analysis and interpretation, (see Clark *et al.*, 1987).

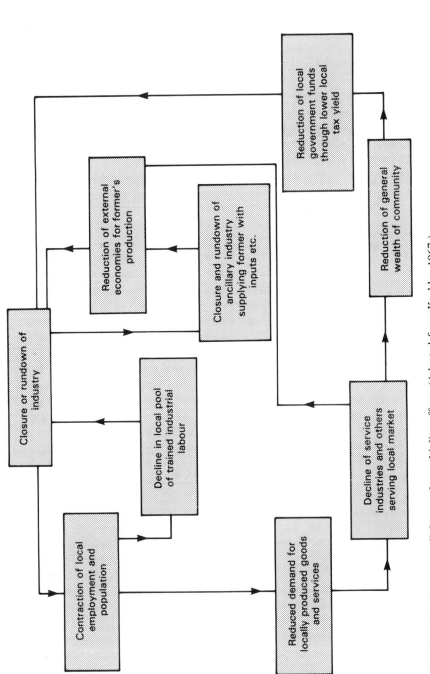

Fig. 10.1 Local economy linkages: the multiplier effect. (Adapted from Keeble, 1967.)

A number of social audits attempt to quantify issues not normally treated in a standard multiplier framework, such as illness and death associated with unemployment caused by plant closure, and the cost of this to the state (Rowthorn and Ward, 1979; St John's NUM, 1985). Others, while primarily multiplier-based, append a treatment of 'unquantifiable' issues. Examples are the use of interviews to explore the meaning of pit closure in people's lives (Hudson, Peck and Sadler, 1984) and of cases from welfare rights work to show the impact of government policies on sections of the population (Newcastle City Council, 1985).

Needs auditing

A very different methodological approach leading to a different kind of social audit starts not from the kind of economics represented by multiplier models, but from theories of economic and social need.

'Need' is usually regarded as an elusive concept in both definitional and operational terms. (I draw substantially here on Percy-Smith, 1990.) It is often assumed, particularly by conventional economists (and one suspects accountants, if they ever think about it), that needs are inevitably subjective, relative, not amenable to objective assessment, difficult to value because of the absence of prices, and therefore not a usable concept.

Percy-Smith suggests, however, that this is not necessarily the case, and that the concept of need is not inherently 'any more difficult to operationalise than "value-for-money", or "economy, efficiency and effectiveness"'. This argument can be sustained by reference to a growing body of work. An early point of reference is Bradshaw (1972) who proposes a taxonomy of need which distinguishes

- normative need (as defined by experts or professionals)
- felt need (defined subjectively by individuals)
- comparative need (defined in relation to certain standards or averages).

Bradshaw bases his categorization on who is doing the defining of needs, and this is a very important issue for social audit. By contrast Mandel (1986) proposes a perspective on need based on the notion of an economic dynamic in which the development of the systems of production is increasingly able (in principle at any rate) to satisfy a wider range of needs. He therefore proposed three 'levels' in a hierarchy of need:

- fundamental needs: those which must be satisfied for the reproduction of labour power;
- intermediate needs: more elaborate goods and services meeting needs at a more than basic level;
- luxury expenditure.

The categorization is linked to Mandel's view that, as the 'lower' levels of needs are progressively met and the number of needs which fall into these categories expands, so the number of such needs which are met through market and profit-based production and distribution diminishes and direct provision for need expands. This is based on Mandel's view that market-based allocation is essentially a response to scarcity. While this view may give less attention than it ought to questions of distribution and choice, in the context of a highly developed division of labour, it again raises key issues for social audit.

Percy-Smith draws most closely on the work of Doyal and Gough, who propose (1991) a rather different hierarchy of needs, based on the concept of well-being, or 'the ability of people to participate in life'. This suggests certain basic needs, for health and autonomy. In order for these basic needs to be met, a set of intermediate needs must be catered for, including clean water and adequate nutrition, adequate housing, non-hazardous work, appropriate health care and education, secure childhood and primary relationships, significant social roles, and economic and physical security.

One attempt to put these concepts into operation is an innovative project in Leeds which is concerned to find ways in which publicly provided services can meet people's needs more effectively. Focusing on the health and welfare needs of two contrasting communities, the research is trying to identify people's needs, how far they are being met, and what changes would have to be made in order to meet them more effectively. Utilizing Doyal and Gough's conceptual framework, it is attempting to develop operational satisfaction indices of intermediate needs, and, at the same time, the current shortfalls in meeting these.

An important point is that such satisfaction indices and the 'satisfiers' available to meet them are often specific to time, society, economic wealth or culture. There is thus much room for dispute over ways and means of satisfying needs, and the appropriate indicators. Particular groups of people, such as women, blacks, the elderly and people with disabilities, may require specific different satisfiers to achieve any given level of need satisfaction.

The research in Leeds, drawing on Leeds Urban Audit attempts to move forward on some of these issues by bringing together the different perspectives on need identified in Bradshaw's taxonomy: the codified knowledge of experts, professionals and researchers, and the experiential knowledge of people in everyday life. It argues that such 'needs audits' should be an important element in processes of policy formation and delivery of public services, so that disputes between (and within) codified and experiential knowledge should be confronted explicitly and resolved as far as possible. Needs auditing thus takes an important step towards the resolution of some of the limitations of multiplier-based methods, that is how to integrate 'expert' (i.e. codified and frequently quantified and monetarized) data with experiential (often unquantified and monetarized) information.

THE FUTURE OF SOCIAL AUDIT

Social audit has come a long way in Britain in recent years. Indeed, social accounting now merits serious mention in some accounting textbooks (Stevens and Kriefman, 1988). The old model of corporate social responsibility rooted in a consumerist, consensual model of society, has given way to a much more explicitly political project. This development has been closely associated with opposition to deindustrialization and the politics of the Thatcher era, and with the attempt to build a socially just and democratic alternative.

Nonetheless, considerable caution is necesssary in assessing the future prospects for social audit for a number of reasons. Firstly, there are the methodological problems, particularly those associated with multiplier techniques. Some of these may be amenable to pragmatic resolution. For example, it would in principle be possible to reduce the current methodological confusion by establishing 'standard' multiplier procedures for different types of social audit, from industrial plant closures to the role of the local authority as economic agent, however difficult this might be in practice.

But many of the difficulties associated with the local multiplier are more intractable and critics are liable to seize on the technical deficiencies of social audits, particularly where they have themselves been used as a weapon against other policies, as the Sheffield Jobs Audit was used as a critique of 'local Thatcherism'. Moreover, it must be questioned whether multiplier methodology is particularly appropriate to some of the central concerns of social audits, such as gender or ethnic equal opportunity issues, and 'qualitative' employment issues such as skill and wage levels, the social relations of work and the social need for less stressful work (Haringey Women's Employment Project, 1986). Multiplier models do not question the social relations of capitalist production, only the distributional effects of private production for profit.

In this context concepts derived from Marxist political economy provide powerful models which focus on the contradictory class relationships inherent in the production process itself, and the crisis-ridden nature of the process of capital accumulation which manifests itself in sequential booms and slumps. Models such as that of the circuit of capital, which describe economic processes within this framework, deserve exploration as an alternative basis for social auditing, particularly perhaps in contexts such as anti-closure campaigns.

New frameworks for social auditing

There are two ways in particular in which models of economic processes such as the multiplier or the circuit of capital need to be extended if they are to provide an adequate conceptual framework for social and environmental audit.

In the first place, we need models which recognize more fully that there is more to 'the economy' than the formal economy. Figure 10.2 represents one attempt to show how the formal economy (private and state sectors) is paralleled by an informal economy, and by a 'social economy' comprising the voluntary and domestic sectors. This is a key conceptual point, because a crucial role for social audit must be to recognize – in an integral way, not as a conceptual afterthought – the contribution of such 'non-formal' sectors to the productive economy.

Indeed, there is a need to go beyond the conceptual framework represented in Fig. 10.2 and develop a model which shows the interrelationships between the various sectors of the economy, not just that the formal economy is paralleled by others. This more dynamic model would enable us to recognize the integrity of the formal, informal and social economies: for example, the way in which unpaid labour (mostly by women) in the domestic economy is an essential element in the productive economy, reproducing the labour power which the formal economy consumes. Likewise, important trends in the modern economy indicate the essential role of the informal economy both in sustaining the local economies of particular areas and social groups, and in contributing to the circuits of capital dominated by formal economy organizations.

Secondly, our conceptual framework for social auditing needs to advance beyond those models of economic processes which treat the question of the relationship between the economy and environmental systems purely in terms of resource and raw material inputs to the productive process. Our framework must be able to show the effects of resource extraction and of production and consumption processes on the environment. Figure 10.3 shows one interesting attempt to do this in the context of environmental impact analysis.

However, a conceptual framework which is capable of recognizing the complex, contradictory and problematic nature of the environment–economy relationship will need to draw also on 'green' models of political economy. French ecologist and environment minister Brice Lalonde suggests that every citizen has three incomes: one from employment, one a social welfare income from the state, and one 'en nature'. The challenge to 'green' social auditing is to develop operational concepts which bring together these 'three incomes'.

There is, therefore, an important and difficult task of conceptual develop-ment which will be necessary if social audit practice is to be grounded in an adequately rigorous framework. The need at the moment is for testing out of the kind of frameworks discussed above in concrete situations to evaluate their strengths and weaknesses and move towards more operational models.

The social audit process

This raises the issue of another equally important kind of conceptual framework, that concerning the process of social audit. How is the process

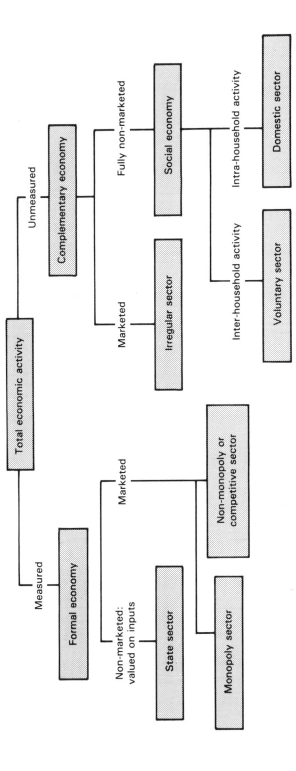

Fig. 10.2 The economy: formal, informal and social. (Source: Wheelock, 1990.)

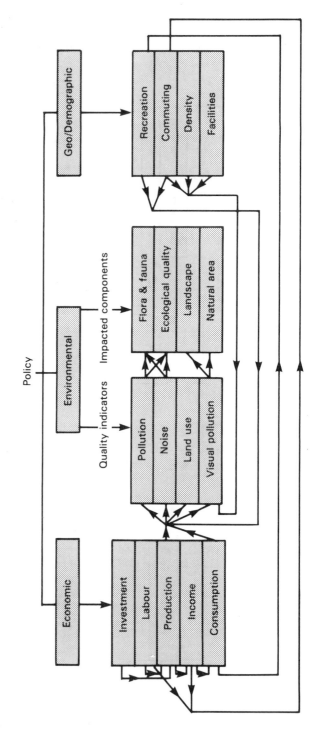

Fig. 10.3 A conceptual framework for environmental impact analysis. (Source: Nijkamp, 1980.)

of social audit to be carried out? A number of basic models may be identified. In the first place, a social audit may be carried out by experts or professionals within an organization. One example would be a corporate social reporting process within a firm (Fig. 10.4). This is, however, a technicist model, in which the objective of the audit is to enable the organization to manage and control its environment. Such an objective is antithetical to many of the principles associated with social audit.

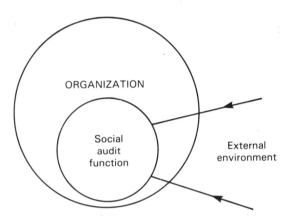

Fig. 10.4 Social audit within firm.

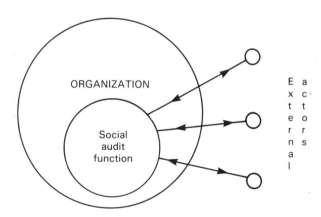

Fig. 10.5 Social audit within firm involving external actors.

A second model (Fig. 10.5) is a more participatory one, in which an organization undertaking an audit seeks the more active involvement of external actors, for example, the customers of a firm, or local interest groups in the case of a local government agency. In this model, however, the audit process still remains in the control of the organization.

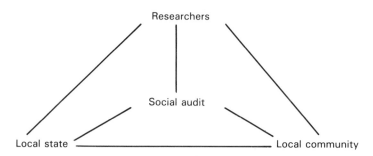

Fig. 10.6 A participatory model of social audit.

A more radical participatory model, such as that of the Leeds Urban Audit locates the social audit process in a more ambiguous position, between the local government agency, the social audit consultants/researchers, and the local community (Fig. 10.6). This model of social audit practice raises several large issues – about the social construction and ownership of knowledge, about 'local community', about the relationship between society and the state. Such questions are inescapably linked to social audit as it counterposes a democratic, public decision-making process to the privatized process of conventional audit.

The politics of social audit

Such questions about the social audit process lead on to a related set of issues about the politics of social audit. We have noted that a fundamental lesson from the history of social audits in the UK is that they have arisen in particular political contexts, from deindustrialization to the defence and revitalization of the case for local state services. Moreover, their success or lack of it has been related not just to the quality of the social audits themselves, but to their position and role within wider political processes.

Particular questions concern the use of social audits in a reactive role against plant closures. Although there are now numerous examples of anti-closure audits, relatively few cases appear to exist where social audits have been associated with, let alone able to claim credit for, a reversal of the closure decision. Given that anti-closure campaigns have to challenge the entrenched power structures of economic ownership and control, this is not at all surprising. However, one obvious conclusion is that, for trade unions, communities and local authorities involved in anti-closure struggles, social audits should represent only one tactic, in association with others such as plant occupation, strike, product boycott or an alternative plan. Another conclusion concerns the need for 'early warning'. Preparation of a social audit well before actual closure, when disinvestment or rundown is beginning, may have more time and scope to influence events. Interestingly, in France and the USA, legislation requires firms to give public notice in advance of impending major redundancies or closures (Rothstein, 1986).

Given these problems, it is worth considering more systematically the strengths and weaknesses of different contexts in which social audits have been undertaken.

The most important context of social audit so far has been the campaign – either in defence of jobs against plant closure or rationalization, or in support of jobs in state services. Such campaigns are likely to stand a greater chance of success, and a greater chance of attracting a wide spectrum of support without unduly compromising on the objectives to be achieved, if they are positive rather than defensive in their orientation. We have noted the difficult questions which arise about defence of existing jobs versus a position which accepts economic restructuring but argues about its terms and implications – a 'restructuring for labour' perspective. It seems likely that this issue can only be resolved in particular circumstances. Where the prospects of new job creation seem unlikely or limited, it may be essential to argue for existing jobs, but where new jobs are in prospect this may be both more difficult and less desirable.

The question of what attitude to take on this issue is partly a question of the process by which the issue is discussed and resolved in a way in which the cohesion of a campaign can be maintained. In this context the adoption of a public enquiry appears to be a very useful mechanism for bringing such issues into the public domain. It is important, however, that such enquiries should be constituted in such a way as to allow a proper debate. It may well be that a local authority is in the best position to convene such enquiries, although other possibilities also exist. However, it is essential that adequate resources of both time and money should be available to enable all parties to make their case to the enquiry, particularly those – such as workers and local people – who may face difficulties in presenting evidence. It is also important that all possible steps are taken to ensure that the company proposing a closure or rundown should feel obliged to participate in the enquiry. It is here that legislation has a role, in providing for early warning to be given of impending plant closure to allow time for action to be mounted, and in requiring disclosure of information by companies.

In any case, social audits will be able to contribute most positively to such campaigns if they are able to deploy methodologies which demonstrate the integrity of economic and social rationales, rather than having to argue a 'social' case against the 'economic' arguments. In this context, an important role undoubtedly exists for using social audit studies to restate a critically supportive case for public sector provision in the 1990s, in the wake of the Thatcherite assault on the state in the 1980s. An important step forward in this direction must be to integrate the better conceptual frameworks for mapping the 'economic space' in which investment decisions should be evaluated, with better approaches to the process of social audit. In relation to, say, the assessment of new transport systems, we need some practical studies which both integrate the role of transport in servicing the domestic sphere into a broader conception of the productive economy, and take forward ideas such as needs auditing in terms of process.

This approach to social audit for the public sector, and particularly for local public services, may be consistent with emerging notions about the role and purpose of the local state. Local government, over the past decade, has had to come to terms with (which does not mean to accept) a progressive erosion of its role as sole, main or key provider across a range of service areas from housing to education and refuse collection. On the one hand, social audit methods may be seen, along with a number of other innovative practices, as means of defending public provision, improving its quality, and if possible retrieving some of the lost territory. But other factors enter into the argument. It is probably the case that the erosion of the forms of public provision to which we have become accustomed has deeper roots than the New Right politics of the 1980s. It seems likely that the expansion of state provision was very closely associated with a particular phase of economic development. With the evolution of the economy beyond this phase, it may be that the basis for the old form of state provision no longer exists, either in material terms or in people's perceptions and wishes. (While there is strong popular support for a National Health Service, there is much dissatisfaction with the way in which it currently works.)

It is in this context that the beginnings of a new consensus may be emerging about a new role for the (local) state – a role which stresses its enabling and facilitating functions among and between a number of service providers rather than its role as an exclusive provider. This argument can have its dangers, and it may be wise to isolate a 'right' and 'left' form of it. On the right, there is at one extreme the notion of local government as merely a board of management which meets annually to renew a series of private sector contracts. Here the state merely 'holds the ring' for the market in traditional neoclassical economic terms. The implications for social audit which this kind of perspective entails are set out by Bruyn (1987), who attempts to define a role for social investment congruent with the New Right thinking of the 1980s, in which government has no role beyond that of enabling industry to become socially self-regulating. Some of the limitations and contradictions of this perspective are well summarized by Owen (1990).

But at the other pole there may be a progressive position which seeks to find new ways in which the local state can pursue goals of both economic prosperity and social justice within the local economy and local society. Social audit can play an important role here, in providing a conceptual framework within which the contribution of particular projects, policies and actions towards such goals might be evaluated, through democratic processes which enable the local state to play a pivotal role in a progressive local politics.

CONCLUSION

The politics of the social audit movement remain at this stage ambiguous. Is the social accounting movement linked to a systematic critique of the capitalist economy, or merely to certain specific aspects of it? Do social audits imply a fundamental challenge to the private ownership and control of the economy, or do they merely seek to contest certain capital decisions, to replace the unacceptable face of private enterprise by capitalism with a human face? The 'community' reference of many social audits is both a strength and a weakness: valuable in counterposing social values to the inhumanity of the market, and as a rallying focus for alliances against closures or in defence of services; but, except in specific communities such as mining villages, oblique to, and maybe sometimes a distraction from, organization and action of a more class-based nature.

The conclusion must be that we must not expect too much from social audit or place extensive reliance on it. Nonetheless, there have been important gains. The social costs of unemployment have been put more firmly on the political agenda, and the legitimate interest of workers and local communities in economic decisions has been forcefully asserted. Social audit has helped to show during the 1980s that an alternative exists to the New Right Project, and can help to build up that alternative during the 1990s.

What are the implications of the social audit experience of the 1980s for the environmental movement of the 1990s? Clearly there is much underlying common ground. Both are linked to a critical politics, and unite in their opposition to the economics and politics of 'the market'. It must be hoped that in the 1990s the essential interdependence of the social and environmental critiques can be recognized. Conventional accountancy attempts to reduce the social to the economic and the economic to the cash nexus. The importance of the social audit movement lies in its commitment to the restoration of social and political control over the economy. This is a commitment which the environmental movement must share. In the absence of a socially controlled economy, environmental concerns are marginalized – both in the Stalinist

East and the capitalist West. Without a sustainable economy, social need cannot be met.

REFERENCES

Audit Commission for Local Authorities in England and Wales (1989) *Urban Regeneration and Economic Development: The Local Government Dimension*, London, HMSO.
Barnsley Metropolitan Borough Council (1985) *Coalmining and Barnsley: A Study of Employment Prospects*, Barnsley MBC.
Barratt Brown, M. (1971) *UCS: The Social Audit*, Institute for Workers' Control Pamphlet No. 26, Nottingham.
Barratt Brown, M. (1984) *The Greater London Enterprise Board*, Social and Economic Study Pack No. 3, Industry and Employment Branch, GLC, London.
Belkaoui, A. (1984) *Socio-Economic Accounting*, Westport, Conn.: Greenwood Press.
Benington, J. (1989) *Restructuring of British Aerospace and its implications for the Welwyn Hatfield local economy*, University of Warwick, Local Government Centre Working Paper.
Bradshaw, J. (1972) 'The concept of need', *New Society*, Vol. 30, March.
Brignall, T.J. and Fitzgerald, L. (1989) 'Rationality and politics in pit closure decisions', *Accounting and Business Research*, Vol. 19, No. 75, pp. 212–26.
Brooke, R. (1990) *The Environmental Role of Local Government*, Local Government Training Board.
Bruyn, S.T. (1987) *The Field of Social Investment*, Cambridge University Press.
Cairncross, F. (1990) 'The environment: an enemy and yet a friend', *The Economist*, September 8.
CAITS (Centre for Alternative Industrial and Technological Systems) (1984a) *Economic Audit: Costs of Closure of the Foundry at Dagenham by Ford*, Polytechnic of North London.
CAITS (1984b) *The Public Costs of Unemployment*, Polytechnic of North London.
City of Cardiff (1990) *An Environmental Strategy for Cardiff*.
Clark, N., Critchley, R., Hall, D., Kline, R. and Whitfield, D. (1987) 'The Sheffield Council jobs audit', *Local Economy*, Vol. 4, pp. 3–21.
Clarke, A. and Cochrane, A. (1989) 'Inside the machine: the left and finance professionals in local government', *Capital and Class*, Vol. 37, pp. 35–61.
Cooper, D., Bird, J. and Sharp, B. (1985) *Report of the Public Inquiry into the Proposed Closure of Polkemmet Colliery, Whitburn*, Lothian District Council, Bathgate.
Davenport, E., Benington, J. and Geddes, M. (1990) 'The future of European motor industry regions: new local authority responses to industrial restructuring', *Local Economy*, Vol. 5, No. 2, pp. 129–46.

Dierkes, M. (1979) 'Corporate social responsibility in Germany: conceptual developments and practical experience', *Accounting, Organisations and Society*, Vol. 4, pp. 87–107.

Doyal, L. and Gough, I. (1991) *A Theory of Human Needs*, London, Macmillan.

ECRA Publishing Ltd (1988–90) *The Ethical Consumer: The Alternative Shoppers' Guide*, Manchester, ECRA.

Edinburgh District Council and Lothian Regional Council (1985) *Rowntree Mackintosh plc, Edinburgh – The Consequences of Closure: A Social Audit*, Edinburgh.

FoE (Friends of the Earth) (1989) *An Environmental Charter for Local Government*, London, FoE.

Geddes, M. (1991) 'Social audit at Kings Cross', *Social Audit Network News* (SANE), Vol. 3.

Glyn, A. (1985) *The Economic Case Against Pit Closures*, Sheffield, National Union of Mineworkers.

Gray, R., Owen, D. and Maunders, K. (1987) *Corporate Social Reporting*, Hemel Hemstead, Prentice-Hall.

Grojer, J.-E. and Stark, A. (1977) 'Social accounting: a Swedish attempt', *Accounting Organisations and Society*, Vol. 2, pp. 349–86.

Haringey Women's Employment Project (1986) *School Meals in Haringey*, London, HWEP.

Harte, G. (1986) 'Social accounting in the local economy', *Local Economy*, Vol. 1, pp. 45–56.

Harte, G. and Owen, D. (1987) 'Fighting deindustrialization: the role of local government social audits', *Accounting, Organisations and Society*, Vol. 12, No. 2, pp. 123–41.

Hird, C. (1983) *Challenging the Figures: A Guide to Company Finance and Accounts*, London, Pluto.

Hudson, R., Peck, F. and Sadler, D. (1984) *Undermining Easington: Who'll Pay the Price of Pit Closures?* University of Durham for Easington DC.

Jefferis, K. and Robinson, M. (1987) 'Social investment production', in Cochrane, A. (ed.), *Developing Local Economic Strategies*, Open University Press, Milton Keynes.

Keeble, D. (1967) 'Models of economic development', in Chorley, R. and Haggett, P. (eds), *Models in Geography*, London, Methuen.

Kirklees, Metropolitan Council (1989) *A Charter for the Environment*.

Kline, R. and Mallaber, J. (1986) *Whose Value? Whose Money?* London and Birmingham, Local Government Information Unit/Birmingham TURC.

Labour Research Department, SCAT and Birmingham TURC (1985) *The Jobs Audit*, Sheffield, Sheffield City Council.

Leeds Urban Audit (1990) *Finding out about your Community: How to do a Social Audit*, LUA, 18 Queen Square, Leeds 2.

Levie, H., Gregory, D. and Lorentzen, N. (1984) *Fighting Closures*, Nottingham, Spokesman.

Lewis, J.A. (1986) 'Assessing the effect of the Polytechnic of Wolverhampton, on the local community', *Urban Studies*, Vol. 25, No. 1.

Lichfield, N. and Partners (1987) *Lambeth Social Audit*, London, Borough of Lambeth.

Mandel, E. (1986) 'In defence of socialist planning', *New Left Review*, Vol. 159, pp. 5–37.

Medawar, C. (1978) *Social Audit Consumer Handbook*, London, Macmillan.

Merseyside County Council (1983a) *The Closure of Smurfit Corrugated Cases Ltd: A Social Audit*, Liverpool, MCC.

Merseyside County Council (1983b) *Metal Box Limited: A Social Audit*, Liverpool, MCC.

Merseyside County Council (1983c) *United Biscuits: A Social Audit*, Liverpool, MCC.

Merseyside County Council (1984) *Cammel-Laird Shipbuilders Ltd: A Social Audit*, Liverpool, MCC.

Newcastle City Council (1985) *Newcastle upon Tyne: A Social Audit 1979–1984*, Newcastle CC.

Nijkamp, P. (1980) *Environmental Policy Analysis: Operational Methods and Models*, Chichester, Wiley.

Owen, D.L. (1990) 'Towards a theory of social investment: a review essay, *Accounting, Organisations and Society*, Vol. 15, No. 3, pp. 249–65.

Oxford City Council (1990) *The Future of Cowley: Report of the Independent Enquiry into the Rover Cowley Works Closure Proposals*.

Oxford Motor Industry Research Project (1990) Cowley Works: Why it matters, why it must be saved.

Percy-Smith, J. (1990) *Auditing Social Needs: An alternative means of evaluating policy.* Paper presented at Local Economy Policy Unit seminar on Social Audit.

Ramsay, H. (1990) 'Defence strategies: local authority and union cooperation in a battle for jobs in munitions, *Local Government Policy Making*, Vol. 16, No. 4, pp. 15–22.

Roa, J., Press, M., Field, P., Douglas, J. and Middleton, J. (1990) 'Curing the tobacco industry', *Local Economy*, Vol. 5, No. 3, pp. 249–57.

Rothstein, L.E. (1986) *Plant Closures: Power, Politics and Workers*, Dover, Mass. Auburn House.

Rowthorn, B. and Ward, T. (1979) 'How to run a company and run down an economy: the effects of closing down steelmaking in Corby', *Cambridge Journal of Economics*, Vol. 3, pp. 327–40.

Schreuder, H. (1979) 'Corporate social reporting in the Federal Republic of Germany: an overview', *Accounting, Organisations and Society*, Vol. 4, pp. 109–22.

Sedgefield District Council and Durham County Council (1983) *Shildon Wagon Works: The Case Against Closure*, Durham, SDC/DCC.

Seeds (South East Economic Development Strategy) (1990) *Green Plan for the South East*.

Social Audit Ltd (1976) 'Social audit on Avon Rubber Company', *Social Audit*, Vol. 2, Nos 3/4.

St John's NUM and Coalfield Communities Action Committee (1985) *St John's*

Colliery, Maesteg: The Alternative to Closure, The Findings of an Independent Public Inquiry, St John's NUM and CCAC, Maesteg.

Stevens, P. and Kriefman, B. (1988) 'Social accounting', *Work Out Accounting*, Macmillan.

Turok, I. (1990) 'Evaluation and accountability in spatial economic policy: a review of alternative approaches', *Scottish Geographical Magazine*, Vol. 106, No. 1, pp. 4–11.

Wheelock, J. (1990) 'Capital restructuring and the domestic economy: family self respect and the irrelevance of "rational economic man"', *Capital and Class*, pp. 103–41.

Chapter Eleven

GREEN INVESTMENT

ALAN MILLER

INTRODUCTION

When looking at the suitability of a company share as an investment, an analyst will consider many issues, including management strength, product sustainability and price/earnings ratio to mention a few, but recently more and more fund managers have been looking at the social profile of a company as an additional investment factor. Considering a company's responsibility and attitude towards social issues is not a new phenomenon, although the upsurge of green issues has heightened awareness of this aspect in investment decision-making.

Ethical investment – more commonly referred to in the United States as socially-responsive or socially-responsible investment (SRI) – is no less hard-headed than any other form of money management. It simply avoids certain investments in favour of those companies making a positive (or, at worst, no negative) contribution towards particular social and environmental aims.

DEFINING SRI

The principle of SRI is essentially a simple one – it is investment based on social as well as economic criteria. SRI has been more clearly defined by Co-op America as:

- the channelling of personal, community or workplace capital towards peaceful, just, environmentally sound purposes;

● the diverting or divesting of capital away from destructive uses.

Just as there is conflict between the positive and negative streams in SRI, there are arguments both for and against SRI. Those who would argue against SRI state:

● that you cannot hope to fundamentally change the ways of a major institution simply by buying or selling its shares;
● that if you are investing your client's money, you should be concerned with making a good return from the markets available and a good return should not be sacrificed for the sake of a clear conscience;
● that with large multinational companies and world-wide trading links, it is not possible to find truly 'clean' companies of any meaningful size.

On the other hand, those who are in favour of SRI state:

● companies which behave in a socially responsible manner will eventually show higher profits and share price, leading to demand for their shares and services regardless of any financial yardstick;
● conversely, companies which pollute or sell harmful products will suffer in the long term.

It must be remembered, however, that if something is a poor investment, for example in terms of risk or bad market choice, then the fact that the investment is socially responsible does not make it any better. SRI is an additional consideration in investment, not a substitute for sound commercial judgment.

GENEALOGY OF SOCIAL INVESTMENT

SRI has a very long history indeed. It can be traced back to Victorian England to social reformers such as Octavia Hill who argued for 'five per cent philanthropy' – the provision of housing for the poor which was of good standard and helped improve their quality of life whilst providing an acceptable rate of return – as well as to the early pension funds set up by Quaker companies which had clauses forbidding investments in such areas as armaments.

Post war history provides the key to the modern day SRI movement. Children born in the 'baby boom' of the 1940s and 1950s grew up in a time of unprecedented change both in political climate, reflected in the 'Cold War' between East and West, and social climate with declining moral standards and traditional values being questioned.

The growth of concerns over social issues crystallized in the 1960's youth culture with 'flower power' and in the growth of the peace movement. This evidenced itself in social pressure in the 1970s over American involvement in Vietnam with 'draft resisting' and shareholder action against companies involved in the war. This was most evident when shareholders in the US giant Dow Chemicals began submitting resolutions expressing concern about the company's production of napalm. It was the Quaker and Methodist Church groups who were particularly active in this action.

It was the Quaker origins of the Friends Provident that led in June 1984 to the new developments in SRI in the UK with the launch of the Stewardship Fund. However, before looking at the UK market, we will consider in detail the US market and how it has influenced the development of SRI world-wide.

SRI IN THE USA

Following the lead given by religious organizations, SRI began to gain momentum in the USA with the needs of dissenting investors increasingly met by mutual funds. The Pax World Fund (United Methodist Church) was launched as the first SRI mutual fund, and by 1975 three other SRI funds had been established – Dreyfus Third Century, Pioneer Fund and Pioneer II.

This concept of SRI offered to provide 'as good a return as more conventional investment, whilst providing an additional service, the selective direction of their assets to companies which perform better according to measurement of corporate social responsibility' (Jeffrey Friedmann, Dreyfus Third Century).

Corporate responsibility is more than just avoiding companies with, for example, South African connections, although in the early days of SRI this facet was evidenced by 'investor boycotts' in the area, but has more recently considered issues as varied as the B-1 bomber to corporate child-care programmes.

There was a dramatic growth in SRI in the mid 1980s, and by 1987 23 states and 91 cities and counties had placed social screens on total assets of $267.9 billion ($70 billion alone from the Californian State pension fund). Furthermore, 140 universities and colleges had taken disinvestment actions affecting $81.2 billion in institutional assets. This growth was largely precipitated by anti-apartheid campaigning which drew public attention to social injustice and led to dramatic divestment in South Africa, with an average of $1 billion per month being divested during 1985 alone. The nuclear reactor disaster at Chernobyl highlighted concerns over environmental issues and provided the SRI market with converts, many of whom were the children of the postwar baby boom which had experienced protest in the 1960s and were now conscious investors with substantial capital influence.

Public interest in SRI continues to grow, with state and local government placing social screens around their investments. In San Francisco, companies with involvement in South Africa will not be considered for government contracts. In Newark, city investment policy includes issues such as equal opportunities and racial equality. Currently there is over $400 billion in securities now being invested with some sort of social screen, a powerful testimony to the strength of SRI.

California has been one of the leading states having an influence on SRI. The two largest pension funds in the USA, the California State Teachers' Fund and the California Public Employees' Fund, decided as long ago as 1979 to adopt a social policy of divestment in South Africa and companies failing to demonstrate equal opportunities.

As a result of the rapid growth of the SRI movement, the Social Investment Forum was set up in Boston in January 1985. Acting to monitor and promote socially screened investment, its members include many organizations who are active in the SRI movement. Historically, the South African issue has been dominant amongst the Forum's members, but it is recognized that environmental issues will replace South Africa as the leading social concern until the end of the millennium. The President of the US Social Investment Forum, Joan Shapiro, has stated:

> The planet's non-renewable resources are at stake. What socially responsible investors can do is work to prevent disasters, encourage good performance and, through their investments, make it costly and embarrassing for companies to violate the environment. We also have to redefine the environment to include not only the natural environment but also the human-created physical environment as well as the environment of our bodies. . . .
> We have to find ways not to destroy our natural environment by appropriately allocating and preserving the resources at hand; learn how to maintain and renew our living environments in an economically, viable way; and monitor what others can do through medicine, health devices and drugs that affect the physical environment of our bodies.

Environmental awareness is another SRI criteria, although it is more of an 'investment' rather than 'divestment' issue. New funds dedicated to environmental issues including pollution and alternative energy sources have been launched to meet the consumer-driven demand for green investment.

Research is, however, the most central challenge in the application of both positive and negative criteria to investment, social investment being dependent upon the availability of extensive and accurate information. Most US funds use external research organizations to maintain the social screens, and with more stringent reporting requirements than in the UK, the information available is greater. The Council for Economic Priorities (CEP) has been a leading force in SRI research for almost 20 years. Its purpose is to research, collate and publicize the facts behind corporate and government programmes to reveal how they actually affect people. CEP, in its first major study in 1970, reviewed the paper industry which led it to conclude 'that doing business conscientiously with respect for the environment and employees, does not indicate a likelihood of lower profits'. In fact CEP has in its studies proved that the most socially responsible corporations are often those with the greatest profitability. CEP has now produced over 100 publications covering issues such as air and water pollution, occupational safety, nuclear energy, toxic waste disposal, military spending and armaments.

Not only is there a wealth of research available to the conscious investor, but in addition to investing in quoted companies through the mutual fund medium, it is also possible to invest directly in the community. Investment in community development projects is achieved by hundreds of small loan funds that provide resources for a wide range of community needs, including low-income housing, worker cooperatives and local economic revitalization projects, which cannot qualify for credit through traditional financial institutions. One rapidly developing area is community development loan funds. Whilst there is no shortage of worthy projects to support, generally loan funds have a shortage of lenders. Most funds seek a minimum loan of $500–$1000 for a period of at least one year at interest rates from 0% to slightly below money market rates.

Despite the apparent speculative nature of such lending, community development loan funds have experienced a much lower default rate than most of the commercial banks. An example of this is one of the first community loan funds, the Institute for Community Economics Revolving Loan Fund, which, as at the end of 1986, had written off only $2500 out of $11 million, the rest having been successfully repaid.

The concept of SRI is well accepted in the USA, and has influenced to a considerable degree developments throughout the world.

SRI IN THE UK

Wealthy individuals have for many years been able to match their investments with their social conscience, as indeed have many social and religious bodies so done. However, in the UK, the concept of 'ethical' investment (as SRI is more commonly known in the UK) has been extended to the smaller investor with the launch of the Stewardship Fund in June 1984. When the fund was launched, it had as much to do with the Quaker origins of the Friends Provident as any commercial judgment.

Since that time a substantial number of ethical funds have been launched, all applying some sort of social screen on investment. Some funds operate more exclusion criteria than others (although, for example, tobacco producers and armaments manufacturers are almost unanimously vetoed) and some funds take a more rigid view of individual criteria than others. In addition to this somewhat negative process, most funds attempt also to place emphasis on positive aspects – for example, actively supporting companies recognized as being protective of the environment. The launch of most of these funds in the last three years is evidence of the increasing demand from large and small investors alike for opportunities to invest in a socially responsible manner. The full range of currently available stock market based socially responsible investment outlets is detailed in the appendix to this section of the chapter on pp. 253–5.

Bromige and Partners were pioneers in the field of ethical investment. Having provided an ethical portfolio service for private clients for some years they launched the Ethical Investment Fund in January 1986. It is generally accepted that the social criteria of this fund are the most stringent of all the ethical funds. Not only concerned with human welfare issues, with bans on investment in South Africa, alcohol, tobacco and gambling, it extends the social screen to animal welfare with avoidance of companies involved in the production of animal-tested cosmetics and pharmaceuticals as well as fur trading. With environmental issues of major concern to all of us, they have a total ban on the nuclear power industry and positively discriminate in favour of companies producing environment enhancing products and services. They extend their concerns to the human environment, by seeking to invest in companies which demonstrate positive attitudes to their workforces and the local community in which they conduct their business. It is this combination of negative and positive social criteria which underpins the fund's appeal.

When the Ethical Investment Fund was launched in January 1986, David Bromige, the chairman of Fund Managers Bromige & Partners stated in interview:

The Friends Provident Fund has been very successful, attracting over £18.5 million in less than two years. But an increased number of options for socially-conscious investors is needed – and I would expect other organisations to move swiftly into this field and this should result in the force of ethical investment gaining its own momentum.

This was crystal ball gazing indeed! Bromige went on to say:

The increased opportunities will lead many investors to divest unscreened portfolios and reinvest in vehicles more closely matching their ethical criteria. This, in turn, can be expected to result in some share price realignment. In the wake of Bhopal and Chernobyl, obvious present day examples, are companies engaged in the processing of toxic or nuclear materials, whilst many companies with South African interests have chosen, not least because of the share price effect, to cut them.

However, David Bromige did not believe that the case for the Ethical Investment Fund relied exclusively on investment performance. First reaction from UK enquirers was that many claimed they would be content with a slightly lower yield rather than pay the price of supporting companies whose activities they find objectionable. That trend still exists today with a significant number of investors being motivated more by the social dividend rather than the prospect of financial gain.

Any individual or group which truly cares about ethical, moral, religious or political principles should in theory at least want to invest their money in accordance with their principles. Many people consider it immoral to profit through the misery of others, and do not wish to receive dividends from companies whose investment, for example, sustains the apartheid economy. On the other hand one, for example, might approve of a company's positive discrimination policy towards equality of its workers, and wish to protect such a company from undesirable predators.

The concept of ethical investment is shaking off its 'crank' image and gaining wide acceptance in the UK. Already a number of local authorities and trade unions have elected to have all or part of their pension funds invested in accordance with a social charter. The issues are what appeals. Whilst those such as South Africa and armaments have diminished in importance with political changes and the lessening of tension between East and West, it is increasing green awareness of issues such as production of CFCs, tropical rain forests and the legacy of pollution which has led to an increased emphasis on social responsibility.

There are today over 20 ethical/environmental or green unit trusts available here in the UK. Whatever their label, they all share a common purpose – investment with principles. All funds apply a social screen and how far that screen goes is determined by the managers when the fund is established, and how well that screen is maintained depends on the quality of the social screening.

Research methods vary from fund to fund. All funds claim in-house and/or contracted research from organizations such as the Ethical Investment Research Service (EIRIS), whilst many institutional investors such as the local authority pension funds use the Pensions Investment Resource Centre (PIRC).

EIRIS was established in April 1983 and launched in November of the same year. Its publicly stated aims are:

- to provide information on a wide range of issues which will help concerned investors apply positive or negative ethical criteria to investment;
- to identify forms of investment which meet certain non-commercial requirements on the part of the investor;
- to promote a wider understanding of, and debate on, corporate responsibility issues.

EIRIS vets all companies quoted in the FT All-Share Index, and a number of companies in the secondary markets. Their service is available to both individuals and organizations. For a specified fee they will provide an analysis of current investments, a list of all the companies on the FT All-Share Index which meet that particular investor's criteria and factsheets on individual companies. EIRIS publicly state that they do not make judgments about the moral acceptability of the activities of individual firms, or provide any type of financial advice.

EIRIS also publish a quarterly newsletter available on a separate subscription. Various publications concerned with aspects of ethical investment are also available.

Both the Stewardship Fund and the Ethical Investment Fund use EIRIS as a major source for their research, whilst some funds such as the Merlin Ecology Fund supply their own 'in-house' research.

PIRC was set up in 1986 by a number of local authorities to look critically at the way in which local government superannuation fund money is invested. It aims to encourage local authorities to give more regard to the social implications of making pension fund investment decisions. PIRC has its own research base and provides information on company groups in areas of concern to local authorities, whilst using its contacts to provide research on companies listed in foreign markets. In addition it helps the coordination of shareholder action between local authorities who want to use their power as investors to influence company activity, and also provides a consultancy service on various legal and policy issues.

PIRC publish a bulletin every month covering current pension fund issues and also a quarterly journal with articles on key topics. They also provide sector studies (e.g. energy sector) and organize seminars and briefings on a variety of topics.

In addition to the research requirements, many funds maintain an advisory board or committee to ensure that the selected stocks match the social template of the trust. Advisory committees vary in size and style from trust to trust but in the main they exist:

- To consider the social criteria of the trust, and monitor and ensure that its stated principles are being adhered to.
- To ensure that the fund manager only invests in companies which meet the social criteria of the trust. They would also advise him to divest if the holding was found to be in conflict with the social criteria.
- To review specific companies in the portfolio, to examine more closely their corporate and social responsibility.
- To look at current social issues to ensure that the trust remains in touch with current concerns.
- To review the stated criteria, and make recommendations for change or addition where necessary.

CAN SRI FUNDS ACTUALLY PERFORM?

In its first year of operation, not only did the Stewardship Fund outperform the Financial Times Index but it consistently outperformed by a significant margin each and every one of their non-screened funds. The New Alternatives Fund in the USA was the top performing of all mutual funds in 1988, whilst the Medical Investments Health Fund featured in the top ten of UK growth trusts in the year to June 1990.

The 1987 investment returns reflected the market correction on 19 October when the Financial Times All-Share Index dropped a record 237.95 points or 20%. The Stewardship Ethical Fund fell by only 10.5%, although it continued to fall throughout October when a degree of confidence returned to the All-Share Index. For the whole year the Stewardship Fund grew by 20%. In the US, the Dow Jones Industrial Average dropped a record 508.32 points or 22.6%, whilst the leading SRI mutual funds dropped an average of 12.42%. Generally, SRI performed well in a falling market although did not recover as quickly as the indices, reflecting the lack of overall market confidence at that time in the smaller capitalized stocks in which the ethical funds are invested.

CAN THE MARKET SUSTAIN ITS GROWTH?

The modern day SRI market provides opportunities for individual and institutional investment across a wide range of social issues, with social screens based on positive and negative criteria. Companies have started to appreciate their responsibilities to the community in which they do business, to their staff and to their shareholders. Whilst many companies have accepted this corporate responsibility principle with real conviction, many others accept that the influence of the SRI market is such that the very share price and profitability of a group can be undermined. Companies, realizing that government or federal contracts would be denied them unless they conformed with changes in attitudes to important issues such as South Africa or the environment, have been forced to alter their attitudes.

Perhaps the most revealing aspect of the growth of SRI is its increased acceptance amongst the mainstream financial institutions, led mainly by unions and local authority pension funds, joining first in divestment from South Africa, and now adding their considerable weight of influence to environmental issues.

Undoubtedly, divestment from South Africa has been the major force in SRI. According to the Council on Economic Priorities, portfolios in excess of $200 billion were ordered to be free from investment in South Africa, and a large number of US and UK companies sold their operations in that country.

In the UK, there are now signs of a maturing ethical market, with community development loan funds beginning in a small way through some of the more innovative local authorities making available limited funds through the resources of their pension funds. Social banking is a further concept which, although successfully developed in the USA, has not yet come of age in the UK.

The UK Social Investment Forum has been launched in the UK to provide a medium for the socially responsible investor to approach, and to provide a forum for the various and diverse social groups. The founding chairman of the Forum, Alan Miller of Bromige & Partners, states:

> We hope the Social Investment Forum will be an organization which represents the broad spectrum of social investment – both the traditional socially responsive investment funds and the more community based and socially directed investment projects, including community banking and neighbourhood initiatives – SRI in action, as well as acting as an education source to make people aware of the range of socially responsible investment and socially directed projects available.

The mission statement of the organization states:

> The Forum's primary purpose is to promote and encourage the development and positive impact of socially responsible investment throughout the UK. We define SRI as investment which combines an investor's financial objectives with their commitment to social concerns such as peace, social justice, economic development or a healthy environment.

Although the organization is still developing, it is hoped to be representative of the broadest aspects of socially responsible and socially directed investment.

ETHICAL INVESTMENT IN EUROPE

Although green issues have historically been of more importance in mainland Europe, the concept of ethical investment is just beginning to gain acceptance. In countries like Holland, Austria and France, ethical and environmental funds are beginning to be launched although the concept is gaining the widest acceptance in Germany. Environmental rather than ethical issues seems the dominant concern in mainland Europe.

An organization recently launched to foster and support the development of social finance organizations primarily in Europe is the International Association of Investors in the Social Economy (INAISE). Target members are organizations:

> . . . which invest in undertakings of an ethical, ecological, cultural and self-managing nature, including women's undertakings, undertakings of ethnic minorities, in undertakings whose aims are concerned with people with disabilities, healthier living, peace and the Third World, and in undertakings in the social economy generally.

Table 11.1 The 'Valdez' Principles

---

1. Protection of the Biosphere
We will minimise and strive to eliminate the release of any pollutant that may cause environmental damage to the air, water, or earth or its inhabitants. We will safeguard habitats in rivers, lakes, wetlands, coastal zones and oceans and will minimise contributing to the greenhouse effect, depletion of the ozone layer, acid rain or smog.

2. Sustainable Use of Natural Resources
We will make sustainable use of renewable natural resources such as water, soils and forests. We will conserve non-renewable natural resources through efficient use and careful planning. We will protect wildlife habitat, open spaces and wilderness while preserving biodiversity.

3. Reduction and Disposal of Waste
We will minimise the creation of waste, especially hazardous waste, and wherever possible recycle materials. We will dispose of all wastes through safe and responsible methods.

4. Wise Use of Energy
We will make every effort to use environmentally safe and sustainable energy sources to meet our needs. We will invest in improved energy efficiency and conservation in our operations. We will maximise the energy efficiency of products we produce or sell.

5. Risk Reduction
We will minimise the environmental, health and safety risks to our employees and the communities in which we operate by employing safe technologies and operating procedures and by being constantly prepared for emergencies.

6. Marketing of Safe Products and Services
We will sell products or services that minimise adverse environmental impacts and that are safe as consumers commonly use them. We will inform consumers of the environmental impacts of our products and services.

7. Damage Compensation
We will take responsibility for any harm we cause to the environment by making every effort to fully restore the environment and to compensate those persons who are adversely affected.

8. Disclosure
We will disclose to our employees and to the public incidents relating to our operations that cause environmental harm or pose health or safety hazards. We will disclose potential environmental, health or safety hazards posed by our operations, and we will not take any action against employees who report any condition that creates a danger to the environment or poses health and safety hazards.

9. Environmental Directors and Managers
At least one member of the Board of Directors will be a person qualified to represent environmental interests. We will commit management resources to implement these Principles, including the funding of an office of vice president for environmental affairs or equivalent executive position, reporting directly to the CEO, to monitor and report upon our implementation efforts.

10. Assessment and Annual Audit
We will conduct and make public an annual self-evaluation of our progress in implementing these Principles and in complying with all applicable laws and regulations throughout our worldwide operations. We will work towards the timely creation of independent environmental audit procedures which we will complete annually and make available to the public.

Source: US Social Investment Forum.

GREEN OR CLEAN?

To the ethical fund manager, green considerations are an important aspect of his or her social screen, but in the main the ethical fund seeks to avoid contentious areas first and foremost whereas the green fund seeks to promote more the positive aspects in investment. In reality most investors wish the balanced approach of 'green and clean', that is they wish to invest in companies that in addition to avoiding irresponsible actions are also showing positive corporate responsibility towards the environment. The cost of true commitment to environmentalism in companies is high since you cannot hope to change the infrastructure and product line of a company overnight. Following the *Exxon Valdez* oil spillage in the Alaskan sound, the US Social Investment Forum fostered the idea of getting companies to adhere to the 'Valdez Principles'. These principles are effectively a charter for corporate social responsibility and are listed in Table 11.1.

Although there was a significant impact with the launch of this initiative, there has been limited acceptance of the principles by corporations around the world, and a similar initiative here has yet to gain wide acceptance either. Whatever their reasons, it is possible to understand how difficult it is for a company to change its practices or processes – particularly if they are profitable. Social unacceptability that hits the very share price, and the prospect of investor favour for adopting a policy of social and corporate responsibility towards ethical and environmental issues will hopefully convince company groups to embrace real social change.

The accountability of companies to their shareholders is absolute, but the information relating to a company's social and environmental policy is not provided in the annual report and accounts. Introducing a requirement for companies to state their social policy, and not just details of their charitable and philanthropic donations, would enable shareholders to decide for themselves if a company was truly socially responsible.

By introducing a statute-backed environmental audit, the reports and accounts of a company group could and would present a true picture to the would-be investor. That way, it would be possible to see not only the financial reward of investing in a company, but also the social dividend – the knowledge that you are doing your part to improve the quality of life – not only for now but for the future of life as we know it. Social investment has come of age.

APPENDIX: ETHICAL AND ENVIRONMENTAL FUNDS AND SERVICES IN THE UK (as at 31 December 1990)

Taking into account the portfolio management services available, there are 30 ethical/environmental alternatives for the retail investor.

Unit trusts

Fund name	Launch date	International/UK
Abbey Ethical	10/87	UK
Acorn Ethical	11/88	Int.
Allchurches Amity	02/88	UK
Buckmaster Fellowship	07/86	Int.
Clerical Medical Evergreen	02/90	Int.
Cooperative Insurance Environ	05/90	Int.
Eagle Star Environmental Opportunities	06/89	UK
Fidelity Famous Names	06/85	UK
Friends Provident Stewardship	06/84	UK
Friends Provident Stewardship Income	10/87	UK
Friends Provident Stewardship North America	11/87	Int.
Jupiter Tarbutt Merlin Ecology	03/88	Int.
Medical Investments Health Fund	04/87	Int.
NM Conscience	10/87	UK
Scottish Equitable Ethical Unit Trust	04/89	UK
Sovereign Ethical	05/89	UK
Target Global Opportunities	11/87	Int.
TSB Environmental	06/89	Int.

Pension funds

A number of funds can be linked to pensions:

Abbey Ethical
Clerical Evergreen
Eagle Star Environmental
Friends Provident Stewardship
NM Conscience
Scottish Equitable Ethical

Additionally, there is a further fund offering pensions only:

Fund name	Launch date	International/UK
Commercial Union Environmental Exempt	12/89	Int.

A number of funds are linked to insurance products, namely:

Eagle Star Environmental
Fellowship (linked to General Portfolio)
Friends Provident Stewardship
NM Conscience
Scottish Equitable Ethical

A number of funds offer a Personal Equity Plan facility:

Coop Environ
Eagle Star Environmental
Friends Provident Stewardship Income
NM Conscience
Sovereign Ethical
TSB Environmental

Additionally, there are three further funds offering PEPs only:

Fund name	Launch date	International/UK
Allied Provincial Green	07/89	UK
Dominion Ethical	07/88	UK
Henderson Green	05/89	UK

Three bond funds are offered:

Fund Name	Launch date	International/UK
Ethical Investment Fund	01/86	Int.
Exon Managed Fund	06/87	UK
Homeowners Green Chip	11/89	Int.

One investment trust is offered:

Fund name	Launch date	International/UK
Merlin Green Investment Trust	12/89	Int.

Four portfolio management services are offered:

Management Group	Launch date	International/UK
Bromige & Partners	01/84	Both
Leopold Joseph Ethical Portfolio	09/89	Both
Merlin Jupiter Green	N/A	Both
New Life Financial Services	N/A	Both

POSTSCRIPT: USING ANNUAL REPORTS FOR ETHICAL DECISION-MAKING

Rachel Griffith

For most investors, ethical or otherwise, the annual report is the prime source of information on what a company gets up to. However, the amount of information given varies enormously from company to company. This makes it extremely difficult to use the annual report to make consistent judgments on the ethical acceptability of companies.

The annual reports of most companies generally give a comprehensive description of the principal activities, primary products and services of the company. This information can be useful for the investor who is concerned about issues like alcohol, gambling or tobacco which are related to a company's main activities or products. It can also help inform investors who are looking for companies with a main activity that they regard as positive, such as the production of safety or environment monitoring equipment.

For specific details, and consistent data, the directors' report is the most useful section of the annual report. In particular, information regarding the company's political and charitable donations is often used by ethical investors. For investors who are concerned about a company's overseas operations the geographic breakdown of turnover and profit (where provided) can be useful, as can the list of overseas interests that is sometimes provided.

This is about the limit to the use an individual investor can make of an annual report. One of the big drawbacks is that the information obtained from annual reports is often not consistent across all companies on non-financial grounds. This makes it very difficult for an individual to use this information to compare companies. For researchers trying to get consistent information across a large number of companies the main use of the annual report is to verify information from other sources or to indicate potential areas of concern.

IMPROVEMENTS ON THE EXISTING FORMAT

Even with regard to a company's activities the annual report has limitations. Companies are not required to disclose their involvement in anything except their 'main' activities. A large company may, for instance, have several subsidiaries that produce a significant amount of alcoholic drinks but not mention it in their annual report.

It would be useful if UK companies were required to list their major markets, products and customers as US companies often do in their 10-K forms (required for purposes of stock exchange listing). This could include the requirement to say where any one customer, or class of customer, accounted for some given percentage, or a given amount (say over 20% of business, or over £100 million). In fact, some UK companies do already provide this sort of information voluntarily.

Current legislation calls for companies to report donations made to political parties or to individuals or organizations whose activities are likely to affect the outcome of an election. However, there are other ways in which corporations provide financial support to organizations of a political nature. These include corporate membership or donations to groups like the Economic League, or the British Industry Committee on South Africa (BICSA) which many would regard as political. While some companies do volunteer this information it is not available on a consistent basis and therefore is of limited use to the ethical investor.

More information on charitable and other donations would also be of interest. This could be accompanied by an explanation of how and why these particular donations were chosen, for example the percentage of profit donated, and details of how, and to whom, these contributions were made. Were members from the management, employees or from the community involved in deciding where the money should go?

Companies are required to give general statements on their health and safety policies and on their policies with regards to disabled employees. However, these are usually very general statements of policy and do not contain any details which would be of use to the ethical investor.

A more detailed history of the development of the company may be of interest to ethical investors, as would a more detailed breakdown of turnover by geographic area of origin as well as the commonly given breakdown by destination.

PROSECUTIONS

Many investors, not only ethical ones, would be interested in knowing when a company in which they invested had broken the law. Prosecutions under certain Acts are already a matter of public record. For example, most prosecutions carried out under the Health and Safety at Work Act 1974 and related legislation are publicly available through the regional offices of the Health and Safety Inspectorate. Details of prosecutions carried out by the National Rivers Authority (NRA) can be obtained from the local NRA offices. There is a range of information on other types of legal infringement that can also be obtained from various sources. The problem, however, is that this information is generally not kept centrally, is not given by the parent company, and is often expensive to obtain.

Companies could include information in the annual report on prosecutions which had occurred during the year, as well as any outstanding cases. The sort of information that would be useful to the ethical investor includes: the amount fined, the number of persons affected (if relevant), a brief description of the incident, the name of the company prosecuted (if it was a subsidiary or associated company) and the date of incident.

Most US companies give details of prosecutions which materially affect the business. This means that small legal disputes regarding contractual matters do not necessarily have to be reported. However, in the UK it would also mean that the Health and Safety and NRA prosecutions mentioned above would not have to be declared as the fines are generally quite small and would therefore be immaterial to the business. Any legislative requirements would therefore have to be carefully drafted so as to ensure that the issues of concern to shareholders were reported on. They would also have to be realistic in terms of the sheer amount of information that will fit into the annual report format. This highlights one of the greatest difficulties in matching the information needs of the ethical investor and the reporting capabilities of companies. It is entirely possible that a company could have a very large number of prosecutions against it in any one year and that this would take up a lot of room in the annual report. However, this is just the information that investors need to assess a company's commitment to any stated policies in these areas. One way of resolving this problem would be to require the full listing of prosecutions to be given in a separate document filed along with the annual report, much as is currently the case for reporting on subsidiary companies. The annual report itself could then include a summary of the prosecutions along with a reference to the fuller listing.

EMPLOYMENT POLICIES AND CONDITIONS

Since information on employees' pay and conditions is only available from the company itself this is an area where great improvement in reporting requirements is possible. Currently there is little, if any, information contained in an annual report that can provide guidance to the ethical investor. While companies are required to give the total number of, and total pay of, employees in the UK, this figure is rarely broken down into full- and part-time, which makes it difficult to interpret. The information could also be broken down by sex, ethnic origin, and whether or not disabled.

Nearly all companies now have computerized personnel records. Parent companies may not keep these records centrally, but with modern technology this could be achieved, for UK employees at least, over a fairly short time period. Given this, a number of statistics on the composition of the work-force could be calculated quite simply. These statistics would be useful indicators, particularly when looked at over a number of years, of such things as the company's commitment to the welfare of its employees and equal opportunities.

Companies are also currently required to give details of the pay of directors and senior employees paid over £30 000 annually. This requirement could be extended to include all employees. This would mean that the number of employees paid within given wage bands (e.g. under £5000, between £5000 and £10 000, etc.) would be detailed providing useful information for investors concerned about low pay, or about the distribution of pay between different grades of employee. A listing of the unions recognized by the company, along with the number of employees belonging to each one, would also be of interest to some ethical investors.

Other information which could provide an indication of employment conditions includes: number of days lost through strikes or industrial disputes; number of days lost through sick leave; numbers of employees being seriously injured or disabled while at work; the rate of turnover of employees. Further information which could help the ethical investor to form a picture of working conditions would include whether or not child-care facilities are provided, if the company offers mid-career break opportunities, and what the maternity and paternity benefits are. In addition the average number of hours worked and holiday leave given are an integral part of employees' conditions. It would also be useful for companies to provide information on their training policy and programmes in general, and in specific a breakdown of employees in management training schemes by sex, ethnic origin, and whether or not disabled, giving the number of hours spent on any such scheme.

ENVIRONMENTAL IMPACT

Environmental audits are becoming more commonly talked about by British industry. As yet there are no agreed standards on how an environmental audit should be conducted, and there is no process by which to ensure their independence, although in due course they may well give rise to the inclusion of useful and accurate information in annual reports.

Currently, the information needed to evaluate a company's environmental impact is not only not reported, but is often not known to the company itself. For example, we have often found that companies using wood products are unaware of the source of the wood, and even whether or not it is a tropical hardwood.

Most companies could provide information on their consumption of energy and any measures being taken to reduce it. Besides a general discussion of the company's efforts the actual amount of energy consumed (in therms) would be informative. This could additionally be broken down into electricity, gas, coal, oil and other forms of energy. Such information would help investors to asssess the company's contribution to greenhouse gas emissions. The actual amount, either monetary or in therms, of energy saved due to improvements made by the company over the past five years would give a good solid basis on which to make comparisons of companies' efforts in this area.

For investors concerned about the use of road transport, information on the size and make-up of the car and goods vehicles fleet owned or leased by a company would be useful. In addition, information on the relative use of rail transport and on incentives to employees to use alternative types of transport would give an idea of what the company was doing to reduce its usage of the road network.

The use of ozone depleting chemicals is an area that many ethical investors are concerned about. A major international agreement, the Montreal Protocol, has identified a number of chemicals which are thought to be the most damaging. Under the Montreal Protocol signatory countries have agreed to reduce, and eventually eliminate, their use of these substances. When agreements of this importance are reached it would be realistic to require all companies to report on their use of the substances affected. Another agreement of this type is the 'Redlist' of substances issued by the Department of the Environment as being those that are most harmful to Britain's aquatic environment. Additionally, there are several European Community agreements, such as the one on dumping of waste in the North Sea, which could also be included in this category. It would be useful if companies had to detail any efforts they were making to replace hazardous substances. In a similar way, information on what licences are held, such as those for animal testing, and any measures being taken to replace animal tests would be of interest to many investors.

In fact, many companies do now put in their annual report a description of the efforts they are making to replace certain substances or practices with more environmentally friendly ones. However, these descriptions often lack a consistent factual basis. It is these facts that an ethical investor needs in order to make an informed and independent decision.

CONCLUSION

So, we see that, although a company's annual report can be a useful starting point for an ethical investor, or his or her adviser, it at present generally contains only limited information on many matters that are likely to be of concern. Much additional, and more consistent, information could reasonably be provided, either in the annual report or on request by shareholders.

Part Four

THE FURTHER DEVELOPMENT
OF GREEN REPORTING

Chapter Twelve

DEVELOPING GREEN REPORTING SYSTEMS: SOME PRACTICAL IMPLICATIONS

BRIAN ING

INTRODUCTION

In this chapter of the book, we attempt to provide those who are required to perform green reporting (as defined elsewhere in this book) with a practical approach. It is our view that green reporting is not straightforward and is not merely confined to producing numbers. There is, with time, as new issues are discovered, and old wisdom amended, a changing reporting requirement. Hence, this chapter stresses the importance of considering organizational factors when undertaking green reporting. It is the organization of the green reporting which will determine its veracity and its success.

The first section of this chapter concerns itself with trying to define the problem for the environmental reporter. This part of the chapter may seem to be a collection of a hundred and one reasons why green reporting cannot be performed. If that is the impression it must be stressed that it is not the view of the author, but the result of the feeling that a true appreciation of the problems involved is required before a practical solution is proposed.

The next section concentrates on the organizational aspects of installing green reporting. This section indicates the need for many parts of the organization to be involved, from the most senior manager to many of the employees. We do not consider that by appointing a person to be responsible for green reporting and expecting that person to get on with it in isolation will, in general, succeed. We also discuss briefly the accounting for costs involved in improving the environmental impact of the organization and measuring the benefit of green reporting. It is a common experience with the pioneers of green reporting that they have benefited financially from doing so. This has occurred despite the obvious extra costs and sometimes the overlooking of commercial opportunities. We feel that it is important that an organization does measure the costs involved in green reporting and the benefits obtained.

We proceed then to indicate the mechanisms whereby data and information can be gathered for the purposes of green reporting, including the provision of advice on MIS amendments as well as a consideration of some behavioural points on data gathering.

The final section discusses the role of the accountant in environmental reporting, and provides a few cautionary words and final conclusions.

GREEN REPORTING – THE CHANGING REQUIREMENT

Green reporting covers a whole variety of issues and topics, many of which are not directly related. Some issues are of a high but transitory public profile whilst others are fundamental and long-term but occasionally receive little attention. We do not attempt to provide an all-encompassing definition of what green reporting means given the disparate collection of issues that need to be covered. What we do suggest is that the following breakdown of main issues is a useful conceptual framework within which to work:

- Use of scarce resources
- Pollution
- Social impact
- Global warming.

For all the groupings above, there is the common factor that the issues and their relative importance (both in fact and in perception) are constantly changing. New issues arise as our knowledge of the impact of our commercial operations on the environment improves. Established and accepted opinions need modification as further investigation is performed. Even where the information is available it is sometimes not widely known until a pressure group is formed to publicize the result, sometimes a considerable time after the original discovery.

We will now discuss each of the main groups of issues in more detail in turn.

Use of scarce resources

A continuing environmental issue has been the use of scarce resources. Since

Forester's modelling of the world economy in the 1970s, many people have considered the impact on economic growth and social well-being of the use, including the expanded use, of scarce resources. These resources can include fuel, special carbon fuels, the heavy metals and vegetable resources such as paper. Many organizations base their whole rationale for existence on the consumption of such resources and as such have received odious comment in the media. The issues that need to be reported on by organizations using scarce resources must include:

- Efforts to substitute more available resources
- Improvements in the efficiency of using the resources
- Recovery and recycling of these resources.

In terms of an organization these efforts need to concern the R&D function looking at different processes and materials, the purchasing department which may be able to obtain the same resources at higher purity with less waste, the operations or manufacturing part of the organization considering efficiency, and the marketing department with their efforts towards recycling and recovery of the goods. An example in the latter case concerns the manufacturers of glass bottles for soft drinks which are faced with the dilemma of public concern over the wastage of the resources that went to make the glass (although sand is fairly common the energy required to convert sand into glass is very expensive) against the economics of collecting and recycling it. The R&D department and operations department can also be heavily involved in looking at the processes for recycling resources. The impact is organization-wide and needs coordination to achieve benefits, both in terms of a reduction in the use of scarce resources and also in reporting the success of efforts made in this direction. Some of the reporting will be quantifiable, e.g. x million pounds turnover using x tonnes of resource in 1991 against y million pounds turnover and proportionately less resources used in 1992. This is relatively easy, but what of the efforts being undertaken now to achieve the reduction in future years? The information provided can at best be qualitative or even restricted by commercial, competitive considerations.

Pollution

Poisons and chemical pollutants can have an impact at the plant or factory, where measurement of the levels of pollutant is relatively easy, or their impact can be further away where additional problems arise. For example, the lead in petrol causes little environmental problems at the refinery; however, when used in the car it can cause considerable problems in city streets. Again with petrol, the carbon monoxide and nitrous oxide emissions from the exhaust can vary with the particular car which is burning the petrol. This is outside the control of the companies which supply the petrol but obviously they have an interest in persuading us all to use environmentally better cars (whether by more efficient engine design or by cleaning up exhausts using devices such as catalytic converters). The reporting of the success, or otherwise, of these initiatives requires data external to the organization producing the pollutant. On the same issue, the organization which is heavily using transport, especially road transport, would wish to consider reporting its use of road transport and its efforts to minimize the environmental impact of that use. Some pollutants are long lasting and cumulative in their effect: the reporting of these needs special care.

There are also some pollution effects which are not felt locally to the source of the pollution. The classic example of this is the blame for the acid rain affecting the forests in Scandinavia and western Germany which is ascribed by some to the emissions of sulphur dioxide from the coal-burning electricity generating stations in the countries further to the west. This international dimension to pollution problems needs to be recognized even in reporting which is primarily designed to be read within the locality causing the pollutant to be added to the ecosystem.

Within the UK there is a principle that in cleaning up pollution incidents and long-term pollution from continuing operations, the polluter should pay for the cost of the cleaning up. It is important that organizations who are causing pollution should report publicly how much they are paying towards eliminating the nuisance. One would expect to include in this the costs of any effluent or gas scrubbing facilities already paid for and included in the operation as well as the fees being paid to external agencies.

Social impact

An organization or operation will have impacts on people and society in general. We can see effects arising from the particular product or process, both effects on the local community and other effects on special interest groups.

Turning to the less than welcome effects that could be caused by a product, we must look at the impact on various groups of people. Of major concern is the harm caused to employees. Most industrial nations now have well-established health and safety at work legislation which attempts to minimize potential danger caused to employees by industrial processes. Some well-established industrial operations are still finding unexpected effects and so it is incumbent on them to monitor and understand changing research. In newer established businesses there is more chance of unexpected effects being discovered. For instance, we have a continuing debate on the health effects of working with computer equipment, especially video terminals, and the effects these cause through eye strain, radiation or even repeated stress fractures (RSF) for those undertaking considerable keyboard input. An organization can survey its current state of protection provided for employees from the harmful effects of the product or process that they undertake but we anticipate that all organizations must expect that unforeseen effects will be uncovered in the future.

Not only are employees affected by the products and processes made by an organization, but so too are its customers. Product liability legislation is increasing throughout the commercial world and we anticipate that organizations will have to report publicly their current exposure to such legislation.

There are others, too, neither employees nor customers, who could be affected by the organization. These constituencies need determining and the effects understood.

Obviously in public reporting there will be a natural tendency to place emphasis on reporting the effects of the main business of the organization. However, subsidiary businesses (and not necessarily subsidiaries in the legal financial sense) will have the potential to have far more damaging side effects out of all proportion to their relative size within the main business.

The effect on a local community of a sizeable operation can be quite extensive. There is obviously the possibility of pollution, whether by chemicals or by noise from the operation. However, there are also beneficial effects to the local community which must be offset in any balanced environmental report. An organization provides employment and economic input to its local community, and can provide synergy with the local businesses. Not only does it directly provide employment and economic well-being, but also, by providing opportunities to other organizations either as suppliers or purchasers and distributors of its product or service, it can benefit the local economy out of all proportion to its own investment. This, however, may of course also lead to increased traffic volumes and noise in the local community.

A well-meaning organization can provide other less tangible benefits to its local community. For example, good architecture and good environmental, in the house-keeping sense, control of its operation can provide a pleasant operating and living environment for those close to the operation. The organization can also be involved in local community projects and these should also be reported. Again, all of these beneficial and deleterious effects from the operation will change with time, with volume and with economic conditions, therefore reporting them requires up-to-date information and interpretation.

There may also be other effects on special interest groups. We can illustrate this by considering how some organizations have needed to report on, and be aware of, their use of animals for research purposes. Other special interest groups (e.g. the disabled) may also have a particular interest in an organization's impact on their members. The organization may also offer sponsorship and scholarships which may be beneficial to the local community or to the nation as a whole. These aspects all need to be covered in a balanced environmental report and as such this requires an appreciation of all that the organization is doing.

Global warming – the greenhouse effect

At the time of writing there is still some debate between scientists on the exact causes of the reduction in the ozone layer. In addition, an increase in average climatic temperatures is predicted from other effects in the upper atmosphere. That it is happening is still debated by some and the extent to which each of the various causes contribute will continue to be discussed. This in itself poses a problem for the green reporter. Many 'green' documents and claims carelessly mix the two problems of depletion of the ozone layer (which mainly affects the level of ultraviolet rays reaching the earth) and the greenhouse effect which will probably lead to global warming. Should companies be mostly concerned with the use, or otherwise, of ozone reacting chemicals such as CFCs, or should they be concerned with the carbon dioxide being produced by their organization? The choice, of course, depends on the extent to which either of these are in any sense a major outcome from the organization's operations. However, the relative importance attached to reporting either of these two contributions to the reported global warming also depends on future assessments of the effect and impact of the two causes. In order to report, the reporter must have set in train data-gathering mechanisms. To be able to report on a whole year in a consistent manner requires the mechanisms to be designed and installed well in advance of that year. The green reporter will always be catching up with now accepted truth.

The difficulties in green reporting

The preceding few paragraphs indicate the great range and variety of topics to be covered in green reporting. We would like now to summarize what we see as the main difficulties in principle that this implies.

The first difficulty is that, unlike the preparation of a balance sheet and profit and loss account where all items being reported are on a common basis, i.e. a unit of currency, the issues which need to be covered in an environmental report require that each issue be reported separately using a reporting mechanism suitable for that individual issue. You cannot simply add up all the different impacts in an algebraic manner and obtain a number at the end which says, if positive, this organization is environmentally sound, and if negative there is cause for concern. Mathematicians would say the financial world is 'univariate' whereas the environmental report is 'multivariate'.

Actually the distinction is not quite as strong as that. Consider those organizations trading extensively in many currencies. There are detailed and accepted accounting rules for converting all the different units of currency into a common one so that a single profit and loss account and balance sheet can be reported. However, this example does show the quite complex rules necessary to be able to consolidate together information which is actually quite similar. To do the same for green reporting would be far more complex and we suggest it should not even be attempted.

Another difference between environmental reporting and financial reporting is that the former has both quantitative data, i.e. tons of waste products per year or per million pounds of sales achieved, and also qualitative data such as 'the plant bordering on a residential area has been tidied up and scrap material cleared away in this financial year' or 'we have commenced an R&D programme to eliminate our need to use such and such a chemical, the manufacture of which is causing concern'. The qualitative information can be as important as the quantitative information.

A further difficulty in adding together the environmental effects is that some are contradictory – the operation may have improved one measure of environmental friendliness at the expense of another. For instance, the removal of a particular pollutant from the effluent from a factory may require the use of a chemical which is produced, say, in an operation where there are reported carcinogenic effects.

We have in environmental reporting also to contend with our very limited experience in the area. Contrast this with financial reporting developed over at least one hundred years of intense commercial activity which has honed and refined the content of a financial report. The audience for financial reporting is also well educated in the process and the conventions used, and so is well placed to interpret the information. Even so, misinterpretations are often made by readers of company accounts.

In the field of environmental reporting, even in its infancy as it now is, we can see some special difficulties:

- Actually collecting the information is a problem, given that we have not done so in the past. What is peculiar about a lot of environmental reporting is that, because it cannot be merged into one unified measure, much of the data that is held and kept for environmental reporting will be disaggregated and as such will need special care.
- There is also the problem of presenting the information. We need to develop standard presentation criteria so that different organizations in allied businesses can be seen to be reporting in a similar manner. We need to ensure that the presentations are truthful and not misleading.
- Once the information is presented it will need care in its interpretation. We must encourage commercial journalists to take a lead in assisting the general public to make proper interpretations of the reported information, and for them not to use it as a basis for scare stories. It would set back environmental reporting severely in a particular industry if the first member of that industry to publish was the subject of unwarranted criticism through misinformed interpretation and adverse commentary.

In summary the preceding paragraphs have demonstrated that environmental reporting is not easy. It is a quickly changing field, not only in the expectations of the audience for the information, but also in the basic information to be reported as new environmental issues become more researched and well documented. However, although we have demonstrated that environmental reporting is not easy, that does not mean that it should not be undertaken. Indeed, it is our view that its importance is such for the community as a whole, and also for the commercial well-being of the organization making the report, that environmental reporting systems and procedures within organizations are now urgent.

ORGANIZATIONAL IMPLICATIONS

We have already demonstrated that green reporting is a variable target as issues and priorities change. In this section of the chapter we discuss the implications that this has for the overall organization and for those parts responsible for the green reporting.

Overall and central managment department

Before we turn to the organizational impacts of environmental reporting, we stress what must seem to be for most readers a statement of the obvious. That is, before an organization is to report publicly on environmental matters, it is necessary for that organization to have environmental policies and objectives. The setting up of these policies and objectives must be undertaken at a senior (i.e. board) level and individual job specifications will need enlarging to include the extra environmental responsibilities.

In order to be able to respond to changing issues, it is necessary for the organization to set up a mechanism for monitoring the debate over green issues. Sources of information should include:

- News reports.
- Publications, press releases, speeches and other material from environmental pressure groups.
- Policy statements from official departments (including supranational bodies such as the European Commission, the United Nations and its agencies, and national, regional and local government). These policy statements should be retained for future reference.
- Published regulations relating to the environment and energy usage. In the UK this would include Acts of Parliament, statutory instruments, regulations published by government agencies (such as the Health and Safety Executive and the National Rivers Authority). Care should be taken that a full range of these regulations is monitored as some regulations covering issues which apparently do not refer to environmental

matters may include subsidiary matters which do have environmental impact.

- Scientific and technical journals covering the organization's field of operations. These journals should include the prominent medical and the more populist technical journals (a good example of the latter would be *New Scientist* amongst others).
- Court decisions (especially compensation and damages claims against companies). It would be advisable to monitor decisions in courts other than the national ones – for instance, within the UK the decisions of the European Court, leading commonwealth countries and the United States should be monitored.
- Statements of intent by political bodies (parties and other pressure groups) which could affect future legislation or, if not directly leading to legislation, could affect the climate of opinion on environmental subjects.

The above list is quite extensive but is not complete. Particular organizations will have specific sources of information peculiar to them (trade associations, consumer groups). The monitoring of all these sources is, we contend, beyond the scope of a single individual. There are two reasons for this assertion: one is the sheer volume of material to be monitored and the other is the various technical disciplines required to be able to interpret the material.

Defining the needs in a large organization

For a large organization we suggest:

- A central group (the word committee is an anathema to us with its implication redolent of inaction and procrastination) which is headed by a senior executive who is respected as not letting detail escape from control.
- This central group will include sufficient representatives of the major business functions (including marketing/PR) and technical areas to be able to cover the operations of the organization. (In very large or diverse organizations it may be necessary to cascade the group into various plants and areas of operations.)
- The group will identify, and regularly review and update, the list of issues affecting the organization, the current state of legislation, possible future legislation and public opinion.
- The group will document which parts of the organization are affected by the issue and in what way. It is possible that different parts of the organization will have dissimilar, even opposite, impacts from a particular issue.

The documentation of the issues and its impacts will be sensitive and will need adequate security (a subject for a book in its own right). Suffice it to say that control should be exercised over distribution, copying and destruction of old versions. It will be necessary for parts of this list to be known by executives responsible for operations and units within the organization. In order to be able to prepare this list we suggest that:

- All the sources of information that need monitoring should be identified.
- Members of the group, or others reporting to them, should be assigned to monitoring the sources against the defined list of issues and should report through some mechanism to the other members. A suitable reporting mechanism could be a pro forma report for each relevant item spotted or a monthly summary report.
- The leader of the group will need to report to the most senior management of the organization any significant new issues or changes of concern.

The group should also be tasked with responsibility for ensuring that the relevant people within the organization are kept fully briefed on all salient issues (managers through the usual reporting structure, staff perhaps through in-house magazines, memos or whatever is most effective).

To be effective as a group they must have the support and commitment of senior management. We are all aware of non-operational tasks that need to be undertaken in an organization, but which are often seen to be counter-productive by those not convinced of the necessity for having the function (e.g. internal audit, quality assurance and even, in some cases, personnel organizations). The ability of the group to report directly to the chief executive is a valuable privilege which, if not unduly exercised, can be essential for its successful functioning.

Such groups can be organized in large operations although the more efficient ones may encounter difficulties in finding the necessary spare managerial resource. Indeed, some organizations may find the monitoring costs unacceptable and would prefer their managers to contract out the monitoring of the issues. This may be the only solution for the medium to smaller company but would still be too expensive for the small operation.

The smaller organization

A small operation may already rely heavily on outside business advisers to monitor legislative and commercial changes that affect the business. Quite often the most influential external adviser is the company's professional accountant. The accountancy profession is already organized to be able to monitor developments in certain fields (e.g. taxation, accounting standards). Keeping up to date is achieved by professional (typically monthly) journals, attending externally organized conferences/seminars and lastly, but probably most importantly for those in the smaller practices, by purchasing loose-leaf reference material with a regular update service. We see all three routes as being valid for the practising accountant in keeping abreast of environmental issues and we hope others will see the commercial opportunities in publishing reference works and organizing conferences in this area.

It must be stressed, however, that for an organization which contracts others to monitor the changes in legislation and environmental affairs, the responsibility for failing to meet the legal requirements still rests with the management of the organization.

Recording the position

This chapter is concerned with environmental reporting – the actions to be taken to improve environmental impact are not the subject of this book. However, we would hope and expect the monitoring of environmental issues, and in particular the negative effect poor environmental image can have on an organization's commercial prospects, to lead to effects to improve the situation in respect of all the issues identified as being significant for the organization.

Having identified the issues, we turn to the organizational impacts of reporting the environmental impact of the organization. We start with the apparently mundane, but nonetheless important aspect of obtaining reportable data.

Environmental data can be of various forms, not necessarily comparable with one another, and not necessarily quantifiable. Considerable care is required in ensuring the accuracy of the data before it is reported. We advise those responsible for environmental reporting to consider:

- Data verification when it is recorded, either by repeat observations by someone else or by independent observation (naturally, statistical sampling can be used to demonstrate the veracity of quantifiable data).
- The use of an external review to verify the data. (We choose to avoid the word audit for this as it could be confused with the financial audit – we discuss 'environmental audits' later in this chapter.) This is particularly useful for qualitative data, including changed workforce attitudes, and for confirming changes of practice (e.g. avoiding chemicals which have been tested on animals).
- Collecting data solely for another's use can lead to reduced data accuracy. Try and make the data collection an integral part of a task for other purposes. For instance, the monitoring of the fuel efficiency of the transport fleet could be related to a key objective of the transport manager, and this should ensure that the data captured is accurate. The transport manager may want to see fuel efficiency in terms of miles per gallon: the environmental report may want to include figures on tonne miles or goods value miles per

gallon. Nevertheless the recording of fuel consumption and miles covered is required both for operational management and environmental reporting.

If it is not possible to integrate the data collecting with operations and, consequently, data collection is performed – apparently – for its own sake, it is necessary to consider other ways of checking and improving the validity of the data. Spot checks have their place alongside proper managerial supervision, but employee motivation can be improved by such means as:

- selecting people for these tasks who are committed to environmental issues (but obviously avoid those who will be so committed that they are liable to leak adverse information before the organization has a chance to rectify the situation);
- giving status and internal publicity to the data collectors: a feature in the in-house staff magazine (with a reinforcing message from senior management on the importance of the task) is one way of improving the perceived value of the task to the employee;
- and, following on from the above, include the employee's name and/or photograph in external environmental reports.

We have already commented on the nature of environmental reporting data, i.e. it is often disaggregated, qualitative and, sometimes transient. This should be contrasted with financial data where, so long as a common unit of currency is used, it is possible to manipulate the data in many ways to produce reports. For public reporting this has led accountants to devise statements of standard accounting practice. Given the nature of the environmental data, there is even greater scope for choice of presentation of the data. Until such time, if ever, that standards exist for reporting on environmental matters, it will be necessary to control both the accuracy of the data and the way it is manipulated to produce the reported figures. Year on year consistency will be required if comparisons with previous years are to be useful, and it will be necessary for the organization to institute the necessary controls on procedures to ensure such consistency. We would expect at least:

- a senior management review committee to examine draft environmental reports;
- a statement of policy that environmental reports shall be honest and not deliberately set to deceive;
- an independent internal check on the data-gathering to ensure the measurements are comparable, or if they are not, that this is recognized, from one period to another.

Operations (including manufacturing) departments

It is expected that within the operations area, more perhaps than in any other, considerable data will need to be collected to assist in environmental reporting. We are aware of the increasing requirements already for data collection within manufacturing operations to support new manufacturing methods. There are also statutory requirements for data collection, for instance, in the accidents and injuries book. We do not see the imposition of more data collection requirements to be a problem in principle, but we can understand the 'groans' of those in manufacturing of yet another request for more and more data.

We see that in the operations area it is particularly important to train the supervisor in the necessity of collecting accurate and verifiable data for environmental reporting purposes. This we feel should be coupled with training in other management disciplines such as concern for spills, wastage, inefficient use of material and reduction of the scrap rate. By integrating environmental issues with business objectives at the shop-floor level this training will have an effect which can be seen in the improvement in the quality of data recording.

We would also anticipate in organizations where trade unions are integrated within the management structure for consultation purposes that the trade union representatives will be involved in the installation of data collection mechanisms for environmental reporting. We would also expect that in those organizations union representatives will request that they see the results of that data recording. In general, if there are problems within the operations which the data recording provides evidence for, these need addressing before the explicit data is available. We can see the union representatives requiring improvements in local environmental matters (especially those within the working space of their members) as part of a negotiated settlement.

We do see that the operations area is one where it is easiest to set clearly defined objectives for improving environmental performance within an organization, and, indeed, within this area of the organization we would expect that the quantitative evidence of actual performance should be relatively easy to obtain.

Sales and marketing departments

We see the sales and marketing department playing a key strategic role in the changes to the business arising out of heightened environmental conscienceness and changes in the market-place. Sales departments may need green facts and data in promotional sales campaigns. They should also provide the key feedback from the customer and potential customer base to those within the organization taking strategic decisions on the business. Not only will the sales department need information and training in the use of information, but also it should become a key part of their training to be sensitive to their customers' environmental concerns so that in their direct contact with the market-place they are not upsetting new sensibilities.

Purchasing departments

The environmental impact of the manufacture or obtaining of supplies may reflect badly on the organization using the supplier. Indeed, replacing an internal manufacturing process which produces pollutants by externally procured supplies may not reduce the adverse publicity.

It will be necessary for purchasing departments to add to their buying criteria (e.g. price, delivery, quality, certainty of supply) a consideration of the process whereby the supplies are acquired. This may require more technical/ manufacturing expertise than is commonly found in purchasing departments.

Research and development departments

We see quite fundamental changes to the emphasis and priorities within the research and development department, with a long-term strategy to include green or environmental effects in the selection of R&D priorities. We expect particular care to be taken in the case of those products which produce waste and an emphasis on the development of new processes in products which use particularly noxious materials in their production. We feel that for the research department to change its priorities to meet the overall needs of organizations trying to respond to greater environmental consciences means that the research and development department needs to maintain a close link with the senior member of the organization responsible for environmental issues.

We could also anticipate the research and development arms of many organizations being asked to provide the interpretation of, and the modelling of the environmental effects of, the raw data being collected in other parts of the organization. This may further lead to changes in the research and development programme with specific projects being included to alleviate those problems highlighted by environmental reporting.

The R&D department will also be required to provide the technical backup to other departments (e.g. the purchasing department assessing the manufacturing processes of supplies).

Transport departments

The transport department could easily become the object of much external criticism as environmental pressure mounts. Indeed, it could be seen to be the villain of the piece given the much larger attention being given to the resource consumption, greenhouse effect and pollution caused by some methods of transport. Apart from the obvious business reasons of efficiency and cost saving, we would anticipate pressures from the environmental lobby leading to many organizations paying much greater attention to good vehicle maintenance, tracking of performance and improvement of efficiency of the transport operation, not only in financial terms but in environmental terms too.

We see emphasis being placed not only on miles per gallon, but also percentage lead-free petrol or diesel (as opposed to leaded petrol) consumption and fuel consumption per tonnes of goods sold. Also the scheduling of deliveries and journeys to avoid congestion and to avoid disturbance in residential areas will be emphasized. Being able to demonstrate this improvement, especially for the latter two cases, will again require the organization to consider how it collects the data to prove that the objectives that it has set itself in this field have been met.

General

Whichever department we are talking about it is important that once it is decided, or it is necessary for other reasons (such as statutory or external pressure), to produce environmental reports the organization should ensure that the trend is in the right direction. The first year's reporting would provide a base line again which future years would be judged and movements in the 'wrong' direction will have a very strong negative impact on image. We have already indicated in the operations area the need to train and motivate supervisors to ensure that the agreed policies and targets are met and we would stress that this applies equally throughout the rest of the organization.

We see the impact of environmental reporting on the organization as a new consideration to be applied in the decision-making process at all levels in the organization. Hence when a decision is required, not only do the people look at financial costs and benefits but also environmental impacts. Environmental impacts should of course, where possible, be accurately determined using conventional methods but decision-makers will be aware that there are many environmental issues where it is not the formal detail that is important as much as how that particular issue is currently perceived.

When considering a decision between two options it will be necessary to consider different environmental impacts, both quantitative and qualitative. We would anticipate that the decision-making process should consider only the difference in environmental impacts, given that the absolute environmental impacts of either of the options may be much more difficult to determine.

In order to make a valid comparison it is necessary for there to be an agreed basis of valuation for particular environmental impacts. Also, it must be clear to all those in the organization which impacts are totally unacceptable. For example, consider an organization which wishes to change its delivery vans from petrol driven to electric. On undertaking the evaluation it might find that it is less able to serve its distant customers with the existing electric van technology, and would obviously have to use contractors for those deliveries. It might also find that the delivery costs are slightly higher, perhaps because electric vans are slower on top of any differences in operating and capital costs. It may, however, find that marketing analysis shows that they will gain not inconsiderably by being seen to be ecologically sound in their choice of vehicles. The basis for making a decision to go to an electric van delivery network requires a trade-off between cost and projected benefits from their marketing improvements. Such trade-offs are not uncommon in business decisions today – indeed as business decisions often involve partly defined data before environmental issues are included, the extra issues should not cause new difficulties in principle.

Despite all the issues and nuances listed above, it is essential to remember the basis of the management process for achieving any objective. The process is often modelled as the following set of activities:

1. Set objectives.
2. Set targets for performance.
3. Plan the activities necessary to obtain the set targets, and obtain the necessary resources.
4. Undertake the task.
5. Monitor progress against plan and target.

In practice, action does not move uniformly through the above steps. Often a step may reveal an infeasibility or difficulty (e.g. in 3 above there may be insufficient resources available) and it is then necessary to return to the previous steps to reconsider. This may sometimes require the agreement of others before the management process can be recontinued. Environmental objectives and reporting are also amenable to this type of management process.

We might envisage objectives along the following lines:

- 'Demonstrate that pollution from the operation is declining within approved standards.'
- 'Obtain a good profile with opinion-forming consumers so that the main supermarket chains will stock us with confidence.'
- 'Demonstrate that we lead on green issues and are not just following and undertaking action merely to comply with the law and accepted norms.'
- 'Minimize green exposure and questioning.'

Accounting for green costs

In many organizations there will be extra costs incurred in improving the green image of a product or the organization itself. These extra costs may well, over a period of time, be more than offset by improved market performance. However, there is a need to report these extra costs in, say, a monthly management reporting cycle.

Who, that is say which particular parts of the organization, should be responsible for the costs? We would propose that the maxim that costs should lie with a department that bears the benefit should be used to allocate some, but not necessarily all, of the extra changeover costs or product costs involved in making an organization or a product more environmentally acceptable. For example, where the marketing department is promoting a change in the production process to improve the marketability of the product, costs should be attributed to the marketing department during the period of implementation.

In general, we would anticipate that the changeover costs would have a separate budget, with all the usual controls one would expect in a financially soundly based management system.

In terms of the published accounts, we would suggest guidance from existing accounting standards. For instance, new development projects to improve products in future financial years should be costed and reported in accordance with the accounting practice already used for other R&D expenditure (expensing existing projects and capitalizing green expenditure, or vice versa, would take some justification). Extra expenditure as a one-off to remove an adverse environmental impact needs to be classified as extraordinary or exceptional.

At the moment we are unaware of any reason for suggesting that there is any need to press for changes to statements of standard accounting practice to take account of any special needs of environmental accounting.

In any environmental reports issued by an organization which includes cost information, the basis of the cost information (i.e. marginal, full absorption) should be specified.

Measuring the benefit of green reporting

The anticipated benefits for an organization undertaking environmental reporting will be difficult to demonstrate. The timing of the benefits will vary: some effects might be immediate whilst others may be part of much longer-term processes. Most of the immediate benefits will be intangible (e.g. image, PR) and their achievement will often be matters of opinion rather than fact.

We stressed earlier the need for an organization to define environmental impact objectives. We feel that the reporting of the extent of meeting these objectives will provide what we call 'immediate measures of performance' of environmental action.

The previous chapters of this book demonstrate that there is a growing interest in the need for organizations to report their environmental impact and that there is, both in the UK and internationally, a trend towards greater reporting, either voluntarily or by making aspects mandatory. We do not see any mechanism for reducing this trend and so we can predict a disadvantage for those organizations which are seen to be slow or reluctant to comply with these extra requirements.

Actual tangible benefits that we foresee are, in the shorter term, the inclusion of the organization on approved lists (and, just as importantly, exclusion from disapproved lists) as potential suppliers and advantaged purchasers.

Longer-term performance will be very much more difficult to distinguish from the effects of other business decisions and operations. We can see long-term effects on market share, profitability (perhaps by having products or services commanding a premium price because of improved environmental impact, as well as improved market share), easier recruitment of staff, improved share price, facilitating the raising of new finance (perhaps through improved investor relations with the institutions, or inclusion on the lists of the ethical investment trusts), and improved value of the business (through the previous effects but also through improved image).

We are aware that there will be organizations that feel reporting their current position which is open to criticism could have adverse effects. We counter by saying that pressure groups and interested parties are increasingly discovering any unsound practices. In general, we advise organizations to concentrate on reporting trends and actions being taken to remedy adverse situations: being forced by outside events to declare will considerably reduce the ability of the organization to achieve credibility in its message of improvements, both current and to come.

However, we are not in a position to demonstrate conclusively that the balance will be a generally beneficial effect: it is almost a matter of faith supported by the evidence of case history.

MECHANISMS

Having in previous sections of this chapter discussed the difficulties and the organizational impacts of environmental reporting, in this section we will try and provide some practical advice on the mechanisms that should be set up to establish environmental reporting within an organization.

Unfortunately we cannot be prescriptive. It is in the nature of environmental reporting that the needs will change with time – and not only in terms of the areas of environmental concern. (Consider the oft-cited case of the introduction of catalytic converters on cars to reduce the nitrous oxide and sulphur dioxide pollutants from exhaust emissions – they also increase the production of greenhouse gases by reducing the overall efficiency of engine units.) We anticipate that there will be a perennial review of the purpose of corporate reporting on environmental matters in general. We already have similar, almost annual, reviews of the purpose of the annual financial reports and statements. There have been major investigations and reports on this topic punctuated by continual discussion of the purpose of these reports. Indeed, in financial auditing circles there is again some doubt as to who the published audited reports are meant for and what reliance can, or should, be placed on them.

What we are recommending in this section is not so much yet another service department adding to the perceived overheads already incurred in personnel, welfare, finance, quality and internal audit departments. Rather we are concerned with how environmental reporting mechanisms should be integrated within the overall structure of an organization. We base this on the trend that we see throughout all organizations to place responsibility for all aspects of a particular operation (be it manufacturing or service) on the line manager in that service or department area. Large organizations do back up line managers with staff functions but these staff functions are becoming more and more of a purely advisory and technical nature, with the management responsibility being vested entirely in the local management.

For those seeking an analogy consider the trend over the last ten years in quality management. The large quality assurance departments in many organizations have been whittled down and quality responsibility devolved to line managers. Indeed, in those organizations which have instituted the quality circles approach the responsibility for quality is now divested to all employees.

We see this devolution to managers as being more important for environmental reporting than for many other of the responsibilities which have been devolved in recent management changes. We feel that a centralized bureaucracy which is remote from the line manager's daily role would mean that the organization would be poorly placed to be able to respond to the fast changing requirements for environmental reporting. We consider that making it a responsibility of the individual who can physically see the operations he or she is responsible for will enable any changes in requirements to be quickly implemented. For instance, the control over the waste of CFC gases in refrigeration manufacturing could have been more easily tightened up by those directly involved who were suddenly made aware of the potential damage of those chemicals.

Having set the managerial approach throughout the whole organization, we see that the most important action to ensure that environmental reporting is well targeted is for the senior executives of the organization to define objectives for green reporting. These objectives must obviously be transmitted to all those responsible for that reporting. We see this as particularly important in an area which can become very nebulous and driven by personal interests. Indeed, we see a particular danger in environmental reporting which we liken to the position of a man who drops a £5 note in a dark street and spends all his time looking under a lamppost, not because that was where he dropped the note, but because there the light is brightest. We can see the danger that managerial action and the subsequent reporting of environmental issues will be concentrated on the easy problem, whilst important (and often more difficult) issues are effectively ignored.

We are all familiar with the standard published financial reports – these would look quite strange to us if they did not have the conventional two-column this year and last year presentation. Within internal management reports one is also used to current month and year-to-date figures as well as previous year and budget comparison data. We see no reason why that sort of presentation will not become the norm for environmental reporting of quantitative data as well.

Understanding the audience

In all reporting matters, be it environmental or financial, it is important to consider the audience receiving the report and what they are interested in. The audience for environmental reports could include the management of the organization, employees, investors and owners of the business, the local community, the community as a whole, special interest groups, pressure groups, and political organizations.

For all reports it is necessary to determine the purpose of that individual report and what it is trying to demonstrate. The presentation style, whether graphics and quality presentation is required and the need for clarity are important issues. We anticipate that in the area of environmental reporting particular care is needed in the use of scientific terms and terminology. Consider carefully the audience for a report. Maybe two different forms of the same information are required for different audiences. There may also be some audiences who require reports more often than others. This is analogous to the internal monthly reports within an organization which itself may only publicly report biannually or yearly.

Whatever the purpose assigned to the report, whatever the matter being reported, whatever the frequency and whatever the audience, we stress that wherever possible a report should be kept as simple as possible. The simpler the presentation and the language the less likely it is to be misunderstood. Environmental matters are in danger of becoming overly complicated.

When considering environmental reporting not only has the content to be decided but also how those reports are to be published. For many consumer products it is important that this reporting information is available at the point of sale. Including it as an integral part of the packaging (even if this has been dramatically reduced as part of another environmental objective) would be powerful. However, environmental results like financial reports should be published in the appropriate public places. We would anticipate that just as financial results are published in the financial press we would expect to see environmental report data appearing there alongside the financial information, but also to be more widely reported and to be included in the popular press as well as the specialist press with environmental concerns. For example, we could see the use of the *New Scientist* as one mechanism amongst many others to get across a message to the technically aware concerned reader. Not only national press coverage but also local press and radio is important because although local residents near an operation may not be interested or able to read a balance sheet, they will certainly be able to see smoke coming from a chimney!

We would anticipate environmental data being included in the general publicity material available from an organization. But environmental reports on paper are not enough. The opportunity should be taken to show people wherever possible what is going on, especially where operations which have a poor public image are concerned. An extreme example of this is the use of an exhibition centre, tours and visits around the site by British Nuclear Fuels Limited at their Sellafield/Windscale operation. Take-home leaflets from such organized visits are a very powerful opinion former.

Quantitative reporting

Where possible it is naturally better to report environmental matters quantitatively rather than qualitatively. Some would go as far as to say that unless you can match your reports to something with numbers it is not worth reporting. We don't take that extreme view though we do recommend where possible the reporting of quantitative data.

The business of financial reporting has been improved considerably over the years so that the reports produced are understandable and concise. We would argue by analogy that the following two key points should be included in any quantitative report. The first is that, wherever possible, ratios should be used to make the data relevant. We are used to costs of sales ratios and asset to liability ratios, and in the same way as the pyramid of ratios is built up in basic managing accounting textbooks we can see similar pyramids being useful for green reporting. It is difficult to be prescriptive for a company but we can see that, say, transport costs can be reported as a pyramid of ratios. Figure 12.1 shows such a pyramid.

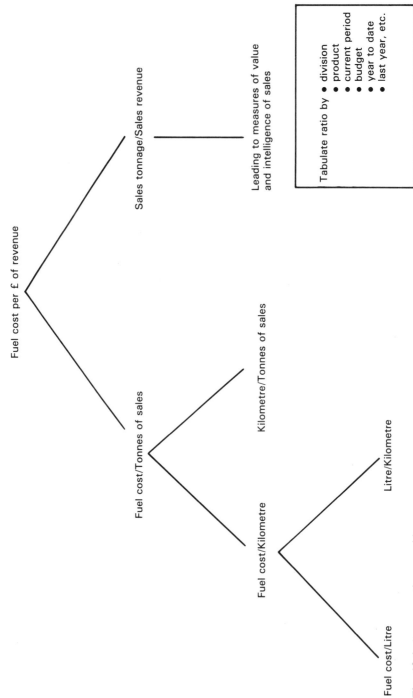

Fig. 12.1 A green ratio pyramid.

As well as the provision of ratio data where possible and obviously some indication of the absolute amount, we believe that trends and comparison figures are also important. It is recognized that some industries start from a poor position in respect of their environmental impact. It is also recognized that to expect an overnight improvement is also economically not realistic. Hence, we strongly urge trend data, showing improvements in the right direction, and where there is a defined objective for that particular issue that the targets are always reported.

If we are talking about externally published reports then it is important that the audience for the report regards the information as credible. Despite their financial rectitude some companies are regarded with deep suspicion on environmental matters by those particularly concerned about those topics. It is important that the reports indicate the credibility and verification of the figures. We could draw an analogy with the financial audit whereby a materiality concept is used to determine to what extent the reported figures should be absolutely accurate. We can see the same materiality concept being applied to environmental figures, but given our comments on the importance of trend information we expect a materiality concept to produce relatively small allowable errors. There is also a problem with verification of transient data. By that we mean data which represents a measurement at a point in time but which it is not possible to repeat at any other time. An example of that would be, say, the biological oxygen deficiency in a sewer outfall from a plant. It would be impossible a day later to go back and verify what the figure was, hence there is a need for credibility and standards in measuring such data. Indeed, we suggest a consideration of outside agencies to actually do the measurement.

Just as in financial reporting, there is considerable scope in environmental reporting for manipulation of the data to provide a much better report. Consider the position of the outfall measurement in the last paragraph. What if that measurement was taken just before the operation starts up each day and before major pollutants are added to the outfall water? We can see that there will be a strong temptation for management to be 'economical' with the truth in their environmental reporting, in just the same way as those companies that have been publishing financial data which in the light of further analysis and subsequent events has been shown to be less than accurate. These companies have found the subsequent exposure to be as damaging – or in some cases more damaging – than reporting the true situation would have been in the first place. We believe the same message applies to environmental reporting, in that, if the data that you are reporting is shown by later examination to have been deliberately less than honest, the embarassment and negative impact on the company is as bad or worse than if the 'truth' had been reported originally. We stress that this is dependent on the recipients of the report, be they the investors looking at the financial report or those concerned with environmental matters looking at the environmental report to apply pressure and public exposure to those situations which do not meet their expected standards.

Reporting on qualitative matters

This chapter is essentially aimed at those of the accounting profession who require practical advice on reporting environmental matters. Accountants are naturally averse to expressing opinion on qualitative matters. Nor do we suggest they should be otherwise. However, as we showed in the earlier parts of this chapter, environmental reporting isn't entirely about hard numeric data but also includes trends, attitudes and opinions.

For instance, we can see that some of the reports will include matters which are pure policy statements, for instance Body Shop with its policy on not using animal testing on products that are sold in their chain shops. Reporting of that sort requires verification of what is actually being implemented. In some cases it is as important in environmental reports as data on pollution levels, for instance. As numerically based professionals we must not be tempted to place undue reliance on quantitative reports in this area. Of course some people would argue that in actual fact many of the accounting reports, and the data therein, are also based on qualitative information and opinions. Even simple matters such as depreciation of fixed assets require an opinion as regards the probable useful life of the asset. Stock valuations are again a matter of opinion in some aspects.

Given that qualitative data attracts greater suspicion from those receiving the information than does quantitative data, it could be advisable to have external people, whose probity and honesty cannot be questioned, involved with the company in demonstrating that the qualitative issues have been iden-tified and correctly reported.

Lastly, it may seem obvious, but we still think it is worth saying that companies should not report an impossible policy objective. This will be seen to be misleading and could in itself result in considerable negative impact for the company concerned.

Systems implications

In this section, we will discuss the implications of undertaking environmental reporting on the systems to be operated within an organization. We stress the conclusion reached earlier that the current state of environmental reporting is such that the requirements of what is to be reported are quickly changing and as such are relatively unpredictable for those preparing the report.

We would be of the view that the rate of change in the requirements for the environmental reports is actually faster than the speed at which most large organizations can change their systems!

Also, the data that is used in environmental reporting needs assimilating, collecting and consolidating into an organization-wide report from data which in previous uses probably stayed locally within the operation which was generating the data. We see this having several implications for systems including:

- Working and connecting operating systems together so that data from one is extractable and assimilable in a central green reporting system.
- The use of fast-build methods to generate the systems to record the new environmental data which is required.
- The need to add to existing systems other facets to cope with environmental needs.
- Particular attention paid to verification and veracity of the data by, for instance, range checks (whether they be static, e.g. the biological oxygen deficiency figures mentioned earlier should not be negative or greater than a certain sum before giving rise to the necessity of checking, or dynamic, e.g. the BOD from one hour to another should not vary by more than 10%). We also would expect there to be consistency in ratio tests of the data. Remember in financial data, purchase ledger and sales ledger information is verifiable for good business reasons by suppliers and customers. Environmental data which is only used internally has no operational need to make sure that it is right.
- Use of cross-checking and cross-tabulation systems to look for relationships in trends. For instance, if one is looking at pollution levels in works effluent, we would expect this to be plotted against production levels and any surprising deviations from the expected tracking of the two sets of data checked.

A further implication for the systems organization from introducing environmental reporting is that there would be new recipients of data from the systems and new types of output. New recipients and wider circulation of reports can put extra workloads onto a system, and even more so new reports or new screen enquiries and new users of the system could also increase the workload. We also anticipate that the hierarchy for financial information will be different from that for green or environmental information, so that reporting lines and reporting systems will need to be designed to meet new users' needs.

Another implication for the systems could lie in the length of time data has to be retained. Because legal actions in commerce are limited by statute, we have retention periods for accounting data which are relatively short. Even so, we are talking about a significant cost, and quite often a considerable volume of data which is stored just in case it is needed in later dealings with customers, suppliers, the Inland Revenue, Customs and Excise or the courts. We anticipate the retention period for environmental data to be much longer than that applied to commercial data. This is because the statute of limitations only applies from the date of discovery of a potential impact.

We also see a need to maintain a database of opinions and comments on environmental matters and issues within the company. This database may be entirely on paper although it should be properly indexed so that future investigations can demonstrate concern and efforts to improve the position in the past.

We are all used to financial reports being produced to a fixed timescale. Indeed, public companies, unless subject to the conditions for a stock exchange listing, seem to those unaccustomed to such procedures not to publish information until a considerable time after the event. We would anticipate that for environmental reporting these long delays will not be acceptable. The matters concerned need to be reported on a timescale and time horizon relevant to the recipient of the information. For instance, a person concerned about airborne contaminants this week because he or she is an asthma sufferer down wind of a particular plant is not interested in information on trends of daily emissions over the last five years up to, say, nine months ago. This will again put pressure on internal systems and communications between systems in an organization.

In summary we anticipate environmental reporting to put volume and especially tight timescale constraints on existing systems which may require investigation and investment to bring them up to their required standard.

Environmental audit

Accountants have a strong view of what the word audit means. Their view of this facet of the English language is probably not shared by anybody else. The financial audit is, of course, nowhere fully defined, but a working understanding has been built up by custom and practice over many years (including many court cases). Although those within the profession know that an audit covers a very limited set of objectives (i.e. checking the true and fair view of figures, not their exact value, and not being specifically designed to detect all fraud), the general public regard audits performed by a firm of auditors as being much more.

When we come to talk of an environmental audit we must stress that we do not see this as the green equivalent of financial audit. A particular way of looking at an environmental audit could be in terms of an environmental impact review of the entire operation of an organization or part thereof. This is more akin to an internal management audit, especially within an American style of internal audit department review. The scope of this chapter does not include providing advice on how such an environmental impact review should be undertaken. It is a specialist subject and it is understood that there are already more than 250 different organizations offering such a service to companies within the UK. It must be said that though many of these 250 companies do provide a useful service, they are not controlled and regulated in the same way that the professional financial audit function is controlled. For the rest of this section in the chapter, we wish to consider only how an external or internal reviewer or auditor can approach the audit of environmental reporting.

We do see considerable merit in drawing strict analogies from techniques employed in the financial area to audit the environmental reports. We see being utilized the same systems audit approach of looking at the way the reported information is derived and checked, whether it be financial or environmental data. We do see the use of the same sort of control procedures and review procedures for ensuring that the report is verifiable. And again, we can see the use of old fashioned 'tick bash' auditing techniques to check the data. What must be clear is that those carrying out such an audit must have some knowledge of the techniques and technologies involved so that the particular areas being reported can be verified. We would strongly recommend that those who are financially qualified should consider adding this type of audit service to their portfolio. And indeed we would suggest that they are best placed to carry out this work so long as the profession over the coming months adopts some basic standards for this work.

We have considered the role of the external or internal reviewer of the environmental data. This should cover what we call the environmental data derived from a proper review of operations, i.e. the environmental impact which is generated within the organization, and also a review of the data from an audit of the total impact arising from the existence of the organization. We do not wish to see a situation where companies which have a particularly environmentally damaging process within their organization, in order to appear to be environmentally sound, subcontract such deleterious work out to another organization. The total environmental impact of an organization must include the environmental impact at their suppliers and also the environmental impact of the use of their products or processes by customers. This is a major difference compared to financial reports whereby the financial impact on the supplier of goods bought into the organization are of no concern in the financial report on that organization.

MISCELLANEOUS

The role of the accountant in environmental reporting

Financial reporting undertaken by accountants at present is subject to complex rules and procedures to ensure, as far as possible, that financial reports are honest and not misleading. These rules and processes are open to public scrutiny and debate to protect the users of those reports. We hold that the users of environmental reports require the same protection. We are not aware of any other professional body who at present can take up the mantle of environmental reporting within a professional environment that ensures their integrity and standards. We suggest that accountants through their professional training should place themselves in a position to oversee environmental reporting. This does not mean that they can be, or even should be, the sole arbiters of environmental reporting. Naturally very few accountants will have the technical knowledge of, say, chemical and biological processes to be able to contribute to some of the interpretative work that is required. However, nor do accountants have the technical knowledge to assess the state of many of the physical stocks listed in financial accounts, but they are able to ensure that proper processes and procedures were undertaken to value those stocks.

Our views on the role of accountants in environmental reporting are strengthened by the repeated use we have been able to make of an analogy between financial and environmental reporting. If our assumption that the accounting profession is the right one to take a lead in ensuring proper environmental reporting is correct, the following are necessary:

- That the professional institutes and associations undertake to add the processing of environmental reporting to professional examination syllabuses.
- That the said associations and institutes prepare baseline standards for environmental reporting. These standards cannot be as prescriptive as the current statements of standard accounting practice since the underlying understanding of the needs are not so well developed. We expect general principles and guidelines to be prepared and these to be interpreted by the respective trade associations for each type of business.
- That accountants in practice should include a consideration of environmental reporting in their own personal continuing professional education programmes.
- That accountants plan and use their professional time, whether in practice or industry, to ensure that they have the time and facilities to undertake these new responsibilties.

Words of caution

We would be misleading readers of this chapter if we did not make it clear that there are some drawbacks to an organization actually reporting environmental data. These drawbacks are inevitable, but we suggest they should be considered, not in the light of how we avoid the need for environmental reporting, but rather in the light of how we can prepare ourselves for the negative side of environmental reporting.

Clearly public perceptions of the environmental impacts of particular products change over time. There is therefore a danger that putting information in the public domain would not immediately give rise to questions but could leave one open to negative comment in the future.

Within mergers and acquisitions work, if a company has information on negative environmental impact which it has not reported, it could find that information used in a dispute on price or warranties after an acquisition.

We also stress that perceptions of what is good performance may well change, and it is important that the reporting be both accurate and well designed. It is necessary to be rigorous in ensuring that interpretations of published data produced by the company are not misleading. For instance, if a particular organization managed to reduce the petrol burnt for each one million pounds of goods sold, this should not be reported as a reduction in fuel consumption unless the improvement in fuel efficiency is greater than the effect of the increase in sales.

We have already mentioned that a change in policy or in operations, whether reported externally or not (given that the keeping of data may force its disclosure in a court case for compensation anyway), implies acceptance that the previous policy was wrong. Naturally, most companies in this situation would indicate that business reasons, i.e. costing saving, better image, better efficiency, were the reasons for change, but care is required.

Lastly, we have suggested throughout this chapter that environmental reporting is in general for the benefit of the individual organization and indeed can make an improvement to competitive position. We, however, do believe that it is not beyond the realms of possibility that specific environmental taxes or duties may force public disclosure of this information.

FINAL CONCLUSIONS

We close this chapter with a few summary messages:

- Environmental reporting systems capable of providing significant quantitative data may be technically difficult to design.
- Presentation is, arguably, more important than any financial information, and effort and time must be expended on getting this presentation right.
- Each individual problem of reporting may be quite simple but it is the totality and the manner in which it is pulled together, and how this varies over time, that can produce the complexities for those designing a reporting system.

- There is a need to understand environmental issues as seen by those outside the organization as well as those inside.
- There is a need to be able to respond quickly as opinions and issues change.
- It is necessary to ensure that every effort has been expended to ensure that the data is right.
- Accountants through their training are ideally placed to play a leading role in environmental reporting. Some, including the author of this chapter, would argue it is their duty to undertake this role.

INDEX

Company names are given in italics; page numbers which are underlined refer to actual examples in the text.